Please return or renew this item before the latest date shown below

City

Leng

Jamieson ©

Gardiner (E)

Bruntem (K)

Donnelly (A)

r|13

2 4 APR 2013

Cuthbertson (N)

−8 FEB 2014

Wilson

Service NP

Pitlair

Argyle

Stuart O

—> HE

Renewals can be made
by internet www.fifedirect.org.uk/libraries
in person   at any library in Fife
by phone   08451 55 00 66

Fife COUNCIL

Thank you for using your library

THE HORSE BOY

A FATHER'S QUEST TO HEAL HIS SON

RUPERT ISAACSON

**THORNDIKE
WINDSOR
PARAGON**

This Large Print edition is published by Thorndike Press, Waterville, Maine, USA and by BBC Audiobooks Ltd, Bath, England.
Thorndike Press, a part of Gale, Cengage Learning.
The text of this Large Print edition is unabridged.
Other aspects of the book may vary from the original edition.
Set in 16 pt. Plantin.
Printed on permanent paper.

LIBRARY OF CONGRESS CATALOGING-IN-PUBLICATION DATA

Isaacson, Rupert.
   The horse boy : a father's quest to heal his son / by Rupert Isaacson. — Large print ed.
      p. cm.
   Originally published: New York : Little, Brown and Co., 2009.
   ISBN-13: 978-1-4104-1589-9 (hardcover : alk. paper)
   ISBN-10: 1-4104-1589-9 (hardcover : alk. paper)
   1. Isaacson, Rowan. 2. Isaacson, Rupert. 3. Autistic children—United States—Biography. 4. Parents of autistic children—United States—Biography. 5. Autism in children—Treatment—Case studies. 6. Horses—Therapeutic use—Case studies. 7. Human-animal relationships—Case studies. 8. Autistic children—Family relationships—Case studies. 9. Fathers and sons—Case studies. 10. Austin (Tex.)—Biography. 11. Large type books. I. Title.
   RJ506.A91795 2009b
   618.92'858820092—dc22
   [B]   2009005102

BRITISH LIBRARY CATALOGUING-IN-PUBLICATION DATA AVAILABLE

Published in 2009 in the U.S. by arrangement with Little, Brown and Company, a division of Hachette Book Group, Inc.
Published in 2009 in the U.K. & Commonwealth by arrangement with Penguin Books Ltd.
Published in 2009 in Australia and New Zealand by arrangement with The Text Publishing Company Pty Ltd.

U.K. Hardcover: 978 1 408 43059 0 (Windsor Large Print)
U.K. Softcover: 978 1 408 43060 6 (Paragon Large Print)

Printed in the United States of America
1 2 3 4 5 6 7 13 12 11 10 09

For my son
And for Kristin, for her unrelenting bravery

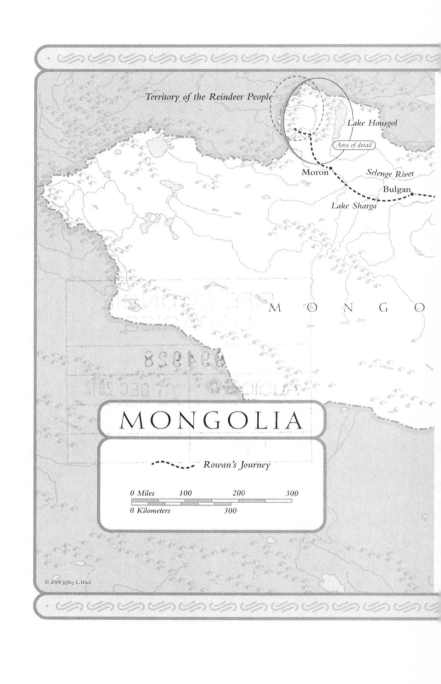

Territory of the Reindeer People

Lake Housgol

Area of detail

Moron

Selenge River

Bulgan

Lake Sharga

M O N G O

MONGOLIA

Rowan's Journey

0 Miles   100   200   300

0 Kilometers   300

© 2009 Jeffrey L. Ward

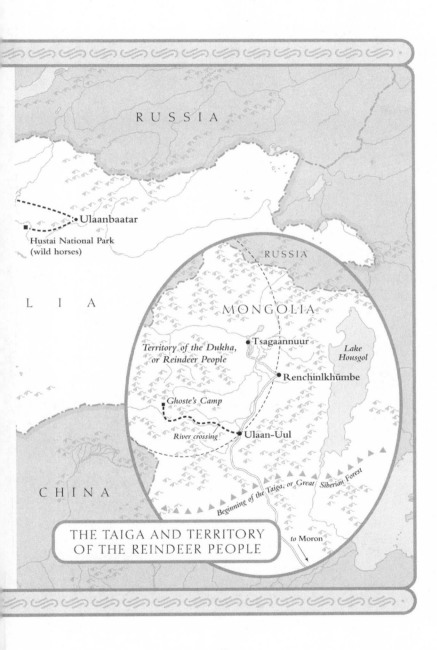

RUSSIA

Ulaanbaatar

Hustai National Park
(wild horses)

L I A

RUSSIA

MONGOLIA

Territory of the Dukha,
or Reindeer People

Tsagaannuur

Lake
Housgol

Renchinlkhümbe

Ghoste's Camp

River crossing

Ulaan-Uul

CHINA

Beginning of the Taiga, or Great Siberian Forest

THE TAIGA AND TERRITORY
OF THE REINDEER PEOPLE

to Moron

CONTENTS

9

PROLOGUE

The horse digs its back hooves into the dirt and gives one last, scrambling effort to reach the top of the rise. I lean forward, taking weight off the horse's straining back, trying not to crush my little boy, sitting in the saddle in front of me, trying not to look down at the dizzying chasm below. For one terrifying moment, the brown-and-white horse slips backward. Then, with a final heave, we are up on top of the high mountain pass.

"Hit Daddy!" My five-year-old son, Rowan, whips round, laughing, and aims a smack at my sore, bleeding lip. I flick my face away to the side. Above us are clouds and cool, rushing air. Behind us, and thousands of feet below, the great Siberian forest, stretching to infinity. To our front, a bare wilderness of mountain tundra.

"Snow!" Rowan points at the wide streak of white still clinging to the higher tops above us, where a pair of ravens fly, cawing madly on the wind. "Get down! Get down and play in the snow!"

Like a normal kid. Almost.

The horse, which Rowan has christened Blue, dips its head, stretching its neck after its effort. Before us rises a great stone cairn set with animal skulls, blue prayer scarves, and prayers scribbled in Cyrillic script on loose sheets of paper weighted down by heavy rocks, fluttering in the wind.

Somewhere in this mountain vastness is the shaman of the reindeer people. Half a year it has taken to track him down. Will he heal my son? Will he even know how?

■ ■ ■ ■

PART ONE

■ ■ ■ ■

1
THE SEVEN-YEAR CHILD

In April 2004 my son, Rowan, was diagnosed with autism. The feeling was like being hit across the face with a baseball bat. Grief, shame — this weird, irrational shame, as if I had somehow cursed this child by giving him my faulty genes, condemned him to a lifetime of living as an alien because of me. Of watching, horrified, as he began to drift away to another place, separated from me as if by thick glass, or the see-through barrier of dream.

I had to find a way into his world, into his mind. I found it, amazingly, through a horse, Betsy.

But let's start at the beginning.

December 27, 2001. A year when the world was still reeling from the destruction of the Twin Towers in New York. My tall, dark-eyed, dark-haired — and eight months pregnant — wife, Kristin, and I were at a friend's house, having tea, when, like something straight out of a movie, she suddenly went pale and stood up.

"Oh God!" she said, looking down over her swelling belly. A pool of fluid lay thick and clear on the parquet flooring.

"Jesus!" I said, and reached for the phone.

One high-speed rally drive up the rainy freeway later (commuters honking and flashing lights at my crazed lane changes), we were being fast-forwarded through reception to an emergency C-section. Kristin was screaming as the contractions began to come so fast that there was no trough between them, only one long, endlessly drawn-out, tearing agony that brought shrieks of an eerie, crowlike intensity from somewhere deep in her suffering body. She wasn't dilating properly, and Rowan was lying breech. We'd meant to have him turned that week. "No time for that now!" quipped the doctor as Kristin was wheeled into the operating room. Then, to me: "Want to watch?"

Out the window went all our holistic natural childbirth ideas. It could not have been more clinical. And I, usually too squeamish to look at blood and guts, found myself watching intently as the doctors sliced Kristin open, moved her innards to the side, and pulled out a blue, surprisingly large human being, my only thought being "Please, Lord, let him be in one piece."

A short time later, while they brought Kristin around from the anesthetic, I stood alone in the private room with Rowan (almost seven pounds, despite being a full month premature), looking down at him as he lay, belly up, wrapped in towels, in a kind of plastic tray. His blue eyes were half open, looking into mine; his tiny right hand clasped around my index finger. The clock on the wall showed a few minutes past midnight.

Which meant, I realized with a start, that Rowan had decided to come into the world exactly seven years *to the day* that Kristin and I first met, and almost — once I'd figured out the time difference — to the very hour that we had first spoken.

Which was surprising, because when I met her, she hadn't wanted to talk to me at all.

"Oh God, another hippy," she'd thought to herself on seeing me, and turned away. It had been in southern India, in the town of Mysore. I'd been hired to write a guidebook to the region. She was there doing research for her psychology Ph.D. I, with hair down to the middle of my back, had been trekking up in the rainforests of the Western

17

Ghats, staying with hill tribes. She had been interviewing Indian girls bound for arranged marriages, trying to find out at what point they put aside their natural sense of what was fair and accepted a system in which wives must bow to their husbands' every whim. Though we had not yet become acquainted, we could not have been more different — Kristin was a suburban girl from California, and I was British, born to southern African parents, brought up partly in the center of London, partly on a remote farm, training horses.

But the moment I saw her, stretched out in a beach chair by the pool of the Southern Star Hotel, all long-legged, tan, and languid, like some fashion model on the beach at Cannes, with strange sparkling lights dancing in her black eyes, a voice in my head, accompanied by an almost physical pull of intuition under my diaphragm, said, clear as day, *That's your wife.*

No, I thought; *can't be.* And I jumped into the water.

But when I surfaced, the voice was still there. *That* is *your wife. Go talk to her. Now.*

In fact, it took a full twenty-four hours before she deigned to talk to me. By then I had only one day left in that town, being honor-bound to move on the next day to continue my guidebook job's busy itinerary. I went into a charm offensive, tinged with desperation, and managed at last to get her to spend an evening with me. Unable to resist the impulse, I told her what the voice in my head had said, bracing myself for the inevitable "You're crazy." Which, predictably, was the first thing out of her mouth.

Then she surprised me. "But then, I'm pretty crazy myself. In fact," she added, "I wouldn't touch me with a ten-foot pole."

It turned out to be quite a story: the previous year she had left her husband for another man, and now she was waiting for that man to leave his wife. Except he was dragging his heels. "I'm messed up," she said. "I'm the first to admit it. But I'm not available."

Which of course for me was like a red rag to a bull.

I pulled out every stop and managed to persuade her to come (along with some friends of hers) to the next big town, where I had a swanky hotel room for free and where we could all camp out. And from that moment, despite some initial resistance on her part, we embarked on seven years of high adventure: through the remoter corners of India, then to London, where she took a year off from working on her Ph.D. to come live with me, then to southern Africa for another guidebook contract, and finally — when she had to return to the United States to finish her degree — to Berkeley, California. We married, and I, being a travel writer and therefore able to live pretty much anywhere, became the ideal academic's husband, following her first to Colorado, where she got a postdoctoral position, and finally to the University of Texas at Austin. Or rather, to the heat-soaked, cicada-singing countryside of oaks and meadows just outside, so that I could indulge my dream of having horses for the first time since my boyhood, which I'd largely spent in the saddle. In fact, ever since early childhood, when my parents would find me out in the horse pasture on my great-aunt's farm, happily talking to the big beasts, I'd been riding semiprofessionally, breaking and training horses of all kinds. Truth be told, I was something of a fanatic.

Meantime, I went back and forth repeatedly between the United States and Africa, researching a book on my family's bizarre connection by marriage to the last hunter-gatherers of southern Africa, the Bushmen of the Kalahari, and writing about their strange culture of healing through the use of trance and their struggles to regain their lost hunting grounds, taken from them to make national parks and diamond mines. Just as the resulting book was published, Kristin announced she was pregnant.

We decided to name the child Rowan, after the tree that, in all the old British folk-tales, is the tree of white magic. Keep rowan wood in your pocket and the bad fairies can't touch you. For a middle name we chose Besa, after a Bushman healer I had become close to. And so it was that, shortly after midnight and two days after Christmas 2001, I found myself, dressed in green scrubs and shower hat, lost in wonder at this physical result of my love for the girl I had seen by a pool in India seven years before.

"Seven years to the day," I whispered aloud. "Welcome to the world, Rowan Besa Isaacson, with your blue, blue eyes. What adventures have you got in store for us?"

We brought him home on a day of rare Texas frost to confront the reality of parent-hood without the help of the sassy but motherly nurses who had looked after us in the hospital — for like most new parents, we knew nothing about child care. We could not believe the gift of this extraordinary little being that was our son. We obsessed about not rolling over and crushing him at night, checking every ten minutes when he was asleep that he was still breathing, worrying that he might not eat enough. Fat chance of that; he barely let the nipple out of his mouth, even when asleep. Like most new babies, Rowan slept half the time, goo-gooed and gagaed adorably the rest of his waking moments, then pummeled away at his mother's breasts like a miniature sumo wrestler before going to sleep again. He didn't cry much. We were amazed at how easy this parenting business was. What was all the complaining about?

Even when Kristin had to drag herself back to work from her short maternity leave, it didn't seem too tough. I'd take a bottle or two of breast milk from the fridge, put Rowan in the baby carrier, and head over to my neighbor's barn, where I was training a young horse, working it in the round pen while Rowan dribbled and giggled and occasionally spit up on my chest. I told myself I wouldn't push him to become a horseman. But I was lying, of course, already imagining how I'd teach him to ride, share adventures on horseback with him. For her part, Kristin, a long-term Buddhist, indulged her own fond images of someday engaging in long spiritual and philosophical discussions with her intelligent, spiritually and intellectually precocious son. Like all new parents, we projected our own dreams and desires onto our kid, and projected hard.

Rowan was an early walker and began to say his first words before he had turned a year. We were overjoyed, reassured by his precocity, flattered to quiet hubris by the reflection of what we fancied were our own superior intellects. We were only vaguely miffed when, instead of enunciating "Mummy" and "Daddy" for his first names, he learned the names of all the *Thomas the Tank Engine* trains. "Hen-*ree!*" he'd say, turning to me with a strange, intense passion and holding up the little green toy engine whose name was indeed Henry. "Hen-*ree!*"

He'd make beautiful patterns of the trains, and of toy animals, spending hour upon hour lining them up in surprisingly coordinated order by size and color on the living room floor. We applauded his aesthetic sense, this early and seemingly instinctual grasp of form, and fantasized about whether he'd end up an artist, like my mother, or perhaps an architect, like my father. When his always obsessive breastfeeding began to be accompanied by strange yogic posturing (sometimes resulting in his twisting right off the nipple and flopping onto the floor, almost tearing poor Kristin's breast off in the process), we nodded sagely, believing that our son evidently had the passionate nature of a writer or explorer. When he started to babble bits of dialogue from his *Thomas the Tank Engine* videos, we smiled, thinking he'd be an early conversationalist.

When Rowan was eighteen months old, Kristin, as a psychologist trained in child development, began to be a little worried. Rowan wasn't pointing. Nor had he added any words to his limited vocabulary, beyond echoing back bits of dialogue from the kids' videos he watched (what autism experts call echolalia). Nor did he show his toys to people, as many infants do. When someone said his name, he would not look around.

Concerned that he might have some kind of speech delay, we contacted the state's early childhood intervention services and organized — responsible parents, you see — a weekly visit from a speech therapist. Rowan ignored the therapist, but after a month or two he could say "It's Woody," when holding up his *Toy Story* doll. He could say *"Toy Story,"* when he wanted to watch the damn thing (about eight hundred times a day). He could say "It's an elephant," when looking at a toy elephant or a live one on the TV screen. But he couldn't say "Mommy" or "Daddy" or "Hello" or "I'm hungry" or "Can I have" or "Yes" or even the usual toddler's staple, "No."

If he wanted something, he grabbed your hand and led you to it: the fridge for food (only crunchy foods, like bacon and apples), the VCR for *Toy Story* or animal documentaries (choose the wrong one and he'd simply scream till you got it right).

Both Kristin's and my parents lived thousands of miles away. "You're too indulgent with him," complained Rowan's grandmothers when they came on their rare visits and saw him ignore us whenever we tried to engage him. "You just let him get away with things. Can't you be firmer?"

"I don't know," said Kristin worriedly. "I don't know."

Then the tantrums started. Not the usual "I'm frustrated because I don't understand/ can't get what I want" tantrums that all kids have. We already had those. Now came something new: a demonic, almost possessed edge, materializing suddenly, out of nowhere. One minute he could be happily lining up his toys or playing with the garden hose (obsessive about water too), or even asleep; the next he'd be screaming, half in rage, half in seeming agony. Sometimes for hours. Why?

Something had to be wrong — but we never considered that it might be autism. I mean, he was so emotionally connected. He looked you in the eye. He came to us, arms outstretched, for hugs. Friends tried to re-assure us: "Oh, I didn't talk till I was four years old." "Cesarean babies are often slower to develop." "Try speech therapy." Well, we *had* been doing that, and it hadn't made any headway with him. We tried oc-cupational therapy. Rowan ignored those therapists too. He raged and cried when made to sit with them, then went back to lining up his animals, his engines, yelling "*Toy Story!*" and "It's an elephant!" but never anything more. Then even these scripts began to come less and less fre-quently. He would stare off into space. Go silent for long stretches of time, until one of the strange, demonic-possession tantrums would descend and consign him and us to an earsplitting, emotionally shattering domestic hell. Our boy, our beautiful boy, was floating away from us, and there was nothing we could do.

Until one night, when Rowan was about two and a half, Kristin went upstairs, got on the computer, and typed in "autism, early signs of." She found a link for "Likely signs that your child has autism," put out by a well-known university, and clicked on it.

There they were:

- Lack of showing toys to parents or other adults
- Lack of gestures: pointing, reaching, waving, showing
- Lack of sharing interest or enjoyment with others
- Repetitive movements with objects
- Lack of appropriate eye gaze
- Lack of response to name
- Unusual prosody (rhythm and intonation of language)
- Repetitive movements or posturing of the body
- Loss of words or other skills
- Babbling instead of talking
- No meaningful two-word sentences by twenty-four months that are unscripted

Rowan had good eye contact. Apart from that, he had every single sign.

2
INTO THE INFERNO

We had a special-needs kid. We had become one of those families.

Kristin went into overdrive, drawing on her psychology-professor credentials to fast-track her way through the maze of Web information, then as now the main source of help for most autism families. Much of the information was conflicting, and piecing together the complex mosaic of things we'd need to get Rowan officially diagnosed and therefore eligible for whatever meager state benefits could be found turned out to involve a nightmare of red tape. We'd need two independent assessments from two different child psychologists, another from a neurologist, and a fourth from the school district's special-education coordinator. All of which would have to be paid for by our insurance, which in and of itself was going to involve — as Kristin found out after the first tentative phone call — any amount of jousting to negotiate. Not that the insurance would pay for any actual therapies. That was up to us. But what therapies, exactly? The Web's autism universe could not have been more confusing. The most effective, it seemed — at least in terms of published data — involved an almost Pavlovian approach known as applied behavioral analysis, or ABA, which rewarded kids with being allowed to do things that interested them and denied them access to those things unless they completed tasks, usually mimicking a therapist who was modeling social scripts like "How are you? I'm fine. My name is . . ."

"It looks like it really works," said Kristin, with the slightly crazed look of one who has spent too long in front of a computer screen. The only problem was that it demanded an in-home regime of forty hours a week with a full-time therapist who would set a daily activity schedule that we must never deviate from, even when the therapist was not there. And which would cost about $50,000 a year.

"Fifty grand?" I was incredulous. "How are we supposed to come up with that?"

"I've sent some e-mails to the special-ed department at the university," said Kristin, her voice wooden. "I can get the assessments arranged for next week, and someone to come out and start ABA."

"But with what money?"

"We'll find it. But damn it, Ru, this is where I'm so mad. It says that the earlier you start the interventions, the better the chance the child has of total recovery, and we've wasted almost a year thinking it was just speech delay . . ."

"Total recovery? That's even a possibility?"

"So the ABA people say."

"But it's a brain thing. I mean . . . I mean, Rowan's retarded. You can't *recover* from autism."

I remembered the autistic kids I'd known as a child in London. I'd been sent briefly to a Waldorf school, where "normal" and mentally and physically handicapped kids had all been placed alongside each other. Two autistic boys stood out in the memory. One, Simon, regularly used to strangle the other kids and had to be pulled off them by force now and then. He'd stand and flap and screech. He had once set fire to the school. The other one, an older boy called Robert, used to get his penis out in the middle of the crowded hallways, masturbate wildly, and shout "Cock-a-doodle-doo!" at the top of his voice.

Would that be Rowan? I looked at him where he was sitting on the kitchen floor — such a beautiful child, with his dark blue eyes containing an inner circle of green, his wavy brown hair, his athletic little body and face full of devilish charm — dragging the cat around by her back legs. Strangely, she tolerated anything he did to her, as did friends' dogs and other pets. He seemed to have a thing for animals, and they for him. I mean, I was good with animals too, especially horses, but not like him. He seemed to have a direct line.

"Apparently they can recover," Kristin went on. "*If* you get in early enough. And those bastards at the county early childhood intervention unit, they must have *known.* I called them today and they as good as admitted it! Said they'd had their suspicions but didn't want to label him! Label him! Ha — didn't want to have to recommend him for more services, more like. Almost a whole year we've wasted!"

"And what about the pediatrician — you'd have thought he'd have noticed something."

"Well, he didn't, did he? We're on our own, it seems."

And we were. As Rowan became more and more dysfunctional, even earning a living became hard. I stopped riding, deliberately keeping Rowan away from horses because he was so unpredictable. Our assumption that Rowan would share a life of adventure with us was firmly dashed. Instead, life had suddenly become a mechanical drudgery of driving from one therapy and assessment appointment to another and dealing with insurance companies, therapists, and Rowan's ever-mounting, inexplicable tantrums. Tantrums on the street, in which his screaming once even drowned out the noise of a jackhammer crew, who downed tools and just stared in awe as Rowan, a tiny human decibel machine, hurled himself to the ground and began to bang his head so hard against the concrete we had to restrain him, head and heels thudding into the hard paving as if he were an epileptic.

Sometimes his rages would be accompanied by projectile vomiting, like that of the child in *The Exorcist*. People would offer to call the emergency services. Or tut-tut their disgust at these terrible parents who let their kid get away with such abominable public behavior, sometimes stopping to tell us we should be ashamed of ourselves, letting a child behave like that on the street or in the store. It was small consolation to snarl "He's autistic — what's *your* excuse?" and see them retreat, embarrassed and guilty. This constant barrage of noise, of emotional violence, of utter powerlessness, had become our whole life. Social life, even our sex life — for we were so exhausted at the end of each day — began to fall by the wayside. The glue of passion that held us together was starting to come undone.

However, through our cyberspace trawling we did discover the likely cause of these strange, overwhelming tantrums — that they were probably neurological in origin; his nervous system was almost certainly overactive. Autistic brains, it turns out, have a much greater number of nerve cells than "neurotypical" brains. The result can be extreme sensory overload. A breath of wind on Rowan's cheek could feel like fire from a flame-thrower. The fluorescent lights of a supermarket or daycare facility could look like lights being strobed at one million times a second. His clothes or bedcovers could suddenly, if the wrong neurological switch was thrown, feel like lead weights or burning napalm. Not that this helped to console him when the firestorms went raging through his brain and body. But it helped us to understand a little what we were dealing with. We and millions of other parents: the past fifteen years had, we learned, seen an enormous, almost 1000 percent, spike in the numbers of autistic kids showing up in the industrialized world. Why?

Many of these were kids like Rowan, with autism-like symptoms but whose profiles didn't quite fit the classic autism model. There was even a new name for their condition: pervasive developmental disorder not otherwise specified, or PDD (NOS). An increasing number of scientists were suggesting that the cause might be a gene-environment interaction: perhaps genetically susceptible children were reacting to an excessive buildup of toxic heavy metals in the environment, especially mercury poisoning, which is known to produce symptoms very close to autism. But no one knew for sure. Dr. Simon Baron-Cohen, the U.K.'s leading autism researcher (and cousin to the famous Borat), described PDD (NOS), with classic British understatement, as "the part of the autism spectrum we understand the least."

PDD (NOS). It sounded so scientific. All it meant was *really like autism but not entirely and so therefore we don't quite know.*

The good news, supposedly, was that if something was caused biologically, it could in theory be treated the same way. Chelation, or the introduction into the body of a chemical agent that would bind to the toxins and take them out with the body's waste, was one treatment offered. We were no strangers to this — by an odd coincidence, Kristin had herself been on chelation treatment for some years, having been diagnosed at age thirty with a rare condition called Wilson's disease, which prevents the body from processing copper. If she did not take zinc several times per day (copper binds to the zinc and then leaves the system with it), she would eventually die of cirrhosis of the liver. So began an endless and expensive round of appointments with specialists — Rowan screaming loud enough to break glass through every second of them — to set up our son for chelation.

Then there were antivirals. Studies suggested that some PDD kids had nervous systems overwhelmed by viral activity, perhaps exacerbated by childhood vaccinations, which caused inflammation of their nervous systems and which, through treatment with antivirals such as Valtrex, the drug used to combat herpes, could be reduced, allowing correct amounts of neurological information to reach the brain. Some parents reported miraculous results.

We had Rowan's DNA tested, and it turned out that he lacked a gene that produced an enzyme called glutathione, which helps the body metabolize toxins. So along with giving him crushed-up Valtrex and rubbing his skin morning and evening with a horrible chelation ointment that stank of rotten eggs and that he violently resisted, we had to give him glutathione daily. As well as a score of other supplements, because chelation took good things out along with the bad. Suddenly we became one of those families with a medicine cabinet stuffed full of vitamins and minerals, pharmaceuticals and sundry homeopathic supplements, all of which had to be consumed daily. To get this horrid cocktail into him required a twice-daily dose of chocolate milk, sugared to the max to disguise the taste — which of course made his hyperactivity and tantrumming that much worse.

But there was one other environmental solution at our disposal, a free and readily available one that Rowan, far from resisting, actually loved: the woods behind our house. Whenever a tantrum happened during daylight hours and we were home, there was one thing I could do: take Rowan out into the woods. Immediately his screams would lessen and out he'd fly, flitting between the trees like some happy woodland elf.

Now, Texas is not without its risks. There's a local saying: "If it doesn't bite, stick, or sting, it ain't from Texas." You don't go wandering blindly into tall brush without a swishing stick to warn the rattlesnakes and give them time to move out of the way. And those aren't the only snakes: cottonmouths in the water, shy but lethal coral snakes under stones, and copperheads disguised among the fallen leaves. We have fire ants, scorpions, and poison ivy, oak, and sumac. Hornets the size of your thumb, killer bees, black widow and brown recluse spiders that, if they bite you, mortify the flesh and leave a gaping, leprous hole. Not to mention prickly pear, pencil cactus hidden in long grass, sharp-leaved agarita. Not a place to let an autistic kid run wild.

But Rowan, as preternaturally agile as he was cognitively delayed, had by the age of eighteen months learned his way around the trails in back of our little red house and was able to find his way back home from any point within half a mile of our door. In the course of that time he had blundered into fire ant piles and had learned, after the swarm had ravaged his fat little leg with searing bites, to leap or avoid mounds of soft red earth. He had come face to face with a couple of snakes and learned to look but not touch. He knew not to put his hand under stones or into holes after the first wasp stung him. It *was* a risk to let him run. But a risk worth taking, because always, within seconds of entering the trees, the screams would lessen, fade, and finally disappear when he found a patch of sand to run his fingers through, a piece of variegated bark to look at, or when he sat down on the trail to become lost in the intricate lattice patterns of a dead yellow leaf.

We had some regular routes: a fallen elm with branches that could be easily climbed; an ancient mustang grapevine, thick as my arm, that Rowan had discovered could be used as a swing; a wide cattle pasture surrounded by a natural parkland of wild pecan trees, where a creek ran sweetly over rocks in a small waterfall and the half-wild cows gathered in a defensive circle and looked at us as if we were aliens dropped from another planet. Here, at least, Rowan was at peace.

Then there were zoos. Austin had two of them, each quite small, each something under an hour's drive from home. We decided to take Rowan there after noticing his intense interest in the wildlife documentaries we sometimes brought home from the video store, not to mention his fascination with any small bug or critter he found crawling around outside. The zoos were an instant success, but he wasn't at peace there. Quite the opposite — he'd enter a hyperactive phase, going everywhere at a hard trot, then stopping and running in circles by a cage of ring-tailed lemurs while a mountain lion that clearly regarded him as prey looked longingly at him through the wire, flicking its tail with hunger. He'd writhe on the ground and babble in front of the bemused peacocks that wandered between the cages. He'd try to climb the fences — he was once halfway up and over a crocodile's enclosure before I grabbed him, much to the croc's disappointment, no doubt — then tantrum violently when prevented, often vomiting or shitting his pants at the same time, so that other parents and visitors would cluck disapprovingly and move away from the noise (Kristin and I were becoming inured to public censure). But he was *into* being there. Animals and nature were what motivated him. That much was clear.

And although now, when he was almost three, he could still barely talk, conversely he also seemed to love words — not to communicate, but the single words themselves, sometimes strung together in half-babbled lists of animals or *Thomas the Tank Engine* train characters. Kristin spent hours each night reading to him. It was impossible to tell how much was sinking in, but it was clear that he loved it, curled up next to her, letting the words flow over him like warm water. Was it just the comfort of having her close, of hearing her voice? Or was his imagination latching on to the story in some way unique to himself? We could not tell.

Then one day Kristin had a brainwave. She got on the Internet and ordered about two dozen animal posters, because animal names seemed to be what Rowan recited most; she ordered photographs of every kind of mammal, bird, and reptile if the image was striking enough to arrest her eye as she trawled the thumbnails. When the posters arrived in the mail, she took them all off to be laminated, and then, one long afternoon while Rowan was at his special-ed class in the local public school (where the teachers regarded him as cute but unreachable), she filled the walls and ceiling of his room with animals.

Rowan was overjoyed, jumping up and down, clapping his hands, and laughing with delight as soon as he went upstairs that night. I went in to check on them later and found him and Kristin lying side by side, looking up and pointing at each picture, reciting the names of the animals together: "Gemsbok oryx, brown bear, redheaded barbet, saltwater crocodile, baby panda, mommy zebra and baby zebra, Siberian tiger . . ."

Within a couple of evenings Kristin was starting to make up stories about the animals each night as they lay there together. "Once upon a time," she began. "There was a little boy called . . ."

"Rowan!"

"That's right, darling! That's you. And one day Rowan was walking in the woods behind his house when he met a very nice gemsbok oryx riding along on a bicycle . . ."

Could you kick-start an imagination? We were determined at least to try.

So between the zoos, which brought out his obsessive side but tired him out, and the woods, which calmed him, absorbed him, and where no one could censure us, we had our points of refuge. Then came the day he got away from me.

It happened after his first applied behavioral analysis, or ABA, session. It was a terrible day. The woman therapist was sympathetic, had autistic children of her own that she had, she said, treated successfully with ABA. But she insisted that in order to concentrate sufficiently to be able to imitate her in simple movements or phrases, Rowan had to be in a closed room with her, with no distractions. No matter how much he cried, threw himself at the door, panicked at this sudden, inexplicable confusion and confinement, he was not to be allowed to go out or pick up a toy or other comforting object until he had fulfilled the tasks prescribed. It was like watching him being tortured. He clearly had no idea what he was being asked to do. At the end of an hour (an expensive hour), the therapist informed us that from now on we were going to have to schedule our lives rigidly with precise activities at precise times, "with no deviation — otherwise it undoes all the good work," including sticking to an hourly chart, to be posted on the fridge, that Rowan and Kristin and I would all do homage to each morning and consult throughout the day so that Rowan would come to understand the meaning of structure.

I could not see how we could possibly adhere to such a schedule. My work didn't allow it, nor did Kristin's. Nor did the reality of leading a life where, because our families both lived thousands of miles away, we often had to get on planes and deal with the vagaries of travel. If there was ever a family that required flexibility, it was us.

And then there was the cost — not to mention the fact that Rowan obviously hated the therapy and regarded it as inexplicable punishment.

When the session was over, I took him for a walk, wanting to clear both our heads. One moment I was sauntering behind him as he trotted along the familiar woodland trail, the next I was sprinting in sudden alarm as he swung unexpectedly left through the trees in a direction he'd never taken before, out of the woods and into the narrow belt of rough pasture that separated our property from my neighbor Stafford's horse pasture. Quicker than I could make up the distance, Rowan was through the wire fence and in among the small herd of four horses, who happened to be grazing right there on the other side. Laughing delightedly, he threw himself onto the ground, belly up, right in front of the alpha mare, the herd leader, a big bay quarter horse called Betsy. I froze. Any sudden movement — his or mine — could spook her and leave him trampled and broken on the ground.

I knew this mare. She was quiet to ride but was famously grumpy toward the other horses, over whom she was the unquestioned boss. The kind who wouldn't think twice about planting two hooves in the face of any importunate herd member or of whisking a novice rider straight back to the barn.

She stood stock-still, as did the other four horses, breathing through her nostrils, unsure whether or not to be alarmed by this strange little human wriggling at her feet. Then she dipped her head to Rowan's soft, writhing form, so close and so dangerously exposed to her hammer-hard hooves. Dipped her head, and mouthed with her lips. The sign of equine submission.

Watching, moving slowly toward her so as not to spook her, I knew I was witnessing something extraordinary. The mare was spontaneously submitting to the child on the ground before her. In all the years that I had been training horses, I had never seen this happen. My son had some kind of direct line to the horse.

And then I cried, the tears coming silent and unbidden on that humid June day, because I thought: "He's got it. He's got the horse gene. But he's autistic. I'll never be able to share it with him. Never be able to teach him to ride. Never share this joy with my son."

It's stunning how wrong a parent can be.

That same month I had to leave home to

accompany a delegation of Bushmen from the Kalahari Desert to the United Nations. These past few years my involvement with these peaceful hunter-gatherers had developed from writing about their plight to full-on advocacy as their situation worsened — there were wholesale evictions to make way for new diamond mines, accompanied by beatings and torture. The group that had been most affected had asked me to help, and over the past year I had raised money to bring a party of six Bushmen to the United States to plead their case before the UN. I had thought that this trip, dropping into the chaos of our new life as autism parents, would only add to our stress. In fact, something entirely different happened.

The Bushmen had timed their visit to coincide with a convention of traditional healers, tribal leaders, and shamans that was being held just outside L.A., up in the mountains of Big Bear, where California's majestic Sierra Nevada comes down to the Mojave Desert. Representatives of tribes from all over Africa, the Amazon, the Arctic, from India, Southeast Asia, and Australasia, from Native America, the Caribbean, and Siberia — from everywhere that the indigenous life still existed — were coming together for this event, aptly called the

Gathering. The Bushmen wanted to attend before heading east to play politics, in order to get a dose of *nxum* (their word for spiritual energy) to ready them for the political tasks to follow. So I made the necessary arrangements, and because it was going to involve spending five days in one place, I had Kristin and Rowan join us there.

I wondered silently if attending this gathering and being exposed to so many healers and shamans might have some beneficial effect on Rowan. During my years of working as a journalist among the Bushmen, whose whole culture revolved around healing through the use of trance, I had seen a number of apparently miraculous healings of various kinds of physical ailments.

In fact, even before working with the Bushmen I'd been exposed to other kinds of natural healing, even though it had never been a subject that had interested me in my youth. The first time had had nothing to do with indigenous tribes or far-flung locations but had happened through horses in, of all places, the tame, semisuburban countryside of the British Home Counties. When I was twenty-five I rode horses for a woman who lived in Berkshire, just west of London. One of her horses was a rare jewel — athletic enough to compete internationally, yet kind enough to look after someone who could not ride and take that person safely around the farm; not unlike Betsy, in fact. One spring this horse got a strange kidney disorder and, though not old, in a matter of weeks became a rack of bones. The vet, completely nonplussed, shrugged his shoulders, said there was nothing more he could do, and suggested we find a faith healer.

I had never even heard of faith healing before, at least not as something that might actually exist outside of stories or movies. But with this beautiful horse dying before our eyes, the owner and I started making inquiries — inquiries that, sadly, came to naught. Eventually, unable to look anymore at the living corpse her horse had become, the owner called the knacker man and asked me to hold the poor beast while the grisly business was done. Now, I had taken horses to be put down before — old arthritic ones unable to hobble out of their stables anymore, horses with badly broken legs. It's always tragic, but there is a sense with horses at this point of old age or injury that they are ready to end their suffering.

This horse was not. When the knacker man appeared, the animal backed off, rolled his eyes, and whinnied. It was as if he wasn't ready to go. He wasn't my horse, so the decision wasn't mine to make — I was just doing as his owner wanted. However, as the man put the gun to the frightened horse's head, I felt wrong somehow. The bolt pierced the brain; the horse went down. It was over. The nagging feeling remained.

A few weeks later, at a party in London, I met a television producer who'd just finished a series. What on? I asked. Animal healers. My heart gave a jump. "Where were you a month ago?" I asked, and I told her our sad story. Then, as an afterthought, I asked if any of the healers had seemed genuine.

There was one, she said — the only one who had not cared whether he got on television or not. A strange little old man in his seventies, she said, who lived in a trailer and mostly healed horses. She and her team had apparently followed him for a year as he laid hands on a valuable thoroughbred brood mare with lymphoma whom the vets had completely given up on. At the end of the year the vets had confirmed that the cancer had gone, inexplicably, and now, she said, these same vets referred people to this healer whenever they thought they could not treat or save an animal.

I got the phone number of one of the vets

in question, who confirmed everything the producer had said. Then I rang several horse magazines and asked if they'd let me follow this healer through some "bullet job" cases and see if the horses recovered. I got the green light from one, rang the healer, whose name was Charles Siddle, and arranged to follow him around for two months, over the course of which I saw him take on several cases: a horse that had burned its lungs in a barn fire, another that had broken part of a vertebra (usually an instant case for the bullet), and another with mental problems — well bred but too vicious to ride. In each case the horse was back in work at the end of a few months. And when I followed up a year later, all were still doing well.

I asked Charles one day what it was, this "energy" that he said he used to heal the horses. He replied, "It's love, Rupert. Just love. Pure and simple."

And with that I thought my strange brush with the world of healing was over. I had written and published my articles and moved on to other stories. Then I began spending time with the Bushmen of the Kalahari. Every ten days or so the clans whose land claims I was following would make a fire and gather round it to clap and sing in polyphonic chant, until, the song and rhythm having reached a certain pitch of intensity, the healers would step into the circle between the chorus and the fire. There, with slow, measured, stamping steps, they would dance, until the trance began to come upon them. At this point they'd reach into the fire, pull out red-hot coals, and rub them on their faces and heads, sometimes even swallow them, to no apparent ill effect. Soon after that the trance would intensify, sometimes with a great roar of pain, occasionally accompanied by a great gout of blood from the nose or mouth. And then they would start to sing, and the healings would begin.

Time and again I saw it: a child with whooping cough, the healer running his or her old hands over the child as it sat wide-eyed in the firelight; an old woman with legs swollen from rheumatoid arthritis, the healer pulling at the pain-disfigured limbs and sobbing as if the pain were being transferred directly into his own body. And then, in the cool light of dawn, the healers and the chorus having kept the dance going all through the night, the child would have stopped coughing, the old woman would get up and walk away on legs no longer swollen.

Once, when I was in the middle of interviewing an old clan leader about his attempts to regain the hunting grounds taken from his people, accompanied by a white South African woman called Cait, who was known to the clan, as the translator, an old, old woman named Antas came swaying across the dunes. She was singing to herself and — despite the fact that an interview was in progress — walked right into the middle of our group, took Cait around the waist, laid her down in the sand, and knelt over her, singing, moving her gnarled hand in circles just above Cait's abdomen while we all just stared. This was early in my dealings with the Bushmen, so I didn't recognize what I was seeing and thought the old woman was drunk. Later, Cait told me that a few days before, she'd been diagnosed with stomach cancer, but she had told no one outside the family. "Antas wasn't drunk," she said. "What you saw was a healing." When I asked who had contacted this old Bushman woman to let her know of her condition, Cait shrugged. "No one told her," she said. "I haven't seen her for months." Four years later I found out that Cait had never had to undergo surgery. The tumor had simply gone away.

But my most intense experience of all had been with an old healer called Besa — a small, owl-eyed man who hardly spoke and would during his trance take on the movements of animals, snorting like a gemsbok or kudu, then becoming unmistakably a giraffe or an ostrich, using, he said, something of the power of these animals for his ceremonies. One night, while dancing for the woman whose legs were all swollen with rheumatoid arthritis, he put his hands on me and suddenly began to shout, *"Leopards! Leopards!"* in his own language.

Perhaps two minutes later, first one, then another leopard growled somewhere just outside the firelight. I didn't want to believe it at first, despite the fact that all the dogs rushed up growling, hackles up, then cowered, whining. The leopards continued to growl and cough out in the night, too close for comfort, while the old man danced, putting his hands on me, laughing while leopards coughed and growled in the darkness and the dogs whined and howled in rage and fear. In the morning we saw the spoor of the two leopards a mere fifteen yards from where we had been sitting, their tracks crossing and recrossing each other in a circle. Later Besa revealed that he'd been showing me "my animal"; everyone had such a spirit or totem animal, and the leopard was mine. "Be sure to harness it for the good," I was told, for leopard was quick to action but also quick to anger. And prone to being wayward.

Besa and I became close — close enough for me to end up naming Rowan after him. Gradually I came to look at shamanism and nature-based healing not as something exotic, otherworldly, but as something as ordinary and natural as humanity itself. Something that could perhaps work as a complement to Western medicine. So naturally, when Rowan arrived with Kristin at the Gathering, I wondered if anything would happen.

Immediately upon meeting Rowan, the six Bushmen of the visiting delegation dubbed him Little Besa, the older Besa being well known to them too. Touching as this was, however, at first the whole thing was predictably stressful. Rowan ran about among the feathered, painted, exotic delegates from the indigenous world, screaming endlessly and obsessively flinging his Woody and Jessie dolls over his shoulder with such violence that they occasionally brained startled passersby. He ran wildly into the various ceremonies being conducted under the tall California pines and kicked the healers' makeshift altars over, scattering their incense and sacred herbs, while Kristin and I chased after him, apologizing, embarrassed.

Some of the healers were irritated. But others — notably a man from Zimbabwe called Mandaza, a Carib Indian healer from Trinidad called Christo, a Guatemalan Mayan lady called Flore de Mayo, and of course the Bushmen themselves — asked if they could lay their hands on him. "He's one of us," said Mandaza simply, running his hands lightly up and over Rowan's head and down his spine, his gaze reassuring, steady. To my surprise, Rowan, far from freaking out, as he usually did when anyone unknown touched him, sat quietly, giggling, seeming to enjoy himself.

That evening Kristin and I took a walk through the woods, Rowan running ahead of us, chasing little birds that fluttered along the trail, babbling his usual unintelligible nonsense. It took us a moment or two to notice that the babble had all of a sudden changed into a shouted, real word. "Green!"

Kristin and I looked at each other.

"Green!" said Rowan again, from somewhere up the trail. We broke into a run to catch up.

"Green!" He was sitting by an isolated patch of feathery grass cropped short by deer. "Green," he said again. "Green grass."

Lucid speech that was original and not

just echolalia. Simple, but the real thing. Kristin and I were stunned.

Over the next two days Rowan started approaching people and showing his toys to them — appropriate toddler behavior he had hitherto never displayed. He became calmer, less hyperactive. But the strangest thing happened on the fourth day, as Kristin and I took a walk with him through the forest to a spot where a two-thousand-year-old Native American medicine wheel was laid out on the cliff edge above the campsite. Kristin and I were deep in conversation. To my huge relief, she — after some soul-searching — had decided that she didn't think ABA was going to be right for Rowan. Which was fine by me, for I had only agreed to try it further to please her, being convinced somehow that it was the wrong approach for Rowan, and that anyway we couldn't afford it. We were so busy going over it all that we didn't quite catch it at first when Rowan, perched up on my shoulders, suddenly said, loud and clear, "Through the forest to the medicine wheel."

We stopped dead. "What did you just say?"

"Through the forest to the medicine wheel," he repeated on cue.

It wasn't until he'd repeated it six times

that I really believed it. And it wasn't echoing — neither Kristin nor I had talked about
either the forest or the medicine wheel. We'd
just decided to take a walk "over there," and
hadn't said anything about our destination.
How did he know? What was going on? Had
the combined efforts of all those healers and
shamans produced a miracle cure?

No.

When I got back home, after the Bushmen had been heard at the UN and had
gathered the international legal support
needed to return to Africa ready to take
their government to court, I found that
Rowan had slipped back into his old nonsensical babble. His obsessions, his emotional and fecal incontinence (at three he
was still completely un-toilet-trained, despite the best efforts of his parents, his
grandmothers, and even paid professionals),
were all as bad as before, if not worse. There
was, however, one word he'd still been saying each day as he waited for me to come
home: "Horse."

So that evening, in the dying September
light, I took him walking in the woods once
more. Straightaway he headed through the
trees toward Stafford's horse pasture. This
time I didn't try to stop him. As soon as he
was through the fence, he made a beeline

for the old bay mare, the herd leader, Betsy, running up to her. Just as he had six weeks before, he threw himself on the ground in front of her hooves before I could stop him.

And again the miracle happened. Down went her head in voluntary obeisance. She began to lick and chew, spontaneously submitting to my autistic son, as before.

"Horse," he said delightedly as she snuffed at him. "Horse."

Two things seemed to have had a radically positive effect on my son, this extraordinary mare and the shamans at the Gathering. Well, the shamans had all gone home to their far-flung corners of the planet. But Betsy lived just next door. The following day I went over to Stafford's house and explained the eerie connection I had observed between his mare and my son. A southern gentleman of the old school, he gave me the key to his saddle room right then and there.

3
THE HORSE BOY

I broke all the rules. I had to. The first time I took Rowan to the barn to saddle Betsy up, he ran amok, climbing on the gates to the stalls, knocking over bottles and pots, repeatedly slamming the door to the feed room, chasing the black barn cat, yelling, squealing, and swinging his Woody and Jessie dolls around and around in both hands like medieval balls and chains, whapping them into the big brown mare as he ran up and down the barn's central alleyway. She stood like a rock, moving not a muscle, even when he darted in and out under her belly just as I placed the heavy Western saddle (an outsized one with room for us both) on her broad back. He pulled hard on her tail as I was tightening the cinch and grabbed at her lower lip even as I slipped the bit into her mouth.

"Do you want to get up?" I asked him, not expecting a response.

"Up!"

It was the first time I'd received a direct answer to a direct question. I bent down, scooped him up, and put him in the saddle. Immediately the flailing and shouting stopped. His grin was so wide it seemed to stretch off the sides of his face and into the air on either side. I put my foot in the stirrup and swung up behind him, one arm holding his solid little body steady, the other picking up the reins. I clicked my tongue and Betsy walked past the open gate toward the wide pasture dotted with post oaks. Then I paused, reining in for a moment, wondering which direction to take, how far to go.

"Go!" said Rowan, impatient.

"You want Betsy to go?"

"Go!" he confirmed. This was amazing.

"To the pond? Or to the woods?"

"Pond!"

I'd never experienced back-and-forth like this. So to the pond it was, Rowan giggling with delight as Betsy, a big-striding horse, walked briskly out across the pasture. Once at the water, we stopped again. A large blue heron was standing at the far end of the pond. It regarded us nervously for a moment, then flapped its great wings and took off. "Heron," said Rowan spontaneously.

He must have recognized it from books or wildlife videos. But again, this kind of commenting on his environment was new. Completely new. Scarcely able to believe what I was hearing, I turned Betsy around.

"Shall we go back to the barn or to our house?"

"Back to the barn!"

Was this echolalia or a real directive? We set off back toward the barn, the long green pasture stretching away before us. Then an idea hit me. It wasn't safe, but . . .

"Do you want to walk or run?"

"Run!"

Again, this could be echolalia, or did he mean it? Either way, he might as well know what the word meant. "Okay," I said, and clapped heels to Betsy's sides. Taken by surprise, she reared back on her hind legs, then rocketed forward. Rowan shrieked, clung to me, and laughed maniacally as the ground flew by beneath us in a green blur. I prayed to God that Betsy wouldn't stumble, shy, or trip. Seconds later we pulled up at the barn, Rowan's laughter pealing off its metal walls.

"Run!" he ordered me. "More *run!*"

I could hardly believe this, but run we did, Betsy flying joyously forward, Rowan laughing and laughing, his voice high and bright on the dry October breeze. We pulled up back down by the pond. Two crows flapped by, cawing.

"Caw caw caw!" I said. "Crows say caw!"

"Crows say caw."

Betsy shifted from foot to foot, ears flicking, waiting for the next order, ready to turn and fly into action once more. This was the first time I had ridden her. Yet already we had achieved a level of instinctive trust akin to the level you have to have with a horse when flying across the country after a pack of hounds or winning in the jumping ring — a connection that usually takes months, sometimes years, to build.

"How d'you spell *crow?*" I asked, then gave Betsy her head again, and she shot forward. "C-R-O-W!" I shouted as the wind whistled past our ears. We came to a halt in a clatter of hooves.

"Again!" shouted Rowan. "Run again!"

Poor Betsy. She probably hadn't been worked so hard in an age. As we stopped the next time, she was blowing, sweat running down her flanks. Gamely, she still hopped from leg to leg, waiting for the off. But if I ran her into the ground, this would be a short-lived experiment. We'd have to get her properly fit.

"Okay," I said. "Betsy's tired. Let's go

61

back to the barn and give her some food."

"C-R-O-W!" said Rowan.

"Spells *crow*," I said as we walked the heavily breathing mare back up the pasture, letting her stretch her neck. "I didn't think you'd taken that in."

We pulled up at the gate to the barn. "Whoa, Betsy," I said.

"Betsy stop," said Rowan. And then, quite spontaneously, "That was fun!"

I swung down, lifted Rowan down. "More Betsy!" he protested as I put him on the ground. This was more cognitive speech than I'd ever heard him utter. He began to cry.

Betsy stood, not moving a muscle, head down in the submissive gesture she seemed to adopt automatically whenever Rowan was on the ground near her.

"Aah. Don't worry. Betsy's tired now. Look, we'll give her a little bath with the hose, then come back and ride her tomorrow. Then we'll give Betsy some food."

"Give Betsy some food!" Rowan laughed, abruptly changing mood, jumping up and down as I put the saddle and bridle away, hung the sweaty saddle blankets up to dry, and turned the hose on Betsy's sweating flanks and back. Before putting her into her stall to feed her, I made a suggestion.

"Give Betsy a hug and say thank you for letting us ride."

Without hesitation, Rowan opened his arms and hugged Betsy's great brown head, which was hanging low enough for him to reach. Then he gave her a kiss. As he did so, an expression of extraordinary gentleness came over her — a certain softening of the eye, a blissful half-closing of the eyelid with its long black lashes. Something passed between them, some directness of communication that I, a neurotypical human, could never experience. Not this side of the spirit world, anyway.

We watched Betsy finish her grain, then snort, give her solid brown body a shake, and walk slowly back to the pasture where the other three horses in the herd — a sorrel filly called Benally, in fact Betsy's daughter, fully grown but unbroken; a brown-and-white paint colt called Batman; and Taz, a chestnut with white socks and a thick white blaze — all stood watching. As she reached the gateway where they clustered, Betsy's ears went back, and, teeth bared, she ran at them, scattering them, planting two back hooves hard on Taz's rump when he didn't wheel and get out of the way quick enough. It was as if she were saying, "I might be gentle with the kid, but don't think I'm not still the boss of you all!"

Rowan and I walked homeward, back across Stafford's pasture toward the woods behind our house, Rowan sitting on my shoulders and singing the alphabet song (something he spontaneously did sometimes, echoing his Baby Genius videos) with a strange hint of ecstasy in his voice: ABCD, breath, EFG, breath, *HIJKLMNOP*, breath, QRS, TUV, WX, Y, AND Z, breath, *"NOWI'VESUNGMYABC'S . . ."* and from there it faded into autism babble. But a joyful babble, delivered at the top of his voice as he bounced up and down on my shoulders and I picked my way through the grass toward the massed line of tall blackjack oaks that marked the beginning of our home woods. "That was fun!" said Rowan again. Was that from a movie? Or had he thought it up himself? Either way, he was using it appropriately, *telling me what he thought.*

The door into Rowan's world had opened a tiny crack.

At first these verbal leaps forward happened only on or immediately around Betsy. I'd arrive back at the house after riding, breathless with excitement at how much Rowan had talked, commented on his environment, only for him to retreat back into nonsense babble the moment he got through the door. For the first week or so it just didn't translate, and I would — understandably — get a rather deflating "That's lovely" from Kristin, who had not been there to see his progress. The same went for his special-ed teachers when I dropped Rowan off at school. Not that you could really call it school — it was more like glorified day care, with a bunch of autistic and other special-needs kids all crammed into a cinder-block room with no windows, fluorescent strip lighting overhead, and all of them reinforcing each other's arm-flapping, shrieking, and other quirks while the teacher's aides stood impotently by. I felt uneasy about even taking him there, but I had to earn a living, and so did Kristin, whose teaching load at the university was not getting any lighter. However, his teachers, or rather his minders, *did* report that on the days when I had taken him riding early in the morning, before school, he was much less hyperactive, more "compliant," less "oppositional."

His other therapists — twice a week one or the other of us had to drive Rowan thirty miles each way for speech and occupational therapy — reported no positive change at all. Despite their initial confident claims that they'd soon have Rowan responding to yes/no questions and other social scripts like a champ, they now considered him too hyperactive, too distracted and distractible to progress. He'd bounce off the walls, grab, hug, and occasionally push or bite other kids. Once I caught the occupational therapist angrily shaking his arm as she led him to the door at the end of his session: "Well, you're not going to be nice to me? I'm not going to be nice to you!" Rowan looked utterly lost, and tried to run. She pulled him back hard, then turned, noticed me, and with an embarrassed smile told me how impossible Rowan had been that day. I made a note to self — should he stay in the therapy center? Christ, who knew? And as for the tantrums at home, his needs were becoming more complex, yet he still lacked the words to express them. And still the neurological firestorms coursed suddenly and at random through his compact little body any time of the day or night.

But with Betsy he was a different kid. Within a couple of weeks he began initiating word games. Although his language was way behind, we had always read to him when putting him down at night, and he had favorite books, some of which he memorized as small scripts. His current obsession was Dr. Seuss. One gray morning, with the first rains of fall gathering on the northwestern horizon, we rode onto the road outside the ranch gate. I was looking to extend the time in the saddle beyond a few quick gallops around the home pastures. Betsy's walking rhythm, hoof clops ringing in perfect time on the blacktop, prompted Rowan to start waving his arms as if conducting a hidden orchestra.

"Every day from here to there . . ." he suddenly intoned, in rhythm with the hoofbeats.

It took me a moment. Then I realized it was Rowan's version of a Dr. Seuss line. "Funny things are everywhere," I said, reciting the next line.

"Here are some who like to run."

I racked my brains for the next line. God knows I'd only read it about a thousand times. "They run for fun in the hot, hot sun." The words came tripping out. I kept them in time with Betsy's walk. I could see her ears swiveling back, listening to us.

"The moon was out and we saw some sheep." Rowan jumped ahead in the narrative.

I hurried to catch up. Ah, yes: "We saw some sheep take a walk in their sleep."

"By the light of the moon," said Rowan.

"By the light of a star."

"They walked all night from near to far."

"I would never walk."

"I would take a car!" Rowan supplied the last line along with a great peal of laughter.

Did he know it was funny?

It took us an hour and a half to finish that ride, doing the full circle of the country lanes close to Stafford's ranch, the elms and oaks shedding their leaves on us as we clip-clopped along the fence lines, cattle looking at us blankly, horses trotting along the wire, snorting at us as we passed. Rowan just kept talking. I just kept riding. He started to play alphabet games.

"A — armadillo."

"B . . ." I tried experimentally.

"Bear!"

"C," I offered.

"Camel!"

"D."

"Dog!"

And so it went. I was amazed by what he knew. For "I," he gave me "Impala!" For "X," "X-ray fish." I knew that was in one of his language books, but I had never known if he'd been taking it in.

By the end of the ride, he was giving *me* the letters and I had to respond with animals of my own, sweating in the saddle as the humidity intensified and the storm clouds gathered.

That evening the rains broke. Great sheets of water came down as if God had upended a huge, unending bucket from the heavens. You couldn't see farther than a few feet, so strong was the flow. Rowan ran out onto the covered front porch where Kristin and I were having a glass of wine, watching the water come down. A real Texas rain.

"It's raining!" he said.

Kristin and I looked at each other. It was the first time his lucid speech had translated away from Betsy.

Longer rides seemed to be the key. It wasn't really safe to ride on the back roads of Bastrop County — people drove fast, and often drunk, sometimes (I saw this with my own eyes) even with a beer in hand, shooting squirrels out of the trees with shotguns as they drove. So the next day I visited the houses of several neighbors to ask if I could ride on their land, always a good precaution in a state where people do sometimes shoot trespassers first and ask questions later. Almost all of them said yes. And so we started to ride farther and farther afield. Through the groves of wild pecan trees, old campsites of the Comanche Indians that lined the Little Sandy Creek a mile from our house. Out to the open forest of cedar trees and hidden meadows where deer would sometimes leap out from the brakes and go bounding away, tails held high like white flags warning of danger. Out to the wide, rough pastures of prickly pear and mesquite, where once a pack of fleet coyotes fled from us like ghosts, and where the desiccated shell of a dead armadillo lay exposed between the cactus and the grass.

We began to develop a vocabulary of places, or journeys. First there'd be the walk across to the barn itself: "Shall we go ride Betsy?"

"Go ride Betsy!" He still couldn't say yes or no. But at least he could confirm what he did or didn't want to do.

So off we'd go. Scripts emerged for this too. "Put on socks and put on shoes!"

He'd echo this in a musical voice: "Put on socks and put on shoes!" And then we'd do it.

Then he'd go running ahead of me, off the front porch — jump — round the corner to the right, to the woods behind the house where the trail snaked away, down the small hill into the dry creek bed, along the trail to the right. Sometimes red cardinals would explode from the trees, alarmed.

"Look! Bird!"

"Yes! Birds! Cardinal birds!"

Or we might surprise a flight of crows,

70

and once, memorably, a lone, myopic turtle, huge, crawling along doggedly in search of some standing water. "Turtle! Look! Turtle!"

"That's right, Rowan! It is a turtle! Good talking. Good words!" It sounded like I was praising a dog or a horse, but God knows I wanted to give him positive reinforcement.

Then an abrupt left turn by the thorn-laden bumilia and three-leafed wild hop trees, past the wild American beauty bushes, laden with bright mauve berries that attracted songbirds by the flock. And across the deepest part of the dry creek, which sometimes ran with water during a strong rain, to face the steep ascent of the far bank, its red clay and rust-colored ferrous rock exposed to the bright Texas sun by the regular passage of feet and hooves. The distance from this short but challenging climb and the boundary fence of Stafford's property was a mere hundred yards. Yet here, whether I was carrying Rowan's light, taut body on my shoulders or he was stomping along on his own little legs, my son would always tantrum. Because this was the point where the home woods ended and Stafford's property began: a transitional zone. Autists have tremendous trouble with transitions, even simple ones, like leaving the end of the car park and entering the supermarket, or walking upstairs from the living room to the bedroom, let alone the transition from woodland to pasture. Whatever part of the brain deals with the transition from one situation to another becomes easily overwhelmed.

So at this stage in the daily walk to Betsy's barn Rowan would scream, throw himself on the ground, yell, hit his head, until we ducked through the fence onto Stafford's pasture. Then, with a sudden squeal of joy, the screams would end and he'd go running off toward the barn.

If it was feeding time, the horses would all be waiting expectantly in their stalls, Rowan having already briefly chased the feral black barn cat (uncatchable, except by Rowan) and petted Bo, the bird dog, a pointer belonging to Terry, the kindly Texas countryman who looked after the place while Stafford worked in Austin. "I don't know why you git on them damn things," he said about the horses. "One end where the money goes in, the other end you got to pay people to take it away, and in between an accident waitin' to happen."

"Shall we give Betsy some food?" I'd then ask, being all too willing to bribe this astonishing mare into further good behavior if necessary.

"Give Betsy some food!" Rowan would confirm. In fact they'd all get some (though Betsy would always get more upon our return), and then it'd be time to saddle up, while Rowan ran to and fro beneath Betsy's hooves, once again breaking all the rules of equine safety, Betsy, as ever, moving not a muscle as long as he was near.

Then — it was becoming a ritual — I'd say, "Want to get up?" And Rowan would have to say "Up!" before I'd lift him there. Then, "Want Daddy to get up or do you want to ride alone?" and I'd wait until, whether from echolalia or intention, he'd say, "Daddy to get up!" Only then would I swing up behind him.

I made mistakes. Lots of them. The first was trying to assert my will over Betsy. If Rowan was turning out to be some kind of infant horse whisperer, I, for all my previous horse experience, definitely was not. Though quiet to the point of self-negation with Rowan, Betsy was still the alpha mare of her herd, and famously grumpy with adults. Not in a buck-you-off-and-stomp-on-you kind of way, but in a spin-around-sharply-and-carry-you-steadfastly-back-to-the-barn-if-she-thought-she-could-get-away-with-it kind of way. Stafford told me she'd done that, or at least tried it, with most adult riders when they first got on her. Horses like to know where the boundaries are, and like children, they often find out in a way that exercises a little humor at the rider's, or parent's, expense. However, I do like a horse to go a certain way, light on the bit, the action of the legs high and floating. Betsy had been trained in a strictly utilitarian fashion — to clomp heavily forward with no finesse.

On one of our first forays, with Rowan sitting happily in front of me reciting the alphabet, I kept nagging at Betsy, trying to get her to collect, to compress the rhythm of her steps into something more beautiful. She gave her head a couple of annoyed tosses, ears back, warning me to quit. I kept insisting. Suddenly she dug in her back legs, reared up, and spun around in irritation. With Rowan's weight leaning against mine, I didn't compensate fast enough and found myself falling onto the hard top of the road. I had just enough time to roll my body underneath his before we hit. But it was a shock. And a lesson — for us all, Betsy too. She was standing there shivering with nervousness: Did she expect a beating? Was she shocked in some way? Horses are usually pretty happy when they succeed in getting out from between you and the ground and will usually run off bucking. Betsy, however, stood stock-still until I managed to struggle upright and swing us back on board. After that I let her alone.

A few weeks later I fell again. Not because I was fussing at her, but because, as we rode along the boundary fence between Stafford's property and my own, the cinch broke and the saddle suddenly swung around to the side. It was a classic lose-your-life-or-get-really-nastily-injured fall, for one of my feet was caught in the stirrup and I could easily have been dragged. And as I fell, again just managing to twist my body so that Rowan's fall was cushioned, my head slipped under the bottom strand of the wire fence, close by the post.

When horses feel a saddle slip around like that, they usually go into a fit of kicking — a survival reflex against predators like wolves trying to rip open the soft flesh of their bellies. When even a well-trained horse feels something flapping at its belly, such as a slipped saddle, its instinct is to bolt, bucking wildly, until the hated thing has been kicked off and the perceived danger averted. Over the years I'd seen it happen before, plenty of times.

With my foot stuck in the stirrup like that

and my neck more or less wrapped around the metal fencepost, I should have been dead meat. But again Betsy did not move; she just stood there, with that soft look in her eye she always had when Rowan was on the ground near her, until we had disentangled ourselves, taken the saddle off, reset it, retied the cinch, and swung up once more. Had Rowan not been with me, would Betsy have reacted the same way? I suspected I owed my life to Rowan on that one.

I learned to carry diapers, wipes, and spare clothes in my saddlebags for the inevitable accidents. Picture me dismounted, reins held in my teeth, trying to hold Rowan still while executing a midfield diaper and pants change amid the cactus and the oaks. Gradually I expanded the contents of the saddlebags, keeping a supply of toys, drinks, snacks, and even books in them, so that Rowan could get down and play if necessary, or I could even read him a book as we rode. As humid, warm October gave way to chilly, rain-soaked November, we bundled up in rain jackets and waterproof pants and just kept on riding. By now we were practically living in the saddle.

If I give the impression here that because of all the time spent in the woods and on Betsy, I did the lion's share of child care, then that impression is false. Kristin, despite the demands of her job, spent hours reading to Rowan when she got home in the evenings, playing with him, working with him on the floor as he lined up his animals and trains, trying to get him to talk about them, building on the language he practiced continually while on horseback.

And though the time spent on Betsy was pure joy, much of the rest of the time dealing with Rowan and his tantrums and his incontinence was pretty hellish. For both of us, the pressure of continually trying to meet Rowan's needs became so intense that, without a safety valve of some kind, we feared we might not make it as a couple. Fully 80 percent of couples with autistic children break up. It was easy to see why. We had no babysitters, for none of our friends could cope with Rowan, and we had no extended family nearby. But we did have each other. Sitting there one night, stunned with tiredness after Kristin had spent the best part of two hours trying to get Rowan down to sleep, we began to bicker, as was happening more and more often, over who spent more energy dealing with Rowan, me with the hours and hours on Betsy, Kristin with the hours and hours reading and (more often than me) fighting her own exhaustion in trying to get him to go to bed.

Then she had a brainwave. "We need time off," she said.

"Great idea," I said sarcastically. "Where are we going to find the babysitters?"

"We can be each other's babysitters," suggested Kristin. Each of us would get a night off every week, to go into Austin, hang with friends, see a movie, have a few drinks, not drive home, crash on a friend's couch. "That way we can come back home fresh for the fight," said Kristin. "What do you think?"

"I think you're a genius," I said, wondering not for the first time at the wisdom of this woman I had met in India all those years ago. We were going to survive this.

Christmas came and, two days later, Rowan's fourth birthday: a time to reflect. In the eight months since his diagnosis we had been trying all sorts of therapies: chelation, Valtrex, speech therapy, occupational therapy, changes to his diet — just about anything that wouldn't hurt him. Whether these were working or not it was too soon to tell, but there had been no obvious, radical change for the better, except through Betsy and, I remembered, during his brief exposure to the healers and shamans he had met at the Gathering. Admittedly, Rowan had regressed back into his autism after his seemingly miraculous response to the healers, but I could not help but wonder: if he had more regular access to such healers or shamans, might he get boosted again? And then Betsy — without question, that *had* been a miracle. Might there, I wondered, be some way of combining these two things — horses and shamanic healing? Was there a place in the world that combined horses and healing at the center of the culture? A place that understood the interplay between horses and healing better than I could, in my blind-man-stumbling way? Did such a place exist?

The horse itself, *Equus caballus,* had, I knew, evolved during the ice ages somewhere out on the great Mongolian steppe. Some research revealed that the word *shaman* itself, meaning "he who knows," originated in southern Siberia, part of which dips down into the northern part of Mongolia.

Mongolia. The place where, six thousand years ago, the horse had first been domesticated. A country where, I now read, shamanism, along with Buddhism, was the state religion.

What if we were to take Rowan there? Get on horseback and ride across that vast,

79

primordial grassland from healer to healer, shaman to shaman? What if Rowan's autism, instead of shutting down our lives, instead of signaling the end of all adventure, of all fun, could in fact be the gateway to the greatest adventure of all?

What if that was possible?

4
A Time for Dreams

"No," said Kristin, when I came in from riding that cold late-December day and told her of my idea. "No way. Absolutely not. I can't believe you'd even suggest such a thing! You must be mad!"

"Maybe now's the time to do something mad."

"Rupert! We have an autistic child — a child who can't even control his bowels, let alone his tantrums! And you're saying that somehow we're going to fly to *Mongolia,* get on horses, and ride from shaman to shaman? I'm supposed to seriously consider this?"

We went to bed angry with each other and — unusually for us — did not drag it up again the next day. Self-doubt kicked in with the light of morning: how could I be sure this was not all just New Age nonsense on my part? Intuition, however, told me that there was nothing New Age about it. This was something far, far older. The same inner voice also told me not to push it with Kristin, to keep quiet for now. At the same time, that old inner voice, the one that had told me, when I first clapped eyes on Kristin, that she was my wife, told me clear as day that we had to go. As for Kristin, she simply hoped it was all pie in the sky, that I'd find it too difficult to arrange, that the idea would fizzle out.

Instead I began to dream — and to plan. What if we were to start our journey with the shamans of the horse people, who lived on the great oceans of pasture where the horse was born, and then ride up into the forests of the taiga, Siberia, to see the shamans of the Dukha, the reindeer herders, whose tradition of shamanism had been unbroken, I had read, for thousands of years, and whose shamans were considered the most powerful of the region? To travel from the shamans of the horse people to the older shamans of the reindeer people . . .

I made e-mail contact, through the group that had organized the Gathering, with a woman shaman from Russian Siberia and told her my idea, asked her advice. She suggested that in addition to my consulting the shamans of the horse people and the reindeer people, Rowan be washed in sacred waters as we went. She could not suggest particular lakes or rivers, as she did not know Mongolia, but she assured me, in our few brief back-and-forths, that this kind of sacred bathing was integral to all northern Asian healing traditions. So I got on the Web, looked up various combinations of "sacred lakes and rivers of Mongolia," and found that pretty much every lake and river seemed to be sacred. But what about the route between Ulaanbaatar, the capital, where presumably we'd have to start, and the far north, where the reindeer people lived? The Tuul River, which ran through the capital, was certainly deemed sacred, as were the Selenge and other rivers to the north. Then I found reference to an isolated lake known as Sharga, sitting almost exactly midway between the capital and the territory of the Dukha. I wrote down the names, began to dream harder.

Of course, it was only a dream. But most assuredly this dream was better than the other, almost equally unreal dreamtime we had inhabited ever since Rowan's autism had taken over our lives. We had no choice in dealing with his autism, but could we not choose what other kind of dreamtime we inhabited?

For away from Betsy, things were getting

worse, not better. As 2004 turned to 2005, Rowan's tantrums and obsessions only worsened. We had no social life anymore. Except for the riding time, there was little joy. Despite all the therapies, the supplements, the special-education program at our local school, Rowan — for all the linguistic strides he was making on Betsy (and even these were inconsistent, very lucid one day, back to autistic babble the next) — seemed to be getting more, not less, autistic. What if there was never going to be a change? What if we and Rowan were stuck here, in this psychological, neurological no-man's-land, forever? Would Rowan ever turn his head when called? Would he ever take a walk with us without running off? Would he ever say yes or no? Would he ever notice or make friends with another child? Would he ever play appropriately with his trains, his animals, or would he just forever queue them up in lines or spirals, leaning close to squint at them obsessively out of the corners of his dark blue eyes with their strange green inner irises? Was this it?

One evening in March we rode in a red, red sunset that gave way to a cool twilight above which rose a thin crescent moon. Rowan pointed at the white sickle framed between Betsy's ears and said, "Moon."

He had never pointed before. Two years late, but he was pointing.

I stopped Betsy. "How d'you spell *moon?*"

"Muh!" said Rowan, pronouncing it phonetically.

"O," I offered, making the phonetic sound of the long *o.*

"O!" said Rowan.

"O."

"O!"

"En!"

"Nuh."

"That's right, Rowan. M-O-O-N spells . . ." I gave an exaggerated intake of breath to see if he'd pick up the cue.

"Moon!" he said triumphantly.

So perhaps there was hope after all. But it was so slow. I wanted something more radical, something miraculous. Would taking him to the horses and shamanic healers of Mongolia provide that? Try as I might, I could not get the idea out of my head.

March turned to April. After a day of almost nonstop screaming and arm-flapping (what in autism jargon is called stimming, short for "self-stimulation"), I took Rowan down through the firefly-dancing woods to the barn, where Terry — or Uncle Terry, as Rowan had learned to call him — was driving up on his ride-on mower, letting his dog,

Bo, rest his front paws on the steering wheel as if he were driving. We rode hard that evening. Rowan was obsessive, making me gallop over and over again between the barn and the pond, hurling himself maniacally from side to side as we went, until Betsy was worked up into a lather. It was hard to keep him in the saddle, let alone keep Betsy balanced. We thundered up and down, Rowan's elbows jarring painfully into my forearms. He screamed and babbled, twisting his body into weird, rigid shapes completely out of sync with the mare's rhythm. It was heartbreaking, as if he had regressed into some bubble-world where once again I couldn't reach him. Finally, for fear of pushing poor Betsy too hard, I insisted we stop.

"More run! More Betsy!"

"Betsy's tired, Rowan. Come on, that's enough, we have to stop now."

The wailing, back-arching, and shrieking began as soon as his feet touched terra firma. I left him there, trying not to shout at him. I wanted to hit him in moments like this, my hot, sudden anger fed by distress and powerlessness. I walked away, carrying Betsy's heavy saddle over my arm, breathing deeply to let the emotion subside. Coming out of the tack room, I saw Rowan stop screaming, sit up, walk over to where Betsy still stood, not moving a muscle. He opened his arms, hugged her right foreleg, kissed it, and said, "I wuv you, Betsy."

It was the first time he'd ever said the words. He had never spoken them to Kristin or to me. Betsy's eyes half closed as he held on to her. Then Rowan came bouncing over, smiling, took my hand, and led me home across the pasture.

That summer we got one thing right. We took Rowan out of the school where his behavior was getting more and more autistic and, by a series of happy coincidences, managed to invent a better plan. At a hippy commune called Greenbriar, three miles down a country road from us, there lived a woman, Katherine, who had her own autistic son, a twelve-year-old boy whom I had met a few times and who seemed in many ways "recovered." Katherine was getting her Ph.D. in clinical psychology. She had also spent ten years as a special-ed teacher and had evolved a way of working with her son through the use of rapid-fire questioning that had led the boy faster through reading, writing, and arithmetic than any over-pressed public school could ever hope to. Her philosophy, though it included some ABA techniques, was the opposite of the hard-core ABA approach. Instead of forcing children to comply, using time with favorite activities as a reward for completing boring tasks, she felt it was more effective to teach them from within the context of their loved obsessions. If they wanted to be taught in a tree, she would teach them in the tree. If they needed to be taught in the pool (Greenbriar had a lovely shaded swimming pool), she'd teach them there.

Greenbriar was on two hundred acres of woodland, providing the type of natural environment in which Rowan thrived. I asked Katherine if she would take on Rowan as a private pupil and she agreed. We worked out a daily schedule for him — two to three hours of academics, using Katherine's own methods, and the rest of the day out walking the trails with a man called Camilo, who had worked with autistic children before, who also lived at Greenbriar, and whose daughter could act as a kind of older sibling to Rowan. I also volunteered to teach other Greenbriar kids two days a week — history on one morning, and riding on another.

When Katherine's son came out to ride with the other Greenbriar kids, I noticed that as with Rowan, Betsy would drop her head and start to lick and chew. And although she was sometimes difficult with the neurotypical kids, with Katherine's son she never put a foot wrong.

For Rowan, the changes from the new school environment were instantaneous. His stimming and his general anxiety level calmed right down. Now almost five, he began his first halting steps at reading. Camilo spent hours on the trail with Rowan, encouraging him to talk about everything he saw, everything he touched. His language was still very uneven — he could spell certain things, say certain things, but mostly it was babble. Except on Betsy — around her the babble receded, the appropriate speech intensified. So when Rowan got home in the evening, we'd go straight out riding. A few times I even took him to school on horseback.

The neurological firestorms and their resulting tantrums continued. And no one — not us, not Katherine, not Camilo, not the grannies when they visited — could make any headway with toilet training (I was hearing more and more stories about autistic kids who remained untrained into their teens and was bracing myself for this). But at least we were making progress. More important, we had tackled a problem by dreaming up and then putting into place something better.

And if dreaming one good dream could yield such positive results, then why not another? As 2005 turned to 2006 and the green, rainy spring progressed into the deadening heat of a Texas summer, that other dream kept nagging at me. Mongolia. I kept it quiet, not wanting to risk another confrontation with Kristin, who I knew was still dead set against the idea. But somehow this irrational voice kept saying, *Do it.* And if it was going to be done, it would have to be soon: Rowan was growing so fast that in another year or so he might no longer be able to sit comfortably in the saddle with me.

That July I gave a talk about the Bushmen at a local venue in Austin. I had by then formed my own small human rights organization and was raising money to pay the lawyer who was fighting the Bushmen's case in the Botswana High Court. After my lecture a young filmmaker called Michel, who had been in the audience, came forward to offer his services to go to Botswana and try to film some of the abuses the Bushmen were suffering there. A dark good-looking young man with cropped hair, sculpted biceps, and blue eyes shining with altruism, he came out to our place to talk about it. The conversation turned to the

Bushman healers and how effective they were, and so it seemed natural to tell the story about how radically and positively (if temporarily) Rowan had seemed to react to a brief exposure to this kind of healing at the Gathering two years before. Then, glancing half nervously, half mischievously at Kristin, I admitted that I was nursing a dream of taking Rowan to Mongolia, where horses and shamanic healing were combined, and that I hoped to do it soon. Maybe even the following year, before Rowan got too big to sit comfortably in the saddle with me.

Kristin just smiled, said nothing.

Michel offered then and there to accompany us and film the journey.

"I haven't raised any money yet," I warned him. "And even if I do, I doubt it'll be enough to pay someone to film."

It didn't matter, Michel assured me. This was a once-in-a-lifetime thing. And, he pointed out, if there was any change in Rowan, then it would be useful, necessary even, to have a record of those changes. Plus he'd grown up on a horse ranch and could handle the hours, days, in the saddle that the trip would require.

So a few times that fall Michel and I met to discuss how we might begin applying for grants. And almost as an act of faith we started filming Rowan and Betsy together — his language, his mind, continuing to flourish through their extraordinary bond. I began to talk tentatively to Kristin about Mongolia. She refused to enter into any kind of discussion about it, other than a noncommittal "Well, if you raise the money, we'll see . . ."

Meanwhile, as the hot weather came back for a final late-October blast, Rowan and I continued to ride. Betsy had long forgotten her initial grumpiness with me and gave me the most beautiful light, floating ride. Now when I sat back and squeezed my legs, she would dance on the spot for me, Rowan's laughter ringing off the trees. She would jump small logs and fences too, which Rowan adored, shouting "Like a bird!" as she flew through the air with us on board. We had achieved that perfect harmony between human and horse that every rider dreams of — except there were three of us, not two.

"What's that?" demanded Rowan as we rode Betsy through the pecan groves one fine fall day, the ground dark with fallen nuts, the earth showing where the wild boar had rooted them up from the grass, and the cicadas seeming to shake the trees with the

intensity of their song. Overhead, buzzards
— actually vultures, though everyone in
Texas calls them buzzards — wheeled slowly
on the south wind blowing in across the
Gulf of Mexico, straight from Cuba.

"What's that?" asked Rowan again, pointing up at one of the great dark, soaring
birds.

"I don't know, Rowan, what *is* that?" I
knew he knew what it was. Wildlife was his
thing.

"It's a . . ." He gave a sharp intake of
breath.

"A B-U-Z-Z-A-R-D," I answered, spelling
it out.

"Buzzard!"

"Good spelling!"

Betsy snorted.

"Betsy's sneezing!"

"That's right, Rowan — good observation."

"She's having a little sneeze."

"She is. Hey, Rowan, would you like to go
with Daddy next year and ride horses in
Mongolia?"

"Ride horses in Mongolia!"

Astonishing. His language was still so
uneven. At moments like these he sounded
almost fluent, but then he'd relapse into
days of nonsense. This time he was prob-

ably just echoing me, but I took it as a yes.

That weekend Rowan and I rode late, staying out long after sunset and coming home under the silver light of a hunter's moon, the night warm, its gently moving air like kisses on the skin. We came in from the range, up Stafford's long driveway, to find him and his grandchildren sitting out enjoying the honeysuckle-scented moonlight. As we rode up to where they were sitting, Rowan suddenly writhed his way to a standing position, like a little Viking standing on the moving prow of his ship, and at the top of his lungs sang out the ABC song. When he had ended, on a rousing *"Next time won't you sing with me!"* Stafford walked up to us, laughing.

"Well," he said, "I think that's neat as heck!"

The first frosts came. Michel and I, having filmed Rowan for more than a month now, decided to take a trip to interview Dr. Temple Grandin, an adult autist who was a professor of animal sciences at Colorado State University. Dr. Grandin had written a best-selling book detailing how animals and autists thought in pictures and how you could understand the autistic mind by studying animals, and vice versa. There were questions I wanted to ask her about Rowan's strange kinship with Betsy. Michel and I also hoped that an interview with a relative celebrity such as Dr. Grandin might help us find funds for a documentary.

When we met her at the university campus in Fort Collins, Colorado, under the frowning front range of the Rockies, I was surprised — even encouraged — to see that despite her successful academic career and her best-selling books, Temple Grandin was still very autistic. While we were setting up the camera she began obsessively to click a pen that had a little light that came on and went off with each click. "Wow," she said, laughing and looking up wild-eyed after a couple of entranced minutes. "I'd better stop. I'm *really* stimming out on that pen."

She had been, she told us, severely autistic as a child, sitting in a corner rocking back and forth, almost unreachable, eating the wallpaper. She'd been lucky, though, having nannies that played endless one-on-one games with her, insisting that she respond. And at an early age she'd discovered horses. "Animals think in pictures," she told us. "So do I. So do many autists. It means we can't connect to other people, who think differently, in words or other mental patterns. Because animals think the same way — visually — autistic people often connect well with animals. When they're young they sometimes communicate what they want to say to their fellow humans through the medium of an animal, especially an animal they're close to. Autists, if you like, are a connecting point for non-autists to the animal world, and animals, especially for autistic kids, can often be the connecting point between the autistic and the 'normal' human world."

As for why the act of riding seemed to make Rowan's language develop, she said that research had shown that any repetitive rocking motion that requires the person to continually find and refind his balance stimulates the areas of the brain where the learning receptors are located. "Combine that with the fact that being on a horse is just so darned cool," she added, "and it's no wonder kids respond. If only more were taught that way."

I went out on a limb and told her about the Mongolia idea, about Rowan's reaction to the shamans. As a scientist, did she think there could be any merit at all in such a journey? I expected her to say no, or at least to say that she had no opinion either way. To my surprise, however, she asked, "These shamanic ceremonies — describe them."

I cast my mind back to the ceremonies I'd

attended with the Bushmen and described the rhythmic clapping, chanting, song. Dr. Grandin nodded. "That kind of repetitive rhythm — for all we know, that could have the same effect on opening the learning receptors of the brain that riding has."

"So you don't think it's just hokum?"

"How can we know?"

"But you think there could be value in such a journey?" I wanted her blessing, I realized.

"The worst thing you can do is just do nothing. All the experts agree on that, even if they can't agree on much else. Take your son to Mongolia if it seems to agree with him. Make your film. Add it to the archive of what we're learning. Come back and let us know what happened."

Another Christmas came, and I got an unexpected present. To my amazement, the Bushman court case in Botswana was won. The Bushmen could return home to the lands that had been taken from them. Suddenly I could turn my full attention to trying to make the Mongolia trip happen. I sent out a proposal for a book and, despite having several fights with Kristin, carved a huge hole in our bank account by buying four plane tickets, for me, Kristin, Rowan, and Michel, to Ulaanbaatar. Through a series of travel-writing contacts, I also began an e-mail correspondence with a tour operator there, a man called Tulga, who reputedly specialized in unusual, back-of-beyond trips. Though surely, I couldn't help thinking, wasn't *everywhere* in Mongolia the back of beyond? I outlined the journey I wanted to make and asked if he could start trying to find out which shamans we should go to see and if they thought they might be able to help a boy like Rowan. After some initial correspondence, he came back to me saying that he had heard of very powerful healers among the reindeer-herding people in the north. If we could reach one of these shamans, people said, we could expect a result. The only problem was that they lived way up in the Mongolian part of Siberia. And the summer camps of their people, the Dukha, or Tsataan, moved along with the reindeer herds, which were up on top of a mountain range 12,000 feet in height.

There were also nine shamans from elsewhere in the country who, hearing about Rowan through Tulga, offered to travel from their own regions to meet us in Ulaanbaatar, the capital, if we could make it by July.

I looked at a map. Between Ulaanbaatar and the Siberian region were endless miles of open country. I remembered my earlier e-mails with the Russian Siberian healer who had spoken about the efficacy of washing in sacred waters, and did another search to decide which sacred lakes or rivers between the two regions where we would seek out the shamans we could perhaps wash Rowan in. There was the Tuul River again, and the Selenge River, both holy, apparently. I went back over some old notes and found the reference to Lake Sharga, not only sacred but slap-bang in the middle between the capital and the reindeer people. I felt sure that we should take Rowan there. I went back on the Web to find the page again.

It wasn't there. It seemed to have simply disappeared into the Internet ether. One night after Rowan and I came in from riding, Kristin found me hunched in front of the computer, obsessively punching various "Lake Sharga" and "sacred waters, Mongolia" searches into Yahoo and Google.

"Hell," she said. "You're really going to do this, aren't you?"

"You know I am. I mean we. We are."

Kristin sighed, sat down on the floor by my chair. "I don't know, Ru. I don't know if I can do it. Isn't it hard enough just getting through a typical day, let alone going on a crazy journey to the far ends of the earth? This was never my idea. And I hate horses."

Perhaps *hate* was too strong a word, but Kristin had had some bad experiences; during the year we'd lived in England, I had taught her to ride, and she had had a couple of falls. She had never really taken to the sport. I was the horsy one in the family. Now, looking at the prospect of taking a journey on horseback, she balked.

"You don't have to come, you know," I said.

"Oh, right." Her voice was heavy with sarcasm.

"I mean I . . . if you don't come, I won't hold it against you. Christ, it might even be easier, frankly. I can get the money back on the ticket. If you don't come, I won't have to worry about you having a bad time. Or falling off."

"Or getting run away with, or kicked, or bitten, or stepped on, or rolled on, or all the other nice things that go with horses."

"Those too. Seriously — I know this is my crazy idea. You don't have to follow it."

"You're sure you won't hold it against me?"

"Not at all. I know I'm bonkers."

Next day, Michel, riding Taz, joined Rowan and me on a ride over the wide cattle pastures a mile or so from our house. Rowan said, "Run! Go fast!" as soon as Betsy's hooves hit turf, made me search out fallen pecan and oak logs to jump, and laughed hysterically as the good bay mare heaved herself dutifully over. "Jump! Jump like a frog!"

"Hot damn, Rowan," said Uncle Terry when we rode back to the barn. "You bin makin' that Betsy jump?"

"Jump!" confirmed Rowan happily.

At which Terry, ever the gentleman, offered Michel and me each a bottle of his homemade (and super-strong) mustang grape wine. I took one gladly — since Rowan's autism had kicked in, I had, I admit, become something of a functional alcoholic, and had put on the extra pounds to prove it. Michel, a yoga and health junkie, declined. "Well," said Terry stoically, "I just thought I'd offer. I'd rather be stupid than rude."

Words to live by. Still, once I got home and opened the bottle, knowing I'd finish it in one sitting, I couldn't help but wonder if it wasn't I and Kristin who needed healing as much as, if not more than, Rowan.

Next morning there was an e-mail from Tulga saying that if I wanted, he could bring his own son on the trip with us. He had been thinking it over, he wrote, and it seemed that the two boys might get along. I doubted it. Rowan had never made a friend, still could not relate to other children. Kristin read the e-mail over my shoulder.

"All right, Ru," she said suddenly. "I'll come. I don't know how we'll make it work. But if you can pull it off, I'll be there. What doesn't kill you makes you stronger, right?" She laughed. "Who knows, maybe the shamans will be able to toilet-train him."

"No baby goats in the house!" Rowan's voice trilled from the bedroom, startling us to laughter. For his birthday we'd bought him Daisy and Howard, two pygmy goats, a black one and a white one, and he'd been teasing us by bringing them into the house whenever we weren't looking, rolling his head back with laughter when we tried to be stern, repeating to us our *No baby goats in the house* as a kind of comedic mantra.

"It's like he's a born Buddhist," said Kristin. I looked up, puzzled. Over the last few years, Kristin's Buddhist practice had been merging more and more with her academic psychology work. Specifically, she had been conducting research into the Buddhist concept of self-compassion, the idea being to cultivate kindness and forgiveness toward yourself as well as others: no easy task, especially in times of suffering or failure. However, the studies she'd been publishing seemed to show that self-compassion was better for mental health than the conventional psychological wisdom, which equates high self-esteem with positive mental health. Kristin had found that the constant pursuit of high self-esteem becomes, over time, an obsession with feeling special and superior, an emotional roller-coaster that you can never get off. By contrast, self-compassion allows you to look clearly at yourself, forgive yourself, and then make the necessary changes to achieve mental equilibrium. Lord knows, as an autism mom, she'd had plenty of opportunity lately to practice self-compassion. "Not that there is really such a thing as a self at all," she'd say, black eyes twinkling.

"What do you mean, he's a born Buddhist?" I asked.

"It's as if he takes nothing personally," said Kristin. "He suffers in the moment, then lets the suffering go. He doesn't carry on the storyline and make a personal drama out of it, so he doesn't suffer after the fact like 'normal' people do. It's kind of a gift, you know."

It was true: a fundamental lack of ego

seemed to be part of the autism package. In some ways I envied him.

There he was, laughing at us, with us, the little black goat neatly tucked up in our bed, boy and goat staring at us with mischievous, totally infectious humor.

Two days later there was another e-mail. The book proposal I had sent out had been accepted. The trip would not bankrupt us after all. We were going to Mongolia.

PART TWO

5
THE ADVENTURE BEGINS

Rowan sat, nose pressed to the Aeroflot window, watching the patchwork countryside below gradually disappear below the thickening wisps of cloud. *So we were really doing it, then. Would this crazy journey — and yes, it was crazy, desperate even — have any effect on Rowan at all? For the millionth time, all my fears came flooding in. What if he hated it? What if he got sick or had an accident with the horses and we had to airlift him out — would our insurance cover it? What if he got sick or injured and we couldn't airlift him out? What if one of us got sick or hurt? What if the shamans didn't turn up? What if we never reached them? What if we did reach them and they did absolutely nothing for Rowan? Or turned out to be total charlatans? What if Tulga the guide turned out to be useless? What if this was all for nothing?*

Was I a complete fool for doing this —

just on some kind of ego trip, and not doing this for Rowan at all? Did I want Rowan to be healed? Healed or cured? There was a difference. Long ago I'd given up wanting him to be cured. Cured as in not being autistic anymore — for that was part of his essence. But I did want him healed. If there was anything Kristin and I wanted to say to the shamans, it was *Please let him come back toilet-trained.* Please let him no longer be held at the mercy of his tantrums, of his wild-storm nervous system. No longer hyperactive, with that incessant edge of anxiety that was like a fist around the heart, always ready to close suddenly and hard. Could a shaman heal those things? Who knew?

I turned to Kristin. "Are we crazy?"

"Completely. No, let me rephrase that. You're crazy. I'm just along for the ride." She gave an ironic smile. "If it goes great, then great. If not, I get to blame you, so for me it's win-win."

"I am mad, aren't I?"

"Bonkers. Barking. Woof-woof."

"I'm the king of Pride Rock," announced Rowan, turning away from the clouds to bestow his most beneficent beam upon us. He was quoting a line from *The Lion King* — one of his obsessively watched cartoons.

Things were already changing inside him. We had spent the past few weeks in England so Rowan could spend some time with his granny and aunt, and so that he would not be forced to make the long plane journey from Austin, Texas, to Ulaanbaatar in one twenty-four-hour go. While there we had gone up to my sister's place in Wales and found a horse for him to ride, a quiet old gray mare lent to us by Billie, a horse trainer and old friend of the family who ran a riding school in central Wales. "She's called Dottie," said Billie, leading the horse out to introduce her to a jumping-up-and-down Rowan. Like Betsy, she lowered her head to him. Not a complete obeisance, but a similar behavior, and she had not put a foot wrong as Rowan and I took off together across the green Welsh countryside.

That evening, on the hills across the valley from my sister's farm, we went walking to see the sunset. Suddenly Rowan started running in all directions, yelling about a little boy called Buster.

"Who is Buster?" I asked as he tore past me, the evening light golden on his face.

"Buster is a *boy!*"

I looked at Kristin. "Is Buster your friend?" I asked as he came flying back in a wide arc, flapping his arms in imitation of the crows cawing overhead. Rowan had no friends. Had never had friends. I was not even sure he knew what the concept was, quite.

"Buster is a *friend!*" he confirmed, flying past again. "Come on, Buster! Run! Run like Buster!"

Again Kristin and I looked at each other. An imaginary friend. This was something altogether new.

Now as he sat on the plane (I guessed we must be somewhere over Kazakhstan), being an absolute doll, having negotiated the change of planes in Frankfurt and Moscow without fuss, he smiled at me. "Going to Mongolia to see the reindeer people," he started to say repeatedly. "Going with Buster."

I could scarcely believe his calm. I was the one who was nervous. "Look at the clouds," he said. "Like cloud cake." As he played contentedly with a toy lion cub and toy foal on the tray table in front of him, I couldn't stop my fears and misgivings from rising up unbidden once more. What if he hated it? What if he rejected it all? Would he allow the horses of this far place to heal him?

Horses had healed me once. I had had something of a nervous breakdown at age twelve. Several years of bullying at school combined with unhappiness at home had finally taken their toll. I woke up one morning and simply could not get out of bed. When I tried to speak, I cried. And cried. I could not understand it. Nor could I stop it. I ended up in bed for three months. Finally my parents asked me what would get me back on my feet. The answer came immediately. I wanted to ride. I wanted to be able to spend weekends at my great-aunt's farm outside London, which we often visited, and learn to ride. It was not the first time I had asked. Ever since the age of three, I had spent my time at that farm out in the field, talking to my great-aunt's two old, retired hunters, now too arthritic and ancient to work. And they would come and stand by me, happy to be near. Like Rowan, I had an affinity. "He's going to ride one day, whether you like it or not," the great-aunt had said. My parents, urbanites to the core, had resisted the idea valiantly. Until now. Okay, they said. Okay, you can ride. And they booked lessons for me at the local riding school, close to my great-aunt's house.

There's an old English saying: "There's nowt so good for the inside of a man as the outside of a horse." In my case it proved absolutely true. It got me out of bed. It got my depression under control. It got me back to school. It healed my broken self-respect. And I proved a quick learner. Within a year I was ready to have my own horse. My parents, not being rich, wanted me to earn the money. So for two years, from twelve to fourteen, I had a stall in a flea market in London, selling first any old junk I could glean from my neighbors' attics and garages, then graduating to antiques, vintage clothing, collectibles. Even so, when I did have enough money, it was only enough to buy something cheap. The horse had to be athletic enough to hunt and do shows, but at the meager price I could afford the only such horse would be a failed racehorse off the track. And these, as all horse people know, come with one fatal flaw — they are complete lunatics.

Throughout my adolescence, I spent my weeks at school in London and my weekends up in the old, falling-down, unheated farmhouse where my irritable old aunt and I avoided each other as much as possible, following the local hounds in winter and doing horse shows in the summer. A young woman who rented the farm cottage from my great-aunt, who had more horse experience than I, taught me how to ride and retrain my impossibly crazy horse. And I learned to be a better rider because of it. By the time I was twenty I could ride and train anything, and began to train other people's horses for money. Horses had been my savior, my passion, my dream — my life, in fact.

We awoke with ears popping, the plane descending, and Rowan, already awake, kicking his legs out hard in front of him. Luckily these were bulkhead seats, so no one was on the receiving end of the kicks. Kicks of excitement. I looked out the window, following Rowan's gaze.

We were flying low now, the plane beginning to make its descent. Not far below us were mountains. Range after range, their tops covered with forests of pine and aspen, interspersed with high green meadows, some dotted with lakes that winked back at the morning sun. Between the ranges stretched great vastnesses of steppe, unbroken, unfenced grasslands that lapped up to the foothills like still green waters lapping at a mountain shore. There were no roads or buildings. Just a vast landscape stretching out for the eye exactly as God made it.

The plane banked, and amid murmurs of excitement from our largely German fellow passengers we rounded the shoulder of a high, rocky set of hills devoid of trees and saw, for the first time, human habitations. Not houses but *gers* (pronounced *gairs*), round tents of camel felt furnished inside, I had read, with truckle beds, brightly painted cabinets, a wood-burning stove in the center, and a doorway facing, if possible, to the south. From up here they looked like little white dots, but *gers,* I knew from my Web searches and perusals of the Lonely Planet and Bradt guides to Mongolia, could withstand the most brutal of blizzards, could have their walls rolled up a few feet from the ground to provide ventilation on hot days, and could be dismantled and loaded onto a cart in under an hour. A good thing, for most of Mongolia's three million people were still nomads. As the plane dipped even lower we could see their live-stock grazing in free-moving herds around the *gers.*

"Goats!" said Rowan delightedly. "Daisy and Howard! Play with the baby goats."

Two riders cantered leisurely below us, one mounted on a dark brown horse, the other on a gray, and then we were passing over yet another low mountain range, its trees bare and blackened from recent fire, and then, on the other side, a sight so extraordinary in this landscape of empty,

God-given freedom that you could not help but doubt the veracity of your vision for a moment. It was a city. A great, huge, ugly scar of a place belching smoke from power-station stacks, overhung with a yellow-brown haze of smog through which a few small skyscrapers were visible. It snaked its way along a wide valley between high ranges like some sluggish, diseased serpent — repellent, yet somehow also intriguing. What was a city like that — industrial, polluted, vast — doing here?

The flight attendants — the women with hair sprayed into such immobility that it resembled blond and brown helmets, the men somewhere between military and camp — came through to make sure our seatbacks and tray tables were up, our seatbelts fastened. We banked in low for the final descent. I turned to Kristin (Rowan still had his nose glued to the window, looking at the great city and the wild mountains beyond). She smiled and said, "No going back now."

And there we were in Mongolia, debarking from the plane with our five-year-old autistic son. As we walked across the tarmac, Rowan mounted on my shoulders, or rather on my right shoulder, as was his wont, the air close and humid, with a faint scent of wood smoke to it, I offered up a silent prayer.

We filed through immigration, Rowan slumped, bleary, and half asleep on my shoulder. Our bags arrived; I loaded Rowan's weight onto the trolley, sitting him atop the bags, and pushed him out to the arrival area, under the frowning gaze of the uniformed officials, to the reception area. There, tall above the rest of the crowd, were Justin and Jeremy, two friends who had been persuaded to come along and handle the sound and a second camera in case Michel should fall ill. At our request, they had arrived a couple of days in advance to meet Tulga, our guide, and make sure all was well before our arrival.

Justin, a friend of Michel's, six feet tall, handsome, often taciturn, sometimes wickedly humorous, already had his sound boom at the ready. Jeremy, taller still, very lean and dark, with a permanent half-goofy smile on his face, was an old friend. Rowan smiled at seeing a familiar face in this strange place. "It's Uncle Jeremy," he said, waving his toy Simba at him. "And who's that?"

The man he was pointing at stood between Justin and Jeremy. Mongolian, about our age, in a white shirt and khaki pants with a black Australian herder's hat hanging down his back, fastened round his neck with a cord, and a mobile phone in hand, he came forward, hand outstretched. "Hello," he said. "I'm Tulga. Welcome to our Mongolia."

I gave him the once-over and relaxed a little. He had that air of quiet competence you learn, after years as a travel writer, to recognize instinctively. We were in good hands, I could tell.

"Say hi to Tulga," said Kristin.

"Say hi to Tulga," said Rowan.

The man laughed good-naturedly. "This way to the van. The hotel is thirty minutes away."

Michel crammed in with us, camera whirring, while the others piled into the back seats. The morning was gray. Mountains loomed on either side of a long, narrow valley bisected by the tarmac road, which led across scrubby, rubbish-strewn pastures grazed by untended herds of cattle and sheep. Ahead of us rose the city, surprisingly huge, smokestacks and high-rises forming a solid urban wall between the high mountain ridges. Here on the steppe between airport and city, huge roadside billboards advertised women's moisturizer, Scotch whisky, Pampers, vodka. It couldn't have been less like the picture of Mongolia I had conjured in my mind's eye. Or even the rural reality I had seen on the plane's descent. Where were the proud horsemen? The nomads?

"There is UB's biggest power station," said Tulga, with evident pride, pointing to a godawful smokestack. "UB's what we call Ulaanbaatar. It's easier, I think."

"British Airways?" said Rowan querulously. I knew that tone. My stomach tightened. It was the precursor tone to a full-on tantrum. He wanted the British Airways airplane set we'd bought him at Heathrow Airport. It was in the other vehicle with the bags.

"Think we should stop and get it?" asked Kristin, looking worried.

"No," I said, knowing myself for a fool. "At least, not unless it gets really bad."

It got really bad. Really fast. Perhaps it was the fatigue of the journey or the realization that he was in a radically new, really different place, but I could tell that his need for the airplane gift set was really just displaced anxiety.

"Come and have a hug and a cuddle," I said, giving him a good deep squeeze. Rowan, like many autistic people — like me too, actually — likes deep pressure. He slapped me hard in the mouth, arched his back, and yelled, "Airplanes! Airplanes!" Then he took a deep, deep breath, and I knew what was coming: "Gi-*RAFFE!*" pitched at the special über-shriek that grates like a fingernail at the inner wall of the skull.

"Stop the car," said Kristin. "Get him his goddamned plane set."

So we did. And he stopped his tantrum. So much for Dad's psychology.

"We're flying to London, to London Zoo and then to Whipsnade Zoo, to see Lee Lee the baby elephant and Asha the baby rhino . . ."

I saw Tulga sneak a worried look at Rowan, as the reality of what it might mean to have to escort an emotionally and physically incontinent autistic kid for four weeks into some of the remotest parts of the remotest country on the planet sank in. My heart went out to him, as the strange, surreal city flitted by outside the van windows.

Ulaanbaatar was all broken-down concrete apartment buildings, cracked sidewalks crammed with hurrying people in cheap Western fashions, with the occasional traditional robe, or *deel,* of a visiting countryman strolling where others rushed. Cyrillic script on the plastic shop fronts, with occasional English: *Karaoke Bar, Game Arcade.*

A group of knowing-looking, long-haired youths in heavy metal T-shirts hanging on a street corner; bent iron railings and smashed bottles in weed-grown parks; no trees on the wide, traffic-choked streets. The people for the most part looked depressed, unsmiling, but physically robust. We saw no tourists on that drive through this city so incongruously plonked down on the steppe by the Soviets when they ruled here for sixty years during the twentieth century. Indeed, the aesthetic was far more post-Soviet than Far Eastern. Put simply, Ulaanbaatar was a carbuncle on the face of one of the most unspoiled, most intact ecosystems left on Earth. I thanked God we'd be spending only a day or two here.

Yet at the same time the place was not without a certain ruined charm, and Tulga, who confessed "I am city boy," clearly loved the place, driving us by the vast main square in front of the people's palace with its marble parade ground and heavy, Stalin-era sculptures of fierce Mongol warriors on horseback. We then drove by the Natural History Museum — duly noted, for it was only 7 a.m. and we had a long, long day ahead of us. I'd looked the place up in the Lonely Planet and knew it'd have enough taxidermy to keep Rowan fascinated for a few hours. The streets did seem pretty deserted, though, and Kristin said as much.

"Everyone is at Naadam Festival," explained Tulga. "You are probably the only tourists in all UB, maybe Mongolia, *not* going to Naadam!"

Of course, Naadam. I'd read about that in the Lonely Planet too — the annual midsummer cultural festival of wrestling, horse racing, archery, and music. People fly in from all over the world to witness this great celebration of the nomadic arts: the wrestling in the great sports stadium at the edge of town, or the horse racing — races up to an incredible twenty miles long, with eight-year-old children for jockeys — out on the steppe proper. One such horse race was being featured on the TV monitor in the foyer of the ultramodern hotel that Tulga had booked for us. As we filed into the marbled, carpeted interior, the program switched from horse racing to wrestling: men built like small mountains, dressed in almost ludicrously skimpy briefs, knee-high boots, and strange arm coverings, with pointed felt hats on their shaven heads. They looked almost camp, though the force with which they were throwing each other to the ground was anything but.

I proffered my passport to the tall lady in

the business suit manning the reception desk, taking in — as we all were — the strangeness of our surroundings.

For some odd reason the picture had switched to a group of svelte Mongolian ladies in swimwear and rubber caps, doing a fitness routine in a pool.

"Is that part of Naadam too?" joked Justin wryly.

Tulga looked round, saw the screen, smiled. "Ah, no. But we in Mongolia love our exercises."

"Let's go home," said Rowan.

"Let's go see our rooms," I said, sweeping him up, plane and all, and putting him on my shoulders.

"Gotta go ho-*ome*," wailed Rowan as we went up the stairs. Then: "Airport!" he cried in delight as we came onto the landing where our room was and scrambled down from my shoulders. "Airport. Look, like an airport."

And immediately he began playing on the ridged gray carpet of the landing, which did indeed look a little like the concrete runway he imagined as he taxied his plane along the floor, squinting sidelong in that way of his and yelling, "Time for takeoff! Time for landing," while the crew stowed their cameras and sound equipment in one room.

Tulga had the drivers carry our bags up as Kristin and I watched Rowan, both of us still dazed and fearful of what lay ahead. What were we about to attempt?

"Can you keep it down, please?" A European man, German, dressed only in a towel, appeared suddenly on the landing. "It's only seven o'clock, and I'm trying to catch up on some sleep!"

"Airport! Airport! Gi-RA-A-A-AFFE!" Rowan shrieked as we carried him into our room, which had a crimson carpet instead of a gray one. "Fer-ench fry-yi-yi-yi-yiiiiiiiiiiiiies! We gotta go ho-o-*ome!*"

"Is he okay?" Tulga put his head nervously around the door.

"I hope so," I said, looking longingly at the bed. "I really do."

I don't know quite how I had pictured our arrival in Mongolia. Straight off the plane and onto the steppe, I guess, with caparisoned horses waiting for us just beyond the baggage claim, smiling nomads cheering us, shamans dancing and drumming, eagles circling in the sky, the horses, cattle, sheep, goats, and yaks doing some kind of Broadway number in the background and the wolves and bears of the mountain accompanying on sax and trombone. Something along those lines.

Certainly not sitting in a second-rate hotel room (though I could tell that this was upper-end, with its plush red nylon pile carpet), trying to work out if it was possible to get French fries (which I was more or less certain Rowan would eat, although he often went on a hunger strike during the first few days of travel anywhere new) while the room door, which would not shut properly, swung open for the tenth time and Rowan, spotting it, made a break for the corridor, where he ran up and down shouting at the top of his lungs.

We made a strange attempt, as a group — an entourage even, with Rowan as the celebrity — to have breakfast in the hotel dining room. Rowan rolled around on the floor, pretending it was an airport runway, getting in the way of the later-rising guests, taking bites out of the cookies, taking the eggs and rolling them across the floor ("Sorry, sorry!"), and insisting on handling all the pieces of fruit on display, then taking them all and making "a picnic" on the floor, much to the chagrin of the various other Westerners coming in to breakfast and to the utter bewilderment of the staff until Tulga arrived to explain. Then they were sympathetic, but it was clear that we had to get Rowan out and moving.

We had the whole long day to kill. Tomorrow was to be the first ceremony on the sacred mountain, at which, according to Tulga, nine shamans were going to work on Rowan. And the day after that we were setting off into the interior. But meantime, in the present moment — and God knows autists know how to live in the present moment: they put all seekers after enlightenment to shame — we had to figure out what to do with the little devil. His hyperactivity was threatening to explode.

"What about the Natural History Museum?" I asked.

We arrived there just as the doors opened. I carried Rowan into the great marble hall as he querulously asked, "Fly back to London?" and started to cry a little. My stomach tightened, as, no doubt, did Kristin's. Tulga paid for the tickets, while Michel, wanting to record Rowan's reactions to everything, even a mundane museum visit, dived in and out with his high-definition digital movie camera, Justin standing quietly by with his boom, headphones on and mixing board suspended from a strap around his shoulders. They followed us up the wide marble stairway (the building had been built in the neoclassical style). Rowan wailed to go to the airport. And then he saw the first display of taxidermy — a tableau of an ibex family, the great horned males leaping onto a mountain rock while the less spectacularly horned females huddled by admiringly with their young — and suddenly he was scrambling down from my shoulders like an excited monkey, shouting "Ibex!" and we were away.

Rowan took off through the museum at a dead run, stopping before each display of Mongolian wildlife — moose, moth-eaten wolf, elk, reindeer, fox, endless species of worse-for-weather-looking stuffed birds (even penguins, which don't live in Mongolia) with their feathers falling off, wild camels, wild horses, gazelles, huge brown bears, shifty-looking wolverines, faded red foxes, grimly tusked wild boar, tuft-eared lynx, and even a mockup of bare-titted (actually hairy-titted) Neanderthals. At each glass-fronted tableau or case Rowan would stop, the rest of us lumbering to a halt behind him, and shout happily, *"What's that?"*

"A moose," I'd say, if it was a moose.

"What's that?" he'd repeat, and I would confirm that it was indeed a moose, or an ibex (again), or a wolf (again), or a reindeer (again). At which he'd demand a third time,

"What's that?" and I'd confirm the animal species for the third time, at which he'd run on. For three solid hours he ran from display to display, his little Croc-shod feet drumming on the carpet and parquet of the museum floor, the boots of the film crew thumping along behind, to the bemusement of the museum staff and the few visitors who had eschewed Naadam that day to visit the museum. Obsessively, endlessly, he ran from room to room, reveling absurdly in the taxidermy, completely ignoring the admittedly excellent collection of dinosaur bones, exhausting us all. By lunchtime, according to the lady in charge of the ibex room, Rowan had visited that display no fewer than twenty-six times. And counting. But he was showing no sign of tiring at all. So off went the boys and Kristin to lunch and round and round went Rowan and I for a final hour. I finally carried him out screaming, nodding frantically to Tulga's suggestion that we try taking him to Ulaanbaatar's big public amusement park.

"Yes," I shouted above the noise as Rowan, heartbroken to leave all that taxidermy behind, screamed "GI-*RAFFE!*" at the top of his lungs and thrashed about on my shoulders, drumming his heels hard into my rib cage. "Let's just keep him moving."

So Tulga, clearly now in mild shock at the realization of what he was in for for the next four weeks, called his assistant (in fact his nephew Bodo, who had taken the others off to a nearby fast-food joint) on his cell phone and told him to meet us at Nairamdal Park, a short drive away. "He'll like it," said Tulga, brushing a lock of hair away from his worried eyes. "Lots of kids. Lots of amusement rides. You'll see."

Rowan of course screamed bloody murder all the way. Then, when I carried him out of the van and he saw the tree-studded plain stretching away in front of him and the crowds of people moving about, he took off — once again — at a dead sprint. I had put on twenty-five pounds around my middle since his autism diagnosis. Clearly I was going to lose it.

If the people at the airport, hotel, and museum had been puzzled by the sight of a little boy running headlong with a trail of paparazzi-style cameramen on his tail, the patrons of the strange, down-at-heel pleasure park — mostly families out for the afternoon, but with a fair sprinkling of local young hipsters in rap gear or heavy metal T-shirts — stared openmouthed. And who could blame them?

Yet there was none of the brazen, finger-pointing, almost hostile attention I'd some-times experienced in other Asian countries. There was an air of discretion, of dignity, about these people. The men were almost uniformly tall and fit, the women strong-looking, beautiful. They were curious about us — you'd have had to be inhuman not to be, as a five-year-old whizzing about the crowds with a film crew close behind would attract attention anywhere. Yet once the first surprise was over, everyone tolerated Rowan's pushing, yelping, and joyful rush-ing about with a good humor quite at odds with the more usual tut-tuttings or worse that we had come to expect in the United States and Britain, when Rowan was at his most autistic. Here, it was as if we — he — were somehow being *accommodated,* not merely tolerated, despite the spectacle we were making as we thundered about in his wake like photographers behind some di-minutive model or movie star. By the time Rowan had had his fill and had headed back to the van, pausing to examine all the cheap plastic toys being sold by the vendors lining the walkway from the main park to the car park, we were all completely exhausted. We hadn't yet been in the country twelve hours and already Rowan had outlasted us all.

"Wow," said Tulga, giving a meaningful

shake of the head as we piled into the van and headed back to the hotel. "A lot of energy, huh?"

"You don't even know," said Kristin. "You don't even know."

It did the trick, though. By 8 p.m., despite the bass thump from the nearby discotheque, we were all out like lights.

Tomorrow we would meet the shamans.

6
LORDS OF THE MOUNTAINS, LORDS OF THE RIVERS

The day dawned warm and humid, with Rowan sitting bolt upright in bed as the first ray of sunlight penetrated the hotel room's thin red curtain. Kristin groaned. I turned over, wishing myself back to sleep, then remembered the door that didn't shut properly — and in a flash I was out of bed and racing out into the corridor in my boxers to retrieve my escaping son, heading down the stairs at a fast clip toward the reception hall and the street outside. I swooped him up, smiled an embarrassed smile at the girl working the desk that morning, and hauled Rowan back up the stairs, while he wailed, *"Office! Office!"* presumably referring to the reception area, and I wondered whether it might be possible to get any coffee. Then I remembered what this day was: the first day of the healing we had come halfway across the world to find. Or rather, to try to find. Today we were going to meet nine shamans at the foot of the sacred mountain known as the Bogd Khan, just outside the capital.

"Do you want to go see some shamans?" I asked ingenuously back in the room, as I pulled off his pajamas and started dressing him — or rather, trying to get him to dress himself. "Yes please or no thank you?"

"Go see the shamans yes please."

Well, that seemed a good enough sign to be going on with.

"I'll go in search of coffee," said Kristin, who had already put on jeans and a shirt. "Something tells me we're going to need it."

"So," said Michel, coming in with the camera as she went out, "what's the plan of action?"

"Oh, you know, what every family does on a . . . whatever-day-it-is morning — go to a sacred mountain and attend a shaman-istic ceremony."

One of the many surreal things about Ulaan-baatar (and truly, there's enough to keep a German expressionist filmmaker happy for decades) is that the moment you step or drive out of the city — and despite the size of the place, there really is an abrupt line, with buildings on this side, pastureland and mountain on that — you are immediately in the wilderness. We drove through the crowded, dirty city center with its rundown Soviet-era architecture, Internet-age computer, fast-food, and coffee joints, and occasional monolithic statues of Lenin, Genghis Khan, and what looked like unknown Red Army soldiers, out through a strange mix of industrial yards overflowing with old machine parts, stray livestock, and a few traditional *gers* surrounded by wrecked cars, rolls of steel cable, and piles of animal hides, until finally, perhaps half an hour after we'd set out from the hotel, the city simply stopped. In the same way medieval cities in Europe once did: no suburb, no sprawl, just urban and rural bumping heads. The detritus of the city — a drifting vanguard of plastic bags, paper wrappers, old car batteries, and smashed vodka bottles — mounted a valiant effort to colonize the grassland. But gradually the trash petered out, its thinner, more edible bits nibbled on by sheep and goats, and disappeared from view.

The sacred Tuul River appeared — shallow, fast-flowing, full of rocky shoals and islands overgrown with black poplar and birch — and then a thin belt of dark green larch and pine along its banks, and finally a narrow line of wild pasture between the river and the steeply rising mountain wall. The larches and pines spread their branches over moss-grown boulders and *ovoos,* great stone cairns where offerings were made to the local deities. Immediately behind this narrow strip of forest rose the almost sheer sides of the Bogd Khan, Mongolia's most sacred mountain.

We passed the presidential palace, set back behind great wrought iron railings that various people had twisted and bent holes in. Clearly you could make a campfire in the presidential park if you wanted to. Then we hit a roadblock.

"It's because the president of Japan has come in for the Naadam," explained Tulga with a shrug as we came to a halt. He got out to chat with the dour-faced policemen. "It'll take about twenty minutes."

"Rowan hates delays," I said.

"Goooo! *GO!*" wailed Rowan, as if on cue.

We looked around. A little way up the hillside stood a statue — a vast statue, actually. A vast golden statue of a Buddha.

"Let's go check that out," said Kristin.

I had a twinge of worry. It looked just the kind of thing to set off Rowan's obsessive side. As an autism parent, you get a nose for that after a while.

"Oh, come on," said Kristin. "We've got to do something to fill the time. Come on, Scubs." She held out a hand to Rowan, using his pet name. "Let's go see the Buddha."

"Buddha!" Rowan's eyes lit up as he registered the great golden statue partway up the hill. And then he was out of the van and away up toward the monument at a determined sprint, the rest of us — as was becoming usual — lumbering along in his wake. We had made it pretty much to the base of the first golden foot of the Buddha when we heard Tulga calling us back.

"We'd better go," I said. "Can't hang out long at a police roadblock, I guess."

I scooped Rowan up.

"Buddha!"

His body tensed, stiffened, the legs locking, back arching, throat choking with the rising pitch of the scream-rising-to-shriek: "Gir-*AFFE!* Want the Buddha. We'll see the Buddha tomorrow! No more Buddhas *ever!* Frey-ench fry-yi-yi-yeyes! We gotta go ho-*o-ome!*"

As always when the obsessive neurological loop kicked in after the frustration and Rowan seemed caught in a sheer screaming hell of his own creation, a fist closed about my heart. When he was small, looking at

135

him, I had felt I was watching my heart moving about outside my body. Now, more and more it was like a fist closing tight about that heart, crushing it as if a kid were picking up a baby chick too roughly and squeezing the life from it. He was getting strong. It was taking more and more muscle power to hold him, prevent him from spinning out and drumming his head on the pavement, hurting himself. He arched, convulsed, hit himself, hit me, bit at my arms and hands, slapped my face. I wanted to shout at him. I might have, too, if it hadn't been in public, with the cameras rolling. Instead, tight-lipped and British, I turned on Kristin and demanded to know why she had insisted on going to the bloody Buddha in the first place, while my over-grown, massive toddler caught in a larger child's body writhed and screamed in my arms.

Tense, we got in the van as Rowan rolled around screaming for the Buddha. Was he really screaming for the Buddha? Tulga seemed to think so. "He really likes the Buddha, huh?"

We drove the rest of the way in silence. Well, not Rowan. I could see the driver wincing as he tried to concentrate on the winding road, which followed the meandering whim of the Tuul River. "Look!" I pointed out the window, hoping to distract my tantrumming son. "See the water? Want to go play in the water? Have a splash-splash?" He was five and a half years old, and I still talked to him as if he were a little toddler. Sometimes, as now, it really depressed me.

"Play in the water," said Rowan querulously. I caught Kristin's eye. That was unusual, for a distraction like that actually to work.

The van stopped; Tulga threw open the door. We had arrived.

"River!" shouted Rowan, grabbing his animal bag and skipping out of the vehicle and away in the opposite direction from where I could see people gathered by a grove of evergreens whose boughs were all hung with blue silk scarves. Kristin dashed after him.

"Is it okay?" I asked Tulga worriedly. "You did tell the shamans, or whoever is representing them, about Rowan's condition, didn't you? That he can't sit still or anything — that he'll have to run in and out of the ceremony at will?"

"Yes, is okay," Tulga said, though he didn't look too convinced. "I asked before. As long as you can bring Rowan there when the shaman says the spirits are calling. Come . . ."

I took a look over my shoulder and saw that Rowan already had his toy animals out and was splashing them in the shallows of the stream, Kristin and Jeremy watching over him, so I followed Tulga to where the nine shamans and their assistants — perhaps twenty or thirty folk in all — were sitting, chatting with each other on the grass by the trees with the offerings hanging from their boughs. Some were in Western clothing, others in blue or purple *deels* (the traditional Mongolian long tunic, tied at the waist with a broad sash) and fur or pointed felt hats, despite the gathering heat and humidity. I was sweating as I walked. Tulga and I carried offerings of vodka, though whether for the shamans to drink after the ritual or to use during the ritual wasn't clear. I also had money, around $125 for each of the nine shamans that Tulga had told me were going to show up that day. I'd withdrawn the crisp *tögrögs* — a vast fat wad of them — at the hotel cash machine. They felt cool in my sweating palm. Tulga led me past the seated people, nodding greetings and saying, *"Oglooni mend,"* good morning, as they nodded back, raising a hand, often as not with a lit cigarette between the fingers. I saw that some makeshift altars had been set up, with incense burning from small fires of dried cow dung on either side of them. We walked on by until we came to a man sitting slightly apart from the rest of the group. He got up to greet us. Tulga gave a small bow; so did I.

"This Mr. Sukhbat, chairman of the Shamans' Association of Mongolia," announced Tulga, who then briefly introduced me in Mongol. There was a shamans' *association?* The man took my hand. He had a crushing grip and smelled of vodka. Had I fallen into a nest of charlatans? But the man was talking, Tulga translating every few seconds.

"He says he and the shamans are very honored that you have come, have brought your child so far. They say they are very touched that you have put trust — no, that's the wrong word — that you have placed such *value* on their religion, which even their own people rejected for a time. He says because they were . . . *suppressed* under communism, many people forgot shamanism, though it was the original religion of the Mongols. Anyone found with a drum or the other, er, *equipment* was put in the jail. Only a few shamans in the very far places survived. Now they teach others and it slowly comes back again. You are helping this."

Great, I thought. *We're guinea pigs.* I smiled. "Please tell him that we are very honored that he has arranged so many shamans to come and help my son."

The man bowed again and said something in reply. Tulga translated: "He says that this is the largest gathering of shamans in Mongolia since communism. When I first told him of you and Rowan and your coming, he put out the word to his contacts all over Mongolia. They all agree that this is a very big healing, very complicated, maybe very hard for them. So they decide to come, as many as possible. Some today have come two, three, four hundred miles — from the Altai Mountains in the far west, from the mountains near to the birthplace of Genghis Khan in the northeast, from the taiga even, some of them — that's the Siberian forest. All coming from many different tribes to try to help Rowan."

I felt chastened for my skepticism. Then again, I had been around enough shamans and healers (and doctors and therapists, for that matter) to know that a little skepticism was never a bad thing. Well, one just has to react as one reacts. The main thing was that we were here.

"Please," said Tulga as the man shook my

hand again. "He says they are ready to start. I will translate. I have a notebook. Maybe when each shaman is finished I can tell you what they say."

"That'd be very kind. Please tell the chairman thank you again."

And so we walked back past the seated, chatting figures and their altars and incense offerings. Some of them had large round drums laid out on the grass. Rowan was still down by the river, happy with Kristin and Jeremy and his *Lion King* game.

When we got to the place where the first shaman was waiting, Tulga said, "This shaman is Buryat, from the far north, in the taiga, near where the reindeer people are." How appropriate, I thought — for it had been a Buryat Siberian shaman whom I had spoken to by e-mail back when the Mongolia idea had first come to me, three years before. Would we find those elusive forest shamans of the reindeer folk? Would we even get that far? I put the thought out of my mind. We were here now. The shaman, a woman in her late thirties or early forties, was putting on a coat made of deerskins, the fur on the outside, all hung about with little iron objects that dangled from the fur, not unlike matte black Christmas ornaments. As we came near, she donned a headdress to which two small deer's antlers were attached — maral, red deer, by the look of them — and which had a black fringe that obscured the lower face. Two eyes and a nose were embroidered onto the front of the headdress, just above this fringe, which allowed the shaman access to her mouth but was clearly designed to make her blind to the outside world.

Flies buzzed about my head. In the distance I heard cattle lowing. A shadow passed over us and I saw a great raptor (which Tulga later told me was a steppe eagle) fly in and alight on one of the branches of the nearest evergreen, higher up than the hanging offerings. It looked at us with yellow eyes. Behind the shaman another woman, presumably her assistant, stood in a cream-colored *deel* and red head-scarf, holding the drum and drumstick. As we came level she placed these into the shaman's hands, and almost immediately, as the assistant motioned for us to sit on the ground at the shaman's feet, the fur-clad, antlered, blinded figure began to drum and sing.

"She's calling in the spirits now," whispered Tulga.

So it began.

She faced the mountain, the tree where

the steppe eagle sat and watched, and began to sing a long, long prayer, melodic, beautiful to hear. She raised the drum, began to beat a deep, rapid rhythm, then started to whirl it, still singing, still drumming, around and around, bending low to the grass, reaching up to the sky. She turned, faced the north, toward the Siberian lands she came from, and repeated the song, the whirling, drumming prayer. Then all of a sudden she squatted down and said something in a high, singsong voice to her assistant. The woman responded by reaching toward the little altar, flanked by two incense fires, that had been set up facing the mountain and taking a small carton of milk that had been set ready there and pouring from it into a little shallow metal bowl. It was then proffered to me.

"She says you must drink it," said Tulga.

I'd been afraid of that. I'm milk- and egg-phobic. Always have been: milk so grossed me out as a kid that I took my cereal with water, and I've done so ever since. As for eggs, I'd hand over my wallet if threatened with an egg in a dark alley. And here I was in the land of the nomads, where milk, milk curd, and meat are the traditional staples. I took a breath and downed the contents of the little bowl, fighting my gag reflex. It was filled up again immediately. My heart sank, then rose again as Tulga translated: "You have to face the direction of your homeland and say a prayer to the Lords of the Mountains where you come from, for the healing, and then offer this milk to them."

"Lords of the Mountains?"

"Yes, you must pray to them . . ." Tulga fought for a quick contextual translation. "These are the spirits we pray to here. Some of them, anyway — Lords of the Mountains, Lords of the Rivers. Can you do that?"

I turned and faced west. I'd been brought up mainly in London and Leicestershire, neither of which had many hills to speak of. Unless you counted Parliament Hill in London, where I'd spent a lot of time hanging out and smoking dope as a teenager. Well, it could do no harm to pray to the spirit of that beautiful place, surely. And for the past twenty years or so, since my aunt and sister had moved to the Welsh borders, I'd spent quite a lot of time in those high hills and low mountains. I thought of the waterfall I always visited, which I had taken Rowan to a week or so before. I thought of the dry, rocky Texas hill country too, whose rattlesnake-infested uplands rose just west of where we now lived. I said my prayers to whatever lords, whatever spirits presided over those places, and then, as instructed, hurled the milk out of the bowl into the air toward the West, where I came from, where those distant hills and mountains were.

"Okay," said Tulga when I was done, speaking up against the drumming and the loud song of the whirling, dancing shaman. "She says the spirits are here now. You have to go fetch Rowan."

"Okay," I said, quaking inwardly. If he was happy playing *Lion King* with his animals down at the river, no way would he be ready to uproot himself and submit to whatever the shaman had in mind. I jogged the few hundred yards and, sure enough, found Rowan deep in his game, Kristin and Jeremy standing over him, chatting.

"River! More river!" he said as I scooped him up, saying, "Time to go see the shamans."

"First shamans, then more river!"

"Yes, yes — exactly."

I hoisted him onto my shoulders and began the sweaty jog back, Kristin and Jeremy bringing up the rear. I was surprised he wasn't tantrumming again. "Look, it's the shamans," he said as we drew near. Then, as we sat down on the grass by the whirling, dancing, drumming, masked, antlered figure, the shaman herself sat down suddenly and held out her arms.

"He's not good with new people," I said to Tulga as he directed me to pass Rowan across.

"The shaman needs to," said Tulga rather helplessly. So, whispering nonsense to comfort and distract *(Scubby-scubby-scub. You're my scubby-wub. Gonna take a wash in the shaman tub. Scubba-dub-dub),* I passed Rowan over — as much as you *can* pass a fifty-pound, kicking, screaming, and violently resisting child. Still, once in the shaman's arms, to my great surprise, he went suddenly quiet and still. Until the assistant passed her spiritual mistress a bottle of vodka, from which the shaman took a hearty pull, then without warning spat the liquid all over Rowan's face and body. The result was predictable.

"Gi-*RAFFE!* GOTTA GO HO-O-OME! FREY-ENCH FRY-YI-YI-YI-YEYES!"

The shaman passed Rowan back to me. "Can I let him go?" I asked Tulga, trying to keep my voice level. He said something to the shaman's assistant, who nodded her assent. I released Rowan from my grip and he went off at speed, back toward the river.

"You have to stay here. Both parents have to stay here," said Tulga.

"Okay. Jeremy!" I shouted.

"Yo!"

"Take off after Scubby Boy. Make sure he's okay."

"Gotcha."

"You must kneel here," said Tulga. I noticed that the shaman, still singing her beautiful reedy song, had put down her drum and instead held a large and heavy deer's antler festooned with bells and ribbons.

"Lie down like so."

I curled into a ball, not on my side like a fetus, but with my back exposed to the sky.

Down came the deer antler, heavy on my back, the bells jingling. Not hard, not really painful at all. Almost reassuring, in fact, like being thumped on the back by a friend, albeit a friend wielding a large, heavy object.

Then it was Kristin's turn to drink milk, say prayers, cast her milk as an offering to the West, crouch down for the antler thumps, and then both of us lined up to have vodka spat on us too. Most refreshing. Actually, it kind of was as it first burned, then evaporated from the skin. I was amazed that Rowan hadn't had more of a meltdown. Leaving the Buddha had been far worse. Then a small bowl of vodka was proffered to Kristin, and Tulga was suddenly listening intently as the shaman's assistant gabbled what was clearly a complicated set of instructions. Oddly, as he listened, I saw Tulga blush, cast a sidelong look at Kristin, blush again, and nod. Then, almost reluctantly, he turned to her and gave her the small, brimming bowl.

"Er . . . the shaman says that when you were pregnant, black energy entered your womb. You must take this vodka and cleanse the, um, *parts* where Rowan came down."

Kristin looked at him a moment. "You're saying I have to take this bowl of vodka and wash my vagina out with it?"

Tulga looked at the grass. "Um . . . yes, the shaman says is very important."

Poor Kristin. Off she went to the river, Michel filming away. "Don't worry, I'll make sure nothing too personal ends up in frame," he said, grinning to himself.

"Actually," said Kristin as she walked away, trying not to spill the vodka from the shallow bowl, "Rowan was a C-section baby, so I'll wash the scar too."

"Okay," I said distractedly, looking at Rowan, who had returned from the river and forgotten his tantrum completely. He stood giggling up at the lady shaman, still whirling, drumming, and singing away.

"And you'd better PhotoShop out my cellulite," I heard Kristin say as she and Michel marched out of earshot. At least her sense of humor hadn't failed her. Yet.

Next thing I knew Tulga was pulling at my arm. "The second shaman is preparing. You must sit there while he calls the spirits in. I'm going to write down what the Buryat shaman's assistant tells me from her contact with her spirits."

Rowan and I sat down together by the second shaman, a slender young man not yet in his robes and fringed mask. Rowan was now happily playing with his toy animals right there in between the two shamans, oddly at peace. The second shaman donned robes of blue and a mask that hid his face, but no antlers. As we sat, he pulled out a Jew's harp and began to play a strange, rhythmic tune, stopping every few moments to break into a prayer or song, before resuming the doing-doing-doing of the mouth harp. Rowan looked up at the noise, gave a throaty chuckle, and went back to his animals. No drumming this time, but more spitting of vodka and choking down warm, disgustingly sour milk, Rowan screaming as if being tortured during those moments, then going back to his play, the distress of one moment not seeming to affect the calm of the next. Then, as Kristin and Michel came back from the river

(Kristin saying, "I can't believe I just did that"), Tulga — on orders from the new shaman's middle-aged female assistant — pulled me to my feet and made me sit facing the mountain.

"No," he said, "on your knees."

My knees? I had noticed but until this moment hadn't really registered the fact that shaman number two wore a rawhide whip at his belt.

"He's going to whip me, isn't he?" I asked, half incredulous, half terrified.

Tulga gave a nervous laugh. "Little bit. Is important not to cry out."

"Jesus," I said, and took a deep breath.

I've experienced pain before. Growing up riding horses, you take falls, occasionally bad falls. At school the teachers beat us from time to time, especially the gym teachers. I'd been hit in fights, beaten up during a mugging in South Africa, had a hand wound scrubbed clean with no anesthetic in India. But the pain of that lash, delivered full force, took my breath clean away.

One, two, three went the lash across my back. I couldn't cry out, though the pain burned like a branding iron. All I could do was breathe hard.

The shaman moved in front of me, lifted my arms, made me hold them out, palms facing down. Then he whipped me across the back of the hands, across the forearms, across the chest, and — this one just about lifted me out of my skin — across the groin. I managed not to cry out at that blow, but only just.

"Okay." Tulga's voice came in through the pain. "You have to stand up now."

I did.

"And jump — up and down. Yes . . ."

I jumped, feeling embarrassed and at the same time kind of stunned by the pain. More than, say, three of those full-on rawhide lashes in the same spot would break the skin. I could feel the welts rising. "Good Lord," I said, rather weakly.

"Okay," said Tulga, translating for the shaman's assistant once more. "Kristin must come here."

"Oh Christ," I thought. "She'll divorce me."

I told her, trying to make it sound as low-key as possible, what she was going to have to do. To my amazement, instead of refusing there and then, she just nodded, knelt down, and started deep-breathing. *Whack, whack, whack.* The shaman stopped at three lashes, not quite as hard as the ones he'd given me, but hard enough.

"Up, you must get up!" Tulga translated

for the shaman. "You have to jump."

"I can't believe this," said Kristin, jumping two-footed into the air.

"Higher! You have to go higher!"

And so, laughing at the sheer absurdity of it all, laughing through her pain, Kristin jumped, hair flying, knees tucked up high as if she were a schoolgirl jumping rope, as the shaman whipped the ground under her feet: a strange sort of dance, or jump-rope macabre.

"God, I'm so proud of you!" I said when it was done, holding out my still smarting arms. "Do you forgive your crazy husband?"

We embraced, laughing despite ourselves. "I'm so sorry," I half whispered, half chuckled. "Your crazy bloody husband."

She laughed back, the experience too intense for words. I heard Rowan laughing too, and looked around to see that the shaman was rubbing the whip across his back and belly, which Rowan found hilarious, then whipping the ground: a much more humane version of what he had done to us. Then he whirled away again, possessed once more by his gods.

7
MONGOLIAN
BROTHER

Kristin and I sat down on the close-cropped grass, rubbing at our red and purple welts, quite unable to believe what we had just been through. Rowan, content now, lay next to us, playing with his Simba and Scar lions, listening to the drumming as four of the shamans began to limber up with their prayers a little distance from us. The shaman who had just whipped us was staggering, breathing hard, sweating, as his assistant and the first shaman, now divested of her deerskin coat and mask, helped him off with his blue robes. He collapsed to the grass and sat vacantly while they rubbed his palms and shoulders, bringing him back to the present moment. As they did this, both women told Tulga what the shaman's spirits had said to him about us and Rowan, about his condition, what had been coming out through his song, while Tulga, listening intently, scribbled their words down into a little notebook. The eagle still watched from the upper boughs of the larch tree. The day grew closer, hotter.

Tulga came over. "Both the shamans are asking, was there anyone on your side, Kristin, who was like a shaman?"

"My side of the family, you mean?"

"Yes, that's what they are asking. Was there someone who was like a shaman in their state of mind?"

"No, not that I've ever heard of. No."

"It's funny. They are both saying that they are getting information that someone on your side of the family might have been some kind of . . . like a shaman . . . not a shaman, but . . ."

"Someone in the past, you mean? Someone dead?"

"Yes."

"Well." Kristin looked doubtful, rubbing her sore back. The close day, making us sweat, made the welts smart more. "I'm the king of Pride Rock," said Rowan softly, deep in his *Lion King* game. "Well," she said again, "who knows in the past? I mean, my dad's side of the family came from the Greek islands, and others from Scandinavia. I suppose there could have been someone back then."

"You said *like* a shaman," I put in. "Not

154

necessarily actually a shaman, right?"

"Yes." Tulga nodded. "Something like that."

"And this person is a good ancestor or spirit for Rowan?"

"No, the spirit is not helpful, they say. I'm not sure I understand fully. I'll ask them again — hold on."

As Tulga conferred briefly and the shamans up the line began to drum and dance, facing the mountain, Kristin said, "I don't know what he means, *like* a shaman. And you know, a lot of my forebears I know nothing about . . ."

Tulga came back. "I understand better now. They are saying that this person was not so far back. And was maybe a little . . . I don't know . . . oversensitive in the mind? Not so . . . stable, perhaps?"

"I suppose there was my grandmother on my mom's side — my mom's mom. She was manic-depressive. Ended up institutionalized. Maybe her? But I can't think what she'd be doing still hanging around . . . I don't know if I even believe people *do* still hang around. Still, her son was hit by a car and died when he was eight, and that was when her mental problems started. She never recovered from losing him, not seeing him grow. Then, years after that tragedy, my mom married and moved out of the house, and her husband had a heart attack and died. She really lost it after that."

"There are some other things that they were saying too — some things about water, and black energy entering your womb while you were pregnant. I don't understand it fully myself. I will go back and ask them some more. See if I can get a clearer picture . . ."

"Black energy from water?"

There were some shouts from the farther group. "Oh," said Tulga, "they are ready. We must go over there."

"Okay." Once again I scooped Rowan up onto my shoulders.

"Let's go see some more shamans!" said Rowan, from up top. Tulga ran ahead to talk with the shamans' assistants. Four shamans were standing in a line, singing their prayers to the mountains, whirling, drumming, entering their trance. The sound of the four drums together was loud, exciting.

"Just like Bodychoir!" said Rowan, starting to bounce up and down on my shoulders in time to the drums.

"Yes, that's right!" God, I was relieved — he was starting to enjoy himself. "Just like Bodychoir!" And I started to dance underneath him.

Bodychoir was a regular part of our Austin hippy life and something Rowan associated with home: a thrice-weekly dance workshop in which the music started slow, culminated in a chaotic climax, then gradually slowed down to stillness over an hour and a half or so. Kristin and I, both mad dancers, had been attending Bodychoir ever since we'd stumbled into it one evening at a yoga studio when we first moved to Texas. It was one of the few things we could take Rowan to — he loved being bounced on my shoulders as the room swirled around him, pumping his fists to the techno beat. At the end of the dances, when the participants sat in a circle and talked about their experience, Rowan would run around madly, yelling, happy, contained in the safe, tolerant space. Bodychoir, though we seldom made it more than once a month if we were lucky, had been a sanity saver for us.

"Bodychoir! Dance and dance and dance!" trilled Rowan as the drums thundered off the tall larches and the shamans began to sing their prayers to the lords of the forest, river, and mountain. Rowan gave a deep, bubbly giggle, dancing away on my shoulders, and in that moment I knew he was okay. Not just okay — that he had embraced the situation and was, at some

157

level, really at peace with this crazy ceremony we were putting him through. Were we terrible parents for doing this? As soon as Rowan began to dance on my shoulders like that, I began — or rather, dared to let myself *begin* to begin — to let myself think that maybe this was all right after all.

"Yes," I said, feeling a great rush of relief. "Just like Bodychoir."

And with that the shamans' assistants called us over.

If the experience had been loud with the first two shamans, a sensory overload of the kind usually guaranteed to send Rowan over the edge of autistic meltdown, the next hour or so upped the stakes so high that for what seemed an eternity, Rowan had to be held in my lap, in Kristin's, or even in a shaman's while the drum thundered away just inches from his face. At times the shamans — all of whom had traveled up from the edge of the Gobi Desert to enact this ritual on Rowan's behalf — actually placed Rowan under the drum and hammered on it with Rowan caught in a deafening soundbox. Sometimes they accidentally bashed him on the head or body with the side of the drum, or with the drumstick. Sometimes their yelling prayer-song rose to a shriek just inches from his face. Sometimes they would grasp his hand or leg and blow on it, or make him hold a sacred object, their own fist, or mine, or Kristin's closed over Rowan's to hold his hand there. I was on a knife edge the whole time, expecting him to explode at any moment, expecting maybe — no, probably — to have to shut the whole thing down, thank them all for their time, and take Rowan away, apologizing to him for subjecting him to such an extreme situation.

But Rowan, far from retreating into screaming, scared distress, reacted the opposite way completely. Still giggling, he started trying to tickle the first shaman, grabbing at her and saying, "Tickle! Time for a tickle!" laughing uproariously as her prayers echoed off the mountainside and the day grew so hot and close that you could see the sweat pouring down from behind her feathered mask with its embroidered eyes, nose, and mouth. My shirt was stuck to my back. Kristin was wiping the sweat from her eyes. Tulga was squinting the sweat away and trying not to let it wet the page of his notepad as he tried to write down snatches of the shaman's song. Only when it came time to have vodka spat all over him again did Rowan, sweating merrily, scream and twist away, but just for a moment. Next thing he was grabbing at the shaman's mask and headdress, giggling, trying to pull it from her head, so that she jerked back, still in trance, possessed by her spirits yet having to protect herself from the mischief of a child. The mood had changed. Rowan was *enjoying* himself. Against all odds.

As the first of the four shamans yelled her final note and beat her concluding tattoo and we were ushered over to the next shaman in line, Rowan looked at me, gave a squinting smile, grabbed my hair, pulled my head in close, and rubbed my nose with his. There is no higher gesture of affection that he shows his father. Then, giving that throaty giggle again, he let go a great, ripping fart. "Farty noise!" he shouted, at the top of his lungs, then, "More shamans!"

So more he got. And up and down went his mood. One moment he was laughing and grabbing at their masks, their drumsticks, their feathers, their drums; the next he was screaming, twisting away, yelling "Almost done!" or "River!" and then laughing, giggling, and grabbing again, playing with them once more as they yelled and sang and drummed and whirled and laid their hands on him, spat vodka, gave us milk to drink, prayers to say, offerings to hurl westward.

I looked up at the trees flanking the

mountain. The eagle was still there. As I happened to be looking up, carrying in my arms a now fully engaged Rowan over to the next ritual, two big black ravens flew cawing down out of the sky and perched on the same branch as the eagle, a few feet away.

This was odd — crows and ravens usually mob hawks and eagles. Biological competitors, they do not often tolerate each other's presence in the same stretch of sky, much less the same tree or tree branch. Yet here they were, all three tolerating each other, looking down on us as the next shaman, a bearded man from the Altai Mountains, recited his opening prayers, then turned and began to dance and twirl his drum over our heads.

There was something empathetic about this man, though I couldn't quite put my finger on why. Something in his body language. Although he whirled and sang and drummed as energetically as the other shamans had, whenever he came close to Rowan, his movements became quieter, gentle, slow, the way one moves when approaching a nervous young horse or a nervous puppy. His song became soft. Rowan reached out to him. The shaman, singing gently, almost intimately, swung the long ribbons of his drumstick over Rowan's face and back. My son gave another of those deep-throated bubble-giggles and started play-grabbing at the ribbons even as they whisked over him. The shaman sat down, removed his headdress and robe, and smiled, giving Rowan — back now to playing with his animals in the close-cropped grass — a paternal thump on the back and legs.

"He'll be fine," he said. "Just do this once a year for the next three years. This or something like this. He'll be healed."

Somehow, when Tulga translated this, I felt a shift in my chest. Did I dare believe it? I tried not to think about it either way. Tried to stay in the present moment. As if sensing my need to guard my heart, my expectations, the bearded shaman got to his feet and went off to offer his final prayers. I watched him go, wondering if I should allow myself to believe him.

We had been at the foot of the Bogd Khan for three hours now. I was amazed at Rowan's stamina, at our own. The light was shifting. Clouds were gathering; a wind was getting up. A herd of cows came lolling in from upriver, saw us, stood awhile gaping in their bovine way, then ambled off. The eagle and the two ravens continued to negotiate the shared territory of their branch. The long blue silk scarves snaked out from the larch limbs on the cooling east wind. Cars drifted by on the narrow road that followed the riverbank. The shamans who had already performed their rituals sat and smoked and chatted among themselves. Tulga scribbled in his notebook. I went and searched for wild greens for Rowan in the pasture, for there seemed to be something of a lull now, before the final shamans got going. I found dandelion, plantain, wild violet: all edible. He'd eaten more or less nothing but potato chips since his arrival the previous day.

"Hey, Rowan," I said, going over to where he'd been playing by one of the dung and incense-smoking field altars. "Look — Daddy leaves."

But Rowan had put his toys down, his attention drawn instead to another little boy, a Mongolian boy in a baseball cap and shorts, whom I had seen hanging out on the periphery of the various family groups surrounding the shamans. Rowan was hugging the boy, who was perhaps half an inch taller than he and maybe a year older, laughing and grabbing at the boy's cap. The boy, caught between annoyance and acceptance — for he clearly felt the eyes of all the grown-ups on him — stood stiffly but acquiescing. Rowan didn't normally take much interest in other kids. He was the classic autistic "parallel player," preferring to ignore other children while playing alongside them rather than to actively engage.

Tulga appeared at my elbow. "The next shaman is calling in his spirits now. You have to come."

I have to admit that of the eighth shaman, I remember little but a generalized blur. At some point the rising humidity broke, and a light rain washed over us briefly, like a benediction, only to peter out and allow the heat and humidity to come back twice as strong as before. When he was done, this shaman was on his knees with exhaustion, his assistants — two of them I remember, young men who looked like they could be his sons — running off to fetch water for the poor man and peeling off his robes, as he looked about ready to pass out.

Rowan went back to the river and wasn't exactly pleased when I jogged over to get him for the final shaman, but he came with good enough grace, especially because he saw the little boy hanging out near the group surrounding the last shaman, who was warming himself up with prayer, facing the mountain in the now familiar way. And so into the final ritual we went, Rowan acquiescing once more — to my surprise — to being put under the drum, to the noise and drama of it all, giggling and grabbing at the shaman's drumstick and feathered headdress as he had before. I was relaxing now, even though the heat was all but unbearable, for this was, I knew, the final ordeal of this long, long day. We'd been here for what? Four hours by now? Longer? Rowan was being a champ. Just one more to go and . . .

At that moment the shaman reared up and suddenly, before I could stop him, whacked Rowan on the back with the cloths and ribbons attached to the end of his drumstick. Rowan screamed. I lunged at the man, but two of the woman assistants got in front of me, saying, "No, no, is okay, okay!" As they did so, the cloths and ribbons came down a second time, and a third. On the last one I managed to get my forearm in the way and take most of the blow there, which luckily wasn't as hard as I had feared, but it was hard enough. Rowan was yelling blue murder. I gathered him into my arms, feeling like the worst parent on the planet. I stood up, Rowan clinging tightly, as the shaman staggered away, dropping his drum, into the arms of several others, the trance having taken him into sudden unconsciousness. Rowan made not a sound. At that same moment one of the middle-aged women who had been assisting the various groups came over and, without a word, took Rowan into her arms.

Normally he'd never allow a stranger to do that. But he hugged her tight as she crooned to him. The ritual was over, the shaman, singing softly to himself, sitting on his knees, clearly still half in trance. Rowan looked up from the woman's neck and smiled the most extraordinary, peaceful smile and said, "What's that?" pointing at the breast of the woman who held him. "I think it's a person."

At that moment there came a loud clap of thunder from the mountain and the heavens opened. A great sheet of rain. Jeremy, Justin, and Michel went running to cover their equipment. The rest of us just stood, reveling in the sudden coolness, the feeling of warm rain. "Mongolian mommy," Rowan kept repeating over and over, with the most strangely luminous, blissful expression on his face. She kept crooning to him, as if somehow taking on his pain, his suffering. He was already over the trauma of having been struck with the ribbons, though I was still shaking from it, as was Kristin. Then Rowan gave one of his throaty giggles again — it seemed incredible, how adaptive he was today — and as the rain slackened, he wriggled down out of the woman's arms and ran over to the little boy, who was standing shivering slightly in his baseball cap.

"Mongolian brother!" he said spontaneously. The kid looked surprised. A little wary, but he let Rowan hug him again. "Mongolian brother!" Rowan said again. "Come on, let's go to the river!"

Kristin and I looked at each other in amazement.

Of course the Mongolian child didn't understand at all, and Rowan didn't understand that. So after a moment of looking quizzically at the kid, off he ran, back to the river, chirping, "First Mongolian brother, then river!" with Kristin trotting after in the now gentle rain.

Tulga appeared at my elbow. He'd tucked his notebook into his jacket, away from the rain. "I see the boys are getting along," he said. "The chairman of the shamans' association wants to speak to you again before we go. And I've taken a lot of notes from the shamans. They have some instructions for you and Kristin. Maybe later this evening I should come to the hotel and we should sit down and go over what they've said. I have it written down."

"Sure. Listen, who is that boy over there? Rowan just went up to him and called him 'Mongolian brother'! He never approaches other kids like that. Is he the son of one of the shamans?"

"No, that's my boy, Tomoo."

"*That's* Tomoo?" I had forgotten, completely forgotten, that during our e-mail correspondence, Tulga had said that he was going to bring his six-year-old son along for the trip.

"Yes." He pointed. "And there is Naara, my wife," he added. "They arrived while you were with the fourth or fifth shaman, I think." I looked where he pointed. The boy was talking to a small, pretty woman in her thirties by a little hatchback car I hadn't seen when we first arrived, parked away from the vehicles that had brought the shamans.

Before we left, Tulga took me to say goodbye to the chairman of the shamans' association. We sat cross-legged on the ground. The rain had almost completely stopped now. When my thanks had been translated, the man told me, through Tulga, "All the shamans here, they agree that if you do this, a good ceremony like this, once a year for the next three years, Rowan will heal fully. For the next three years — it's important."

"Here in Mongolia?" I asked, wondering how I'd explain *that* to Kristin.

"No." Tulga translated the man's answer. "It can be anywhere — anywhere the shamans are strong. He says he wishes you well, and that he is glad you are going to the reindeer people, because they are the strongest Mongolian shamans of all. He also gives you his thanks. He is honored that you have trusted them to help you. For many years people turned their back on the old religion. You, coming so far, show them that people, even people outside of Mongolia, still value the traditions. He is grateful for that."

The light rain began to intensify once more.

"The gods are happy." Tulga was translating for the man again. "The rain shows that the Lords of the Mountains have accepted for Rowan to be healed. It is a very good sign. Also it's good that no animals came to bother us during the ceremony, and that no large flocks of birds came flying in. Those would have been signs that the Lords of the Mountains were rejecting. But the signs are all very, very good."

I didn't know what to say, so I just said, "Well, thanks. Thank you very much."

"More shamans!" yelled Rowan as I took him in my arms and put him into the van, where the rest of our party waited. *"More shamans!"*

Kristin and I exchanged looks; no words came. It had been too intense for words. It was Rowan who brought us back down to earth.

"Party pigs!" he said delightedly, spotting a bag of candy pigs that my mother had thoughtfully packed for the journey sticking out of the corner of his bag.

"Party pigs," I confirmed, opening the packet for him as the driver pulled away. The eagle and the two ravens, I noted, had gone, flown off, perhaps, with the rain.

Back in the strange, plush red-carpeted hotel room that evening, Tulga sat down and gave us the shamans' reports on Rowan's condition. Rowan, for his part, was passed out in the bedroom. We were all worn out. I'd fallen asleep in my chair on getting back from the shamans; Kristin could barely keep her eyes open. But we made one last effort as Tulga, exhausted himself, sat down with the notes that the shamans' assistants had told him to pass on to us.

"Okay," he said, scratching his head as he marshaled his thoughts. The past forty-eight hours had been as demanding for him as for us, if not more so, as he had had the responsibility of organizing it all. "Okay," he repeated. "The first shaman, the woman from the Buryat tribe up in the north, her name was Gildma. She said, as you know, that her spirits told her a black energy entered Rowan when he was in the womb, when Kristin went into some water. Out in nature. Maybe a lake or river. That is one thing. Then, in addition, there is a spirit, an ancestor, on Kristin's side. So Rowan is dealing with those two things. But she said the black energy can be cleared. I have some instructions for that, which I'll give you when I finish all the shamans' reports."

"And the ancestor on my side," said Kristin. "I just want to get it clear — does the shaman think that ancestor is being helpful or unhelpful?"

"Not helpful."

"And are we talking about an actual family member, from recently?" I put in. "Or a more distant ancestor? And are we talking male or female?"

Tulga took a moment to examine his notes, then: "Both she and the next shaman, who was from the northwest of Mongolia —"

"The one who whipped me," I said, look-

171

ing at the red weals on my arms and thighs.

"Yes, that one," confirmed Tulga. "He also said it was an ancestor — an immediate ancestor, someone close, and female. The first shaman also said it was female. And with a strange mind. That's what she meant when she first said 'like a shaman,' because some shamans have mental problems a bit before they start their training. It can be a sign that they are supposed to be a shaman. Someone in Kristin's family, a woman, not too far back, like that."

Kristin just nodded, taking this in.

"Anyway," Tulga went on, "both the first shamans said they did a lot of work for Rowan to get this spirit out and the black energy out. So then there were the four shamans from Central Mongolia — they are Khalka Mongols. The first one, she called on a Lord of the Mountain from the northeast of the country, which is where Genghis Khan was born. She said the same thing — a black energy hitting Rowan in the womb. The one after her said that a bad spirit was sitting on him, trying to pull him off the ground. That's why he was — maybe you remember — getting Rowan to hold on to the thong, and to a rabbit's foot. He was making him heavier."

"So the spirits wouldn't be able to take

him away?"

"Exactly. So he can't be pulled away. All the four Khalka shamans were doing that work. To keep Rowan here, with us. But the next guy, the one with the beard — he was Durvod, from the Altai Mountains, in the west — he called on the lords of five sacred mountains from there, holy mountains with snow and ice glaciers all year round. He said the problem started three years ago —"

"That's when he was diagnosed," confirmed Kristin.

Tulga nodded. "This man said Rowan will be okay. That the bad energy will lift. He also said that the spirit making trouble was a woman on the mother's side."

"My side," said Kristin.

"Yes. He also said this person was mentally ill in her life. He also said — and two others said this too — that he thinks Rowan will maybe be a shaman."

That was interesting. Were shamans sometimes adult autists? I thought of Temple Grandin's point, that autists could be connectors between the "normal" human world and the animal world, or the world of science or music. Were autists, in traditional societies, sometimes also connectors to the spirit world? I thought of Besa and some of the other healers I'd met, all of whom were odd, spoke in riddles, were "away with the fairies," as the British put it. That wasn't so far from Rowan. Although it was interesting how all of them had integral roles in their communities rather than being marginalized.

Tulga went on. There was a consensus among all the shamans that the black energy in Kristin's womb could be cleared through prayer and the right rituals. And also that an ancestor spirit was trying in some way to take Rowan away. All agreed that a big ritual, to appease the Master of the Waters, as Tulga put it, would be needed at least once a year to counteract this. As for the influence of this strange, probably female ancestor on Kristin's side, there were certain protective rituals we had to do now. Tulga smiled. "The shamans gave you some homework."

The shamans had indeed given Tulga some complex instructions for us, a set of nightly rituals we had to complete as a family as long as we were in Mongolia. There was a bottle of vodka and milk mixed with herbs; we had to clean Rowan's body with this each night, using wet wipes or tissues, and then throw the used cloths to the west (in this case, I would hurl them from the bathroom door to the bathroom wastepaper bin, which we'd worked out lay due west). Then there was a carton of milk with a smaller amount of vodka and different herbs, which we all had to wash in for the next three nights, throwing the used tissues, as with the first mixture, to the west. Then there was a box of matches, which we had to strike and burn that night in a pattern of three times three — three matches at a time, passing the bright burning flame three times clockwise around Rowan's body, just for this one night, until the matches were all used up. And then on top of *that* we had been given a second matchbox, this one full of finely chopped grass or herbs that smelled very similar to American sage and sweetgrass, which the Indians use in many of their ceremonies. Again, this had to be burned and passed three times around Rowan's body, clockwise, every night until we went home.

"Is there a logic to all this?" I asked, somewhat rhetorically.

Tulga gave a tired laugh. "They did not explain. Only said it was important to do."

"But, Tulga." Kristin brought us back to the matter at hand. "They did say today's healing was a success, right?"

"Yes," he said. "They said the gods accepted — the rain, the thunder, these were the signs. Very good signs. The gods have accepted, yes."

Tulga left us alone after that. As we ran a bath for Rowan and began slowly to pack up, for tomorrow we were off into the vast interior, Kristin and I found ourselves too tired to talk more. All the same, it was impossible not to wonder: had the ritual, all five long hours of it, worked? I mean, *really* worked? Would there be any difference at all? Was it all just theater? Was I an idiot for putting any credence in this? Was I in fact putting any credence in it? What did all this stuff about water and black energy mean? What black energy? What water? Kristin and I had been in California when she found out she was pregnant. We'd gone swimming in a mountain lake up by Mount Shasta, I remembered. Was that it? Or was it in Texas — Barton Springs, in the middle of Austin? The Pedernales River, out in the Texas hill country? These were places where we bathed in the hot weather, and Kristin's pregnancy had revealed itself in May, which is water-hole weather in Texas. What did it all mean? And who was this female ancestor of Kristin's with mental illness, supposedly trying to pull Rowan's spirit away? Was this all complete hocus-pocus? Was I a fool for even being here at all, dragging my family through . . . through what, exactly? Or were we exactly where we needed to be?

Rowan had made his first friend, or tried to, at least. That was something completely new. I looked at him, his small chest rising and falling softly in sleep. Maybe tomorrow we would see more changes. Maybe not. What I *did* know is that we were off, into the deep interior, to find the nomads who would take us to the sacred lake and then on up to the reindeer people. Despite all that had happened already, our journey had only just begun.

8
WEST WITH THE RAIN

"That's a total Scooby-Doo van," said Kristin, as we gathered outside the hotel next morning, ready to leave for the great interior.

"More like a pimpmobile!" said Jeremy, as the driver opened the door to the van.

"Check it out!" said Justin, hefting his sound equipment down the hotel steps. "We be pimpin'!"

The van had leopard-skin seats and little pink curtains on the windows. A strange contrast with the fact that it was a military-grade Russian four-by-four, combat khaki on the outside, all Rick James on the inside.

Rowan loved it at first sight. "Leopard spots!" he said delightedly, climbing in.

It was a tight squeeze: all of us crammed into the passenger seats of the pimpmobile, as the vehicle was immediately dubbed, with Tulga riding in front, and a second van bringing up the rear with our baggage, which, with the film equipment, was considerable. How we'd manage when the time came to switch to horses was still an open question. Tulga's wife, Naara, and little Tomoo were going to follow by car and meet us at the nomad encampment where we were to get on horseback for the eight-day ride to Lake Sharga.

"And why exactly Lake Sharga again?" asked Jeremy as the van, driven by a fat, hulking Mongol called Haada, who looked like a wrestler, moved out into the surprisingly thick weekday traffic. The city had filled up again since the Naadam weekend.

"To be honest, I don't quite know," I admitted. "I mean, this whole trip evolved kind of oddly."

I looked over at Rowan, who was staring out the window. "Look at all the people walking," he said. True enough — the sidewalks were crammed with folk hurrying along, as city dwellers do in every country of the world.

"But Lake Sharga," prompted Jeremy. "Seeing as it's such a trek to get there . . ."

"Well, I don't really know why. I thought — in fact, a Russian Siberian shaman I spoke to by e-mail after the Gathering three years ago suggested — that it might be a good idea to wash Rowan in some sacred

179

waters. I got on the Web and found a reference to this sacred lake, midway between here and the reindeer people, whose shamans are supposed to be the most powerful, so . . ."

The driver braked for a horse and cart that was holding up a line of heavy trucks, then sped nimbly and dangerously past them all, narrowly avoiding the oncoming cars as he ducked back into his rightful lane at the last possible moment.

"So you found this lake on the *Internet?*" Jeremy was incredulous. "Do you know anything more about it than that it's supposed to be sacred?"

"No," I admitted. "Not a thing. And funny thing was, I could never find that Web page after the first time. What can I say? I just have a gut feeling about it."

"You and your gut feelings," muttered Kristin, half annoyed, half joking.

The city was starting to give way to industrial yards, *gers,* patches of green here and there, strewn with rubbish, grazed by sheep and goats. We'd be out of Ulaanbaatar soon. Jeremy turned to Tulga in the front seat and tapped him on the shoulder.

"What about people here in Mongolia, Tulga — what do they say about this mysterious Lake Sharga?"

Tulga turned to face us, grinning: "I'd never heard of it before Rupert asked to go there. My wife Naara's cousins, the nomads who are going to guide us in there, don't know anything about it either. They just know where it is. That it's just a lake. Quite far away. That's all."

"So we're going all this way to see a lake that you just pulled out of your butt?" said Jeremy.

I laughed. "I suppose so. Maybe we'll know when we get there."

"Look," said Rowan. "Camels!"

He was right. We had left the city limits — abruptly, as before, the steppe lapping up to the urban edge like a great green-brown sea, mountains in the far distance — and there they were, a line of huge brown wooly camels, plodding slowly and steadily to the left of the van window, out and away into the vastness of the steppe.

How do you count the hours of this kind of travel? Soon after we left Ulaanbaatar behind us, it was as if the great city had never been, was a mere dream of a city amid this all-engulfing ocean of grassland. The road began as tarmac, a straight black ribbon running westward over the grass. Then it became . . . well, not a road. Tar gave way to dirt, which gave way — and this was a

181

major highway, remember — to a series of strange, parallel, almost random tracks torn into the great muddy landscape like scars and gouges left by the passage of some giant beast. Rain squalls came and went. The gears of the van ground loudly, the interior swung wildly, with us in it, like traveling inside a cement mixer, killing conversation. But outside the window was a scene that was utterly timeless. White *gers* with great wooden corrals of goats and sheep; men and women flitting by on horseback, also kids, some scarcely bigger than infants, handling their rough, shaved-maned mounts like circus riders. Cows lumbering across the gouges of the road, udders swinging. Self-governing flocks of sheep and goats on their way from where to where? Modernity intruded only along the narrow strip of tire-torn highway, where trucks ground by, laden with sheepskins and wool, the great loads tied down with tarps, the drivers smoking. Our own driver, intent on the treacherous dips and drops of the road, the crazy randomness of the oncoming vehicles and the faster ones trying to pass, was listening to Mongolian rap, barely audible above the roar of the straining engine.

And Rowan, through all of it, was dreamy, relaxed, stiller and more at peace than I was used to seeing him, bumping his head against the window, eyes glued to the strange landscape passing by.

We stopped sometime in the early afternoon to make lunch and stretch our legs. Tulga told the driver to pull off the road that was not a road onto the wide steppe at an area by a small lake. We stepped out, stiff and aching, into space and silence. Grassland stretching away to far-off mountains. The small lake in the middle distance, gray cranes poised elegantly at its edge. Two horses, one white, one a dark bay, grazing the hummocky, tussocky grass between us and the water's edge. Rain clouds gathering. The other van pulled up behind us, its super-skinny driver, a Jack Sprat to the large guy driving our van, grinning widely as he cut the engine. Rowan went barreling out onto the grass, whose hummocks suggested that in certain seasons this was a wetland, a shallow part of the nearby lake, perhaps.

"Baby frogs!" he said, squealing delightedly. And sure enough, leaping in all directions from his feet, from ours, were scores of little dark green froglets, not long out of the tadpole stage by the looks of them. "Let's catch one," said Rowan. He bent down and deftly picked up one of the little creatures between finger and thumb. Then he looked around him, sighed, and went skipping off over the hummocks. I shadowed him the way I was now so automatically trained to do, little frogs springing off in all directions at each footfall.

Tulga opened the back door of the second van, where a small butane stove was ready for use. Rowan darted about, catching and releasing frogs, as the smell of cooking bacon drifted across the steppe. Then, just as Michel came running up to film Rowan's first foray onto the great steppe, my son stood up, quivering, with that deer-in-the-headlights look on his face.

"Code Brown!" I shouted, which sent Kristin darting into the van to grab the small blue plastic bucket, brush, and two-liter bottle of water we'd put by especially for this moment. She came sprinting over to help, knowing from the slightly trauma-tized tone of my shout that this was, in our special language of autism parenting, a "two personer."

"You have to joke about it, you see," I said to Michel, who stood wincing and looking away as I peeled off the soiled, caked trousers and underwear and Kristin arrived with the necessary accoutrements.

"Gotta get all clean . . ." Rowan whined. He was always distressed when this happened. Yet if these accidents distressed him so, why did he steadfastly refuse to let us toilet-train him?

It was odd, since he would pee in the potty, even getting up in the middle of the night to take himself. Yet sit him down on the toilet seat and he stiffened right up, got that deep-fear look, as though he was terrified — but what of? — and shouted, "Almost done!" Finally, at the urging of several therapists, we had taken him out of his supersized diapers, hoping that the sheer discomfort of filling his underwear several times a day would motivate him to poo in the potty.

That had been three months before. And it had made no difference whatsoever. So now, instead of the relative convenience of using disposable diapers (on a child *almost six years old*), here we were embarking on a journey across the remotest place on earth with an incontinent child and no easy way to clean him and launder his clothes after each accident. We must be mad, I thought, wiping away automatically, then washing his legs down with bottled water. Mad.

I got him clean and Kristin came up with fresh pants and underwear. How long would this continue? Should we just put him back in diapers? That would mean going backward. Every expert we'd spoken to said that if we did that, we'd never get him toilet-trained. In the meantime — a meantime that could very well take years — our job had become ten times harder.

Kristin dressed Rowan, who, the ordeal over, tripped off happily after the baby frogs once more while I filled the little blue bucket we'd brought with water and set to work with a scrub brush on the horrible soiled clothes. Above, in the wide, wide sky, a flight of seven cranes flew over, honking, heading for the small lake. The rain clouds were almost overhead now, the wind growing suddenly chill.

Would Rowan be one of those autistic kids who entered adolescence without being toilet-trained? Or without learning to control his tantrums? Physical and emotional incontinence: were these to define our lives forever? It didn't bear thinking about.

Right on cue, from across the steppe, Rowan suddenly screamed, *"MEERKAT!"*

And just then the heavens opened. Michel, Kristin, Jeremy, and Justin ran for the van, Rowan with them, still screaming for what I guessed must be a lost toy animal. The rain came down in a solid wall. Soaked within seconds, I tipped the dirty water out into the grass and laid the pants and underwear out in the rain to rinse. I started to look for the tiny lost toy among the tussocks of grass, the rain coming down so hard that I had to screw my eyes half shut to stop the water running into them, walking up and down, quartering the ground as Rowan's shrieks — *"MEERKAT! MEERKAT!"* — rose in pitch, clear above the drumming roar of the rain.

I found the toy by stepping on it. I picked it up, retrieved the bucket, brush, and the by now thoroughly rinsed clothes, and went back to the van.

"Yay!" said Kristin as I appeared, sodden but with meerkat in hand. "Look what Daddy found! Now *that* is a cool daddy!" The relief inside the van, the soundbox for Rowan's shrieks, was palpable. Rowan smiled, reached out, grabbed the toy.

"Say thank you, Daddy," said Kristin.

"Say thank you, Daddy," echoed Rowan. Then he looked around him. "Hippo? Hippo? Where's the hippo? Oh, it's gone! The hippo's gone to Greenbriar. Hippo! *HIPPO! HIIIIPPOOOO!*"

"I hate to tell you this." Michel raised his voice above the noise. "But right as he got out, before he went for the frogs, I noticed he had his toy hippo as well as the meerkat. He must have dropped it when he went after the baby frogs."

I looked down at the ground immediately outside the van, now a shallow lake up to my lower calves. Somewhere under those waters was a toy hippo.

I took off my plastic Crocs, and as the rain intensified once more, and to the accompaniment of a new set of shrieks so sharp, so shrill, that they reverberated behind the eyeballs, I began to wade up and down, up and down, feeling with my toes for a toy hippopotamus in a rainwater lake in Mongolia.

Later, when the hippo had been found, the rain had stopped, and we had all eaten, the sun came out and the day became hot. We drove on, back onto the random ruts and scars that comprised the main east–west highway, the landscape becoming increasingly arid and empty, the grass sparser on the ground, more red earth showing between the patches of close-cropped pasture. Sometimes an hour or more would pass without even a *ger* or a lone horseman in sight. Rowan sang to himself, varying between an old folk song I used to sing him sometimes, "Over the Hills and Far Away," and what I eventually discerned was the electroreggae theme tune from the movie *Madagascar.* I tried to sing with him, but he gave a devilish smile and went, "No-no-no-no-no. No singing daddy!"

We made a short game of it, me starting to sing, him shutting me down, as clouds, hills, grassland, mountains passed by. Distant ranges were drawn casually across the far horizon as if God had just made a few casual strokes with a watercolor paintbrush. Sometimes the road, such as it was, smoothed out, and it was almost like driving normally, except for the heat and the dust flying in the windows. Sometimes we lurched and tossed as Haada braked suddenly at a set of particularly deep ruts, throwing us all in different directions. Yet Rowan loved it, laughing delightedly when we were being tossed like human salad, retreating into his meditative song when the going smoothed out, occasionally turning to either Kristin or me for a hug or grabbing my hair for an intense eye-to-eye, forehead-bonking, nose-rubbing moment, then back to himself again. It seemed an age, a month, since we had been with the shamans. Had it been only the day before?

We stopped again in the late afternoon, the shadows lengthening to the golden hour, and took a short break to stretch our legs. Rowan took his toy animals out and set them up in the sandy soil between the tussocks of grass by a marmot hole that doubled, for him, as an animal cave. I was amazed at how comfortable he was in this alien land.

Then a car pulled up, a small hatchback, the kind of small, tough Japanese car that seems to get anywhere on any Third World road, no matter how rough. And out got Naara and Tomoo, Tulga's wife and son. Tomoo carried a toy sword. Seeing Rowan already lying down in the sand, playing with his animals at the mouth of the marmot hole, Tomoo shouted, "Row-an!" and ran across to join him.

Rowan looked up. "Mongolian brother!"

"Tomoo!" said the boy, pointing at his chest. "Tomoo!"

"Tomoo!" repeated Rowan, delighted. And then the strangest thing happened. Rowan got up, left his game, and threw his arms wide. There should have been violins. Tomoo and Rowan ran into each other's arms.

And then, the embrace done, Rowan stepped back, took Tomoo's sword, pulled the plastic blade free of the black scabbard, and said, "Sword fight! Just like a pirate!"

Giggling, he flourished the sword at Tomoo, who immediately parried with the scabbard. For the first time ever, Rowan was playing — actually playing — with another child. Tomoo, smiling now, made a gentle cut, which Rowan parried, and then, squealing with delight, he darted back to the van: "The pirates are running away!"

At a loss for words, Kristin and I gaped as Rowan and Tomoo chased each other, laughing like any two small boys anywhere in the world, round and round the two parked vans.

Eleven hours after leaving Ulaanbaatar, the road finally dwindled into little more than a goat track winding across a highland valley between low, grassy mountains, and gave out at last in a sort of vast natural amphitheater or bowl. There stood three *gers,* and, grazing nearby, several hundred baaing, bleating sheep and goats of all sizes and colors and a herd of horses, similarly harlequinlike to the casual eye, in their checkered black and white, brown and gray, red, bay, sorrel, cream, gunmetal black: every hue of horse God had ever created. Numb by now, we didn't quite take in that we had actually arrived, despite the van's slowing almost to a stop, until Tulga said something to the driver in Mongol, then turned to us, bags under his eyes, and said, "Here we are."

We stumbled out the sliding door into the

surprisingly chill evening, to be greeted by the sound and scent of livestock, rain, dogs barking, children shouting, wood smoke, dung smoke, and a freshening wind, all jostling each other for space in the wide and moving air.

These kinds of arrivals from nowhere into nowhere — they reset the brain, like pressing the button on your internal odometer so that it reads three zeros once again, or wiping a blackboard clean. *What now?* your brain asks. *What now?*

"Horse!" Rowan skipped down and out of the pimpmobile, as fresh as he'd been that morning, and sprinted off through the dying light toward a skewbald horse that stood tethered to a pole between us and the first *ger,* where people in long, coatlike *deels* moved about, shouting to each other above the noise of the goats and sheep, which were being driven down from the mountainside toward their big wooden corral by two small boys on horseback. The tethered horse, skittish-looking, flicked its ears between the sounds of the people it knew and those it didn't — us — and stamped its hooves dangerously as Rowan ran over to it, clearly expecting to ride at once. I lunged at a stiff-footed pace and scooped him up. "We don't know that horse, Rowan. Best wait to say hello till we know it better."

"Horse! Horse! Ride a horse!"

The brown-and-white animal, a handsome beast, nickered softly at him. I could tell it was a high-strung animal, one that might kick, or at least swing round unexpectedly if it felt insecure and knock Rowan down. But then, as the others staggered geriatrically out of the van behind, stretching, yawning, swearing at the cramp in their muscles, the fatigue of the drive, the amazing, incredible beauty of this amphitheater of high grassland over whose encircling mountains the clouds were all lit up pink, blue, purple, and gold with the sunset — the horse took a step, two steps, toward Rowan.

The soft look, the Betsy look, came over its eyes, the lids half closing, the expression gentling. It started to mouth, to lick and chew. Down went the head. Submission: to Rowan, to the little figure standing before it, reaching out with his hand as I crouched behind, restraining, letting him move closer as the horse displayed — as they so often seemed to with Rowan — this strange, voluntary submission to him as alpha, herd boss. Crazy. Yet here it was, happening again. He reached out farther, caressed the velvet nose. Said, "Maybe ride tomorrow," and then, with a joyful skip that made the horse snort, start, jerk against its tether rope, he went sprinting off toward the goat and sheep corral.

As I followed I spotted Tulga out of the corner of my eye, walking toward the *gers,* where big, aggressive-looking sheepdogs were barking, growling, and baring their fangs at him, and shouting the traditional Mongolian greeting when you approach someone's *ger: No-khoi, ko-rio! Hold the dogs!*

Christ, what if one of them bit him? Or Rowan? Better I should be the one to get his leg mauled if it came to that, so I trotted behind Rowan, ready to kick any dog I might have to as Rowan, delighted, came level with the multicolored river of goats and sheep, lambs and kids flowing slowly into the great wooden corral. Rowan and I were greeted with shy nods and half-smiles by the women and children gathered there (the menfolk all seemed to be off at the *gers,* talking to Tulga and the drivers). Rowan, oblivious, started to walk round and round the wooden fence, looking through the pine poles that made up the rails, until he made his way to the opening where a small boy, perhaps only two or three years older than he was, sat mounted on a sorrel gelding, counting off the confusing, shifting heads of livestock as they entered the corral with the professionalism of a Texas cowboy or a Welsh shepherd. Might Rowan be like this someday? He was already inside, among the milling hooves and horns. "Just like Blackie," he said, pointing out a little black baby goat. "Want to hold it. Hold it? Hold the baby goat? Hold it, please?"

Again, this was unusually lucid speech. Not just the usual *"Goat! Goat!"* followed by some nonsensical (except in autism logic) word like *gi*-raffe or *French fries* to communicate his urgency. I looked around at the Mongolian mothers, aunties, and grandmothers who had gathered here to look over the livestock. With no Tulga to translate, I couldn't do much more than gesture, afraid that Rowan would suddenly explode with frustration. It must have shown clearly on my face, for one of the older ladies, a big, smiling matriarch with an air of easy competence, strode in, grabbed a large black nanny goat by its impressively wide horns, and gestured with her head and shoulders that Rowan should climb up and ride.

His face lit up. I grabbed him under the shoulders, hoisted him on board. The broad-backed goat, probably a veteran of many infant rides, stood stoic and patient, not struggling as Rowan took hold of the horns, let his fingers run through its coarse yet soft fur. Then he was off again and clambering over the corral rails to go running back up toward the *gers* and their dogs. I gestured my thanks to the ladies and leaped the fence in pursuit. Rowan, hugely overstimulated, his hyperactivity at full throttle, was running almost too fast for me to keep up with, at least easily. The sun, setting now behind the westernmost mountain, filled the sky above the steppe with one last choir-of-angels burst of pink and gold, then disappeared into a pale, pale blue in which one cold star began to wink. I sprinted after my son, thinking, "Lord, we're really out here. I mean, we're in bloody *Mongolia,* for chrissakes." Outer Mongolia — the official back of beyond.

"Ro-wan!" It was Tomoo's voice, loud and clear. He and his mother must have driven up while we were with the goats.

"Tomoo!" Rowan changed direction and went running, open-armed, toward his new friend.

Did this sudden ability to make friends have anything to do with the shamans? After all, the first contact had happened at the end of the ritual, and now here he was, tearing around playing chase as if he'd been doing it all his life. Like any other kid. Such were my thoughts as, panting, I trotted after them in the rapidly thickening darkness, roaring for one of the film crew or Tulga to fetch me a flashlight, as various people rode up on horseback out of the night to see what all the commotion was about and the drivers fired up their engines and set their headlights on the hillside so the tents could be put up.

The night quickly descended into the special kind of confusion that only a bunch of people setting up camp in the dark in a new place can create. It seemed to take an age to get everything organized: the sleeping tents, the kitchen tent, the food, and then the cook — a rather sullen-looking middle-aged lady who had traveled in the van with the ultrathin driver, said little, and didn't seem terribly friendly — started cooking up rice and noodles by flashlight. Rowan, completely overexcited now, kept running off into the dark, sometimes playing with Tomoo, sometimes off on his own. I could hear hoofbeats and snorting nearby. The families' herd must have drifted down from the heights to come in close to the *gers*. Probably for safety, as it seemed they got their food from foraging on the open steppe, not from being fed grain. Were there wolves up there on the open heights?

"Rowan? Rowan?" I tried to keep a handle

on him as he darted in and out of the darkness. Hopefully he wouldn't blunder into those hooves that stomped and shifted out there, or go too far . . . no, there he was again. "Rowan, you have to stay with Daddy! Rowan —"

It was almost midnight by the time we ate, Rowan scarfing down a huge portion of bacon (was this all he was going to eat for the next three weeks?), and past midnight by the time we finally bedded down, wrapped up in clothes against the rapidly falling temperature. The darkness, now that the vans' harsh headlights had at last been switched off, was utter and complete. The sounds of the night quieted to hushed voices and laughter from the *gers,* distant bleating from the corral, stamping hooves and snorting from the horse herd close by in the darkness. Our tent was in three compartments, one central portion for the bags and on either side of that a separate sleeping chamber that could be zipped up tight. The ground was hard underneath me, but it felt good to be sleeping on the earth.

From the other sleeping compartment, where Rowan and Kristin lay tucked up together, I heard mother and son talking softly together in their own nighttime psalm: "Who does Mommy love?" Then Rowan's response: "Rowan!"

"And who does Rowan love?"

"Mommy!"

"And who does Daddy love?"

"Rowan!"

"And who does Rowan love?"

"Mommy *and* Daddy!"

He giggled softly, relapsing once more into autism babble. But a happy-sounding babble. Soon afterward that also softened and died, replaced by the sound of deep breathing, a slow, rhythmic rise and fall.

We lay on sheepskins, the same ones we would be putting over our saddles for the long, long horseback hours that would start tomorrow. I lay there waiting for sleep to take me, thinking of how Rowan and his autism had changed my whole relationship with riding. Three years before — the year of Rowan's diagnosis, the year he had met the Bushmen and the shamans at the Gathering, the year he had first forged his strange relationship with Betsy — there had been an event, tied to his autism, that had utterly and irrevocably altered the role of horses in my life.

It had happened in the brief weeks between the Gathering and my return home, while I was still on the road, escorting the Bushman delegation to the United Nations.

While en route between California and the East Coast, we had stopped to stay with two Indian tribes in Arizona, the Hopi and the Navajo, so that the Bushmen, fighting for their land down in southern Africa, could meet with tribes here in the First World who had secured their land rights, at least on paper. While we were camped at a place called Spider Rock, deep inside the Navajo reservation, ready to take horses down into the wilds of Canyon de Chelly next day (the Bushmen of Botswana ride like demons, hunting with spears from horseback), a Navajo medicine man had come to visit, saying that he had heard why we had come and offering to make a sweat lodge that very evening, in order to pray for the return of the Bushman land.

So the lodge, white-hot rocks piled on top of each other inside a bender of branches covered with old tarpaulins and buffalo hides, was made, and the Bushmen, myself, the medicine man, and some of the local Navajo stripped down to our underwear and went inside to pray in the stifling, lung-burning heat. After several rounds of chants and prayers in both Dine, the Navajo language, and English, the medicine man, his voice disembodied in the burning darkness, asked if anyone else had anything he wanted to pray for.

"I do," I said. "My son was diagnosed with autism this year. I'd like to pray for him."

So the medicine man led us on another round of chants and supplications to the Creator, to the Great Mother, to the ancestral spirits, while the sweat poured down our bodies and I, under cover of darkness, allowed quiet tears to flow. At the end of the ceremony, as we stood outside under the desert starlight, the cliffs of the canyon dropping away below us into blackness, the medicine man — a sturdy, stocky, long-haired man in his middle fifties, still muscled like a much younger man — asked me a surprising question.

"Do you hunt?"

Yes, I replied, I did, but perhaps not in a way he was familiar with. Then I described the strange, grandly pointless ritual of the English foxhunt: its mad, addictive careen across the winter countryside, the huge fences that had to be jumped, any one of which could mean a broken neck for horse or rider, the fear and the ecstasy, the falls and the injuries, the need for complete oneness between rider and horse, the crazy music of the hounds, belling through the woods and across the fields and pastures in pursuit of their fleet red quarry.

"Do you kill the fox?" asked the medicine man.

"At the end of the hunt, if the hounds catch it, then yes." Although, I added, in America, which has almost as many hunts as Britain does, the landowners, not being sheep farmers, put no pressure on the hunts to kill, so if a fox goes down a hole it is left alone, rendering the American version pretty much bloodless.

"Well, I don't know why," said the medicine man, his voice soft in the darkness, "but I'm getting the message that you have to stop, and that it's somehow connected to your son's autism. Beyond that I can't explain, but Spirit told me this while we were praying for your son, and so I'm telling you."

I stood a moment in silence, feeling a strange emptiness deep in my gut. So much of my life, my identity, had been tied up with hunting. Perhaps because I hadn't been born to it but had had to find my way into it, as a city boy without affluent parents, through the side door, learning to ride on weekends at my great-aunt's farm in Leicestershire, compelled since infancy by some strange, overwhelming urge to get on the back of a horse. I had used hunting as a way to explore the world, eventually even making my living at it, at least partially, whether by training horses for the hunt field or by writing about different hunts all over Britain and the United States for the equestrian press.

You could say I was addicted. There is no adrenaline rush quite like going at a big fence out of rough ground, a fence so big you can't see what's on the other side of it, whether ditch or wire or road or farm machinery or some other hazard. "Throw your heart over first, then follow as best you can," the old Leicestershire farmers used to say. Being that kind of rider, thinking about myself as that kind of rider, had come to dominate my life. I had a lot of ego, a universe of identity, tied up in it.

Truth be told, I had all but stopped riding lately anyway, since Rowan's autism had taken over our lives. But I missed it so. And now I was being told that I would have to give it up completely — the part of riding that mattered most to me. I stood there in the darkness, the medicine man next to me, weighing his words. My heart sank. There was no doubt about it — my intuition was telling me firmly, irrationally, and most damned unwelcomely that this man was right.

"Okay," I said, sighing. "Okay. I'll give it

up, then."

So on to the East Coast and Capitol Hill and the United Nations we went. The Bushmen went home successful, and on my first night back at home in Texas, after Rowan had gone to bed, Kristin told me that he had kept saying "Horse! Horse!" while I was gone. I telephoned a close friend, also a foxhunter, and told him about the medicine man's words. At first my friend was angry, thinking I had now become an "anti," which to foxhunters is high heresy. I assured him I hadn't; this decision was purely personal, impossible to explain rationally.

And as I told him this, a fox — a rare sight in Texas, where coyotes routinely hunt and kill foxes both as competitors and as food — walked out of the nighttime woods and into the illuminated half-disk of yellow cast by my porch light. Standing in that spotlight, it stopped, turned, faced me, took two steps toward me, and began, amazingly, to bark at me. "You'll never believe what's happening now," I said into the receiver, and held it out toward the noise, letting my friend hear the vulpine third party now listening to my tale.

Next day I took Rowan riding on Betsy for the first time, and my entire riding life, my whole relationship with horses, changed forever. A change that had led us here, to the horsemen of the remotest place in the world.

I lay remembering this, listening to the half-wild horses outside the tented darkness milling and snorting softly among themselves, wriggling my back to get more comfortable on the sheepskin that would lie on our saddle next day, when we mounted up and headed off — to where? Toward what further mystery? The steppe lay open before us. Tomorrow we would ride.

9
FITS AND STARTS

Have you ever spent any time in the uplands of Britain? There is a certain quality of light there, diffused through moving cloud, that shifts and changes continually, illuminating different stretches of hillside with an almost ethereal, otherworldly light, like that which shines in through high cathedral windows or stained glass. Beautiful, ever-changing, fey: it's not surprising that the Celts and other inhabitants of these regions have a strong tradition of being "away with the fairies." Or even claiming to see them, for that matter. The quality of the light makes you think of such things. You almost can't help it.

Such was the light I awoke to the next day: low cloud masking the higher reaches of the hills, sunlight breaking through occasionally to etch every detail, every blade of grass on first this piece, then that piece of hillside in fine gold, like a fragment of illuminated manuscript torn from some medieval tome, only for the light to shift once more, the gold to fade to gray, until, half a mile farther along the shoulder of the hill, the fairy spotlight came on once more, gilding grass, rock, a stunted tree in its magical luminescence, causing it suddenly to shine like a jeweled thing, exquisite, only to fade, move on once more. "Just like the Pennines," I thought, picturing the mist-shrouded hills of northern England in my mind's eye. I let my gaze roll over the emptiness of hillside and lowering cloud. Today we'd go into the wild.

A horse's whinny came pealing down the wet-feeling, cool wind. Several horses of different colors stood tied to a long rope suspended between two wooden poles stuck into the turf. A short distance away, a young man on horseback cantered around, chasing other horses with a long wooden pole like a lance, to the end of which was attached a loop of rope. I'd seen this tool before in pictures — it was an *urga,* the Mongolian equivalent of a lasso. As I watched, the young man suddenly galloped off in hard pursuit of a jet black horse that broke away from the rest of the herd and went off at a hard run, trying to escape into the open hills. The young man, flat out in pursuit, stood up in his stirrups, leaned forward from the saddle, thrust the loop end of the lance over the head of the escaping horse, then deftly pulled the noose back, at the same time reining his mount back hard, so that the black horse, caught now, spun round, pulled off-balance by the capturing horse and rider.

Immediately resigned, it meekly let itself be led toward the horses already tied up to the long line between the two wooden poles. Bare-headed and wearing a crimson *deel* and short black riding boots, the young man secured the black horse there, remounted, and went cantering off again, *urga* in hand, to fetch another beast from the milling, restive herd. These, I presumed, were the horses we would be riding today. And for the next few days.

I drifted over to the camp table where Michel, Jeremy, and Justin were blearily gathering around what looked like a thermos of hot tea, shutting out the hoofbeats and the shifting fairy light and the fear of what might be to come in favor of the reassuring simplicity of a mug of hot breakfast tea. Sometimes you need what's familiar to help you face what isn't.

For I was scared. Scared of the sheer size of the place. It made me think of a line in a funny book, *Flashman at the Charge,* a satirical look at the disastrous Crimean War of the 1850s, in which the British showed up confidently to invade Russia, got off their boats, looked around, gulped, and said, *Hmm, big place, ain't it?* I was having the same reaction. Now that I was here, dwarfed by the impossible scale of the place, to say that I felt intimidated would be an understatement. I took my metal teacup and went over to the horse line, where the young herder was just bringing in another horse, a gray this time. Handsome, tall, he grinned at me, dismounted, tied the new horse up alongside the others, gestured to the black horse he'd caught earlier, and pointed at me.

"That's the horse I'm going to ride?" I pointed first to the small, compact beast, then to myself. The young man nodded, then indicated a pile of saddles and bridles lying just off to the side. Among them was the lightweight Western saddle that I'd brought for Rowan and me to ride in together, knowing the Mongolian saddles would be too small to accommodate us both. The young herder went to the saddle, grabbed it, and brought it over, offering me a chance to try the horse out. Good idea, I thought. Tulga and other travelers had warned us that these horses were half wild and prone to test a new rider. Of course, in our e-mails and conversations I'd impressed upon Tulga the need for me and Rowan to have the quietest horse possible, and I trusted these people who lived on horseback to know what horse to give me. But there's no substitute for feeling a horse out yourself.

So the young man untied the black horse, a mare, which I realized, now that I stood next to it, was really only pony-sized, yet with the longer proportions of a taller horse (all Mongolian horses are like this — small horses rather than large ponies). It had a mane hogged short, a broad back, a quiet eye. Solid and dependable-looking, the kind of which the old Leicestershire farmers of my youth would say, "It's got a leg at each corner. A good sort."

I did up the cinch with its complicated Western knot as the Mongolian slipped the homemade rawhide bridle with its jointed, loose-ring snaffle bit over the black horse's head. A simple bit with two rings at the side to attach it to the bridle and a jointed piece for the mouth — archaeologists have found these loose-ring snaffles in graves going back thousands of years — it's the most commonly used bit in any country today. The joints make it sit easily over the horse's tongue. The loose rings, which move as the horse's head moves, allow some play, ideally suited to a quiet, easy-tempered horse. I put my foot in the stirrup, grabbed the horn, and swung aboard. I was on a horse in Mongolia.

I gave the little black mare some leg, asking it to move away from its fellows. It did so, ploddingly, lazily. This was good — the last thing I needed was a flighty, high-mettled animal (though Lord knows horses are perfectly capable of being both lazy *and* flighty, as it suits them). Then again, a slug that I'd have to kick every step of the way across this vast country wasn't going to be much fun either. I kicked again and clicked my tongue, asking for a trot; she went forward readily but quietly. Good sign. I sat back, put one leg behind the girth, and kept the other where it was, asking her to canter. She ignored me, simply speeding up her trot. Maybe there was some other cue, a Mongolian technique she was trained to do. I looked back at the herder, who was watching me with the critical eye with which horsemen always regard each other.

Seeing the question in my eyes and the fast, uncomfortable trot the mare was doing, he opened his mouth and gave a shout — *"Chuh! Chuh!"* — and made a flapping motion with his left hand. I made the cry and flapped the rope, and the little black mare went willingly into a canter. She moved evenly, rhythmically, underneath me, not pulling at my hand or trying to go fast. The right horse for the job.

As we rode, a light, spitting rain began. I turned her back toward the *gers* just as a crack of thunder sounded, a chill gust blew out of the south, and suddenly it was raining hard. These sudden, heavy storms seemed to be the pattern here. As I cantered up to the *gers* — everyone else had run for the tents — the handsome young herder who had given me the horse stepped out of one of them and beckoned me inside. I reined the black horse in, jumped off, tied her to the hitching pole outside the front door that the young man was pointing at, then followed him through the low door into the *ger,* leaving the poor mare to drop her patient head and turn her cold backside to the rain.

Entering the *ger* was like entering another world. No, it *was* entering another world, another world completely, from the thick, almost sickening smell of the goat stew steaming away on the metal stove in the center of the round tent to the beautiful, delicate yellow-and-blue pattern work painted on the dresser that stood to the rear of the *ger* and the two wooden beds on each side. A rifle hung over the dresser, and there were various framed photographs of horses with child jockeys and men in *deels* standing proudly by, some of which had medals draped over them.

Sitting on one of the beds was a handsome, strong-looking middle-aged man in riding boots, a dark red *deel,* and, somewhat incongruously, a porkpie hat like the kind worn by English horse dealers of the old-fashioned, slightly gypsy sort. Next to him was his wife, also middle-aged and handsome — the same strong-looking woman who had held the goat for Rowan to ride the evening before. Across from them, separated by the stove and a low table with small stools to sit on, was the tall young herder and his pretty, broad-faced wife. They all smiled, we exchanged greetings, and then the older man took a small book out of the lining of his *deel* and placed it on the low table, motioning for me to sit on one of the stools and doing the same himself. I looked at the book — a Mongolian-English phrasebook and dictionary.

A bowl appeared at my elbow, full of a sharp-smelling white liquid.

"*Airag,*" said the man, and motioned for

213

me to drink.

I'd been afraid of this. *Airag* is the famous fermented mare's milk that is the staple of both survival and pleasure out on the Mongolian steppe. I looked at it, white and milky in its bowl. A thin sheen of fat — tiny yellow bubbles of it — floated on the surface. I fought back the urge to turn and run screaming into the rain, extended my hands, bobbed a grateful head, and drank.

I wish I could be one of those travelers who says that everything exotic tastes great. But some things just don't. I've eaten mopane worms out in the Kalahari with the Bushmen, and they taste like . . . well, worms. When I ate flying ants with them, they tasted every bit as horrid as I expected them to. But I choked them down with a smile. And did the same now, *choke* being the operative word.

"Mmm," I said, handing the bowl back to the patriarch and smacking my lips. "Delicious."

He smiled, nodded, and took a sip himself. Well, I thought, knowing I'd have to drink again and again as long as I was sitting here, at least there was a slight buzz attached to it, a small kick to mitigate the yuck. I felt the warmth; my body was unused to alcohol at such an early hour. I came out of my reverie to see that the older man had opened the phrasebook on the little table and was pointing to a sentence printed there. I leaned over. *Ah Tavtaii moril.* Welcome.

I picked up the phrasebook and leafed through until I found *bayarlaa,* thank you. I leafed through some more pages till I found the words *tand ikh,* for "very much," and then gestured what I hoped was to be understood that I felt honored, which I did. Tremendously. They were going to guide us, take care of us on this crazy journey. Damn right I felt honored. The *airag* bowl, having made the rounds of all four other people in the *ger,* came back to me. Sighing inwardly, I took as deep a draft as I could. If I was going to have to drink this horrible essence of throw-up, I might as well get as much buzz as I could in the process. The rain drummed hard upon the felt roof of the *ger.* I looked up and passed the bowl back to the old man, feeling a little tipsy now. Was all *airag* this strong, or did it vary from batch to batch?

"Boroo," said the younger man this time, phrasebook in hand. Rain.

I reached out for the book, wondering if it would be all right to make a joke. My mind had somehow — perhaps the alcohol had something to do with it — leaped to a memory of an old Monty Python skit where someone is trying to get a cup of tea or something in some Scandinavian country with the help of a guidebook (I've probably got the skit muddled; cue millions of Pythonologists all crying, *"Wrong!"*) and ends up saying: "I'm sorry, but my hovercraft is full of eels."

I guess it was the *airag*. I paged through to the "useful everyday phrases" section and yes, there it was, leaping right out at me: *Ogonuu jorlongiin tsaas*. Could you give me the toilet paper?

A moment of incomprehension from the weathered, lined face above the *airag* bowl. Then suddenly his eyes twinkled, and all four people at the table roared with laughter. The ice was broken.

The patriarch leafed through the book and found *Taksi duudarai,* please call me a taxi. To which, rising to the challenge (as the *airag* came round a third time), I replied, *Khaan kheregtai jorlong,* where is the lady's toilet?

Much laughter and a fourth (Lord have mercy) round of the fermented mare's milk, as the old man pointed to *Namaig khuleej uzeerei,* wait for me!

Then, becoming serious again, the patriarch asked his son to bring him a paper and pen. He pointed at me and said, "America?"

I nodded. He made a motion that, in my tipsy state, I interpreted as "Draw a map of it, then," which I did. He nodded, evidently pleased, grabbed the phrasebook, and showed me *dachka,* daughter. He pointed at himself.

"You're a daughter?" I asked, confused. He pointed at himself again, and his wife, then the word. "Your daughter!" I said, getting it.

He nodded, leaned forward, all horse smell, sweat smell, tobacco smell, and said, clear as day, "Los Angeles."

"You have a daughter in Los Angeles?"

He nodded, though whether I'd got it right or was projecting something hugely wrong I had no idea. So on the makeshift map I had just drawn, I put a large blue circle, colored it in, and wrote *Los Angeles* next to it, and showed him. "Los Angeles."

His eyes lit up in satisfaction. *Dachka,* he said again — *daughter* — and pointed there. Could he really have a daughter living in L.A.? Was this *ger,* sitting here amid all this wild, open, utter remoteness, actually connected by family ties to the glitz capital of the Western world? Why not? Why not, indeed.

I drew another circle on the opposite

217

coast. New York. Then, way down in the south of the central bit, I drew a third circle: Austin, Texas. I slapped my chest a bit too hard (the *airag* again) and leafed for one last time through the little book. *Damoy*, I said. Home.

There followed a bit of languageless small talk. The old man pointed proudly to the photographs of horses with medals draped over the frames, in which I recognized the two small boys I'd seen riding around the camp. So he bred racehorses, and the grandsons were the jockeys. I was impressed. Would Rowan ever be able to ride by himself like that? I wondered. It was my dearest wish.

I pointed at the rifle hanging on the back of the *ger* and made a poor approximation of a wolf howl, putting a question mark at the end of it. Affirmative nods all round, confirmed by the tall younger man's pointing to the words *chono,* wolf, and *galisatsb,* hunt, in the little dictionary. Poor wolves, I couldn't help thinking. Though if I was living out here with only my livestock to support me, I'd probably hunt them too. The *airag* came round a fifth time. It wasn't tasting any better, but my buzz was thickening. I noticed a sound. Or rather, a lack of one. It had stopped raining. Surely Rowan and

Kristin must be up by now. I stood up and bowed, because I did not know how to say "I really ought to go check on my wife and child" in Mongolian. But mutual understanding seemed to flow.

The older man and his wife nodded amiably while the younger man got up and opened the door to look outside. The clouds were lifting off the hills. There was a warmth floating in on the wind, replacing the chill. The black mare pricked her ears at me as I stepped outside, untied her, swung into her wet saddle, and, with a smile and a wave from the tall young man, set off at a canter back to our tents. The horse went noticeably better for me, I noticed, getting the feel of me just as I was of her.

I reined in by the tents to find Justin, Jeremy, and Michel happily breakfasting on hot bacon-and-egg sandwiches, but no sign of Kristin or Rowan. I led the black mare over to our tent and there heard the sound of singing and giggling.

"Mommy have a sing."

Then Kristin's voice: "Sing, sing a song. Make it simple, to last your whole life long . . ."

I recognized it — the Carpenters.

Then Rowan's voice, perfectly on key: "Just sing, sing a song."

Then both together: "La la la la la, lala la lalala . . ."

I knelt down. "Knock-knock."

Kristin unzipped the tent. "Oh, thank God, Ru. We've been lying here for an hour — he's insisting on singing this over and over. I'm starving."

"Sing! More sing!" said Rowan.

"No one's brought you anything to eat?" Annoyed, I looked over at the guys, chatting together at the breakfast table. "Hold on."

I strode over, the black mare following obediently. "Hey, Jeremy!" My ire fell on him because he was a friend rather than someone who had just come in to help record the journey. "What are you doing just standing about stuffing yourself? Didn't you think to check on Kristin and Rowan? This isn't a vacation . . ."

I heard myself, then stopped, embarrassed. God, I could be a jerk sometimes. After all, where had I been? "Sorry," I ended lamely. "But she's been in there an hour while everyone else has been having breakfast and —"

"No need to say another word." Jeremy put down his plate and went over to the kitchen tent. "I'm on it."

"Thanks," I called after him, feeling stupid and a little drunk. "An egg sandwich or something. And some bacon for Rowan."

I went back to the tent, where Rowan was still making Kristin sing the same few lines of the song, over and over. "Breakfast is coming. Hey, Rowan, do you want to go for a ride? Look, a new horse. She's called . . ." I fished for a name. "Blackie!"

"Very inventive," said Kristin, crawling out of the tent.

"Want to take a little ride?" I asked again, ignoring her.

"No! No ride! Want Mommy to sing. Sing! *SI-I-I-I-I-I-ING!*"

The tantrum came down like rain, like thunder. Back arching. Scream rising to shriek, head suddenly thrusting forward. Rowan started to hit his head with his hands, hard. I picked him up, keeping my face well back so as not to get my nose broken by his flailing arms and legs, and dragged him away to the van — out from which popped Tomoo.

Rowan's tears, his thrashing, stopped as abruptly as they had begun. "Tomoo!" he said, suddenly delighted, and slipped down from my arms and up into the van where his toy animals were waiting, as if nothing had been wrong at all.

I took Blackie's lead rein back from Tulga as he went off to organize the guys, and squatted down as light rain began to fall, watching the two boys play with the lions and other African animals from Rowan's bag.

Kristin drifted up to join me, and I let Blackie graze on the end of the lead rope. Rowan played king of Pride Rock on the leopard-skin van seat while Tomoo flew Rowan's toy British Airways airplane overhead. Not a squeak from Rowan about that, though usually he was a pretty poor sharer.

After ten or fifteen minutes of this, I said, "Don't you want to come play with Blackie? Blackie the horse wants to say hello." Rowan ignored me. I let a few more minutes pass, then repeated the request. No response. Don't be pushy, I told myself, though of course thinking, "What if he refuses to get on a horse at all — what then?" Blackie flicked her ears forward, snuffled at him. Rowan grinned, squinted autistically down his nose at her, holding his head at an odd angle. And there it was again, the horse's head going down, the licking and chewing, the voluntary submission. At least Rowan would be safe with the horse. "Want to give Blackie a hug and a kiss?" Rowan did so. Blackie's eyes half closed in pleasure, her lower lip dangling. Rowan squatted down, began to stroke her fetlock and pastern.

"Look," he said. "She's got a leg, and a hoof . . ."

"That's right. She's a nice horse." I was aware that I sounded patronizing, as if I had an agenda. Rowan must be picking up on it — you can never fool a kid, autistic or not. "Want to go for a ride?" I tried to sound innocent.

"No *thank you!*"

Rowan got to his feet and darted back into the van. I let it go a few more minutes, then suggested, "Want to go for a ride with Tomoo?"

Tomoo looked up, hearing his name. I gestured toward the horse. He nodded, put the plane down, and let me lift him up into the saddle. Rowan sneaked a look. "Come on, Rowan. Let's have a ride with Tomoo."

Rowan said nothing but didn't protest as I reached in, pulled him away from his animals, and swung him up behind Tomoo. He gave him a hug, using his forearms because his hands still clasped two toy lions, and off we went, the two boys sitting comfortably together as if they'd been friends for ages, not just a day, and Rowan treating the situation as if he'd had friends all his life, not just for one day. We went down to the goat and sheep corral, now empty, the men having discreetly slaughtered whichever beast they had marked out. But as we approached, for some reason Rowan stiffened and started to wail: "Van! Van!"

So I turned Blackie around, and back to the van we went, Rowan whining, his voice rising toward tantrum. God, what a morning this was turning out to be. Back at the van Rowan yelled, "Down! Get down!" so I lifted him and Tomoo off Blackie's back, and into the van they hopped.

"Ah, Rupert." Tulga appeared at my elbow again, gliding up silently. "I think the feast is getting ready. The family is asking for you to come to the *ger.*"

"Feast?" asked Kristin, who had been sitting on the van's step all the while. "What kind of feast?"

"Oh, delicacies of the steppe," said Tulga disingenuously.

"I think I'll stay here," said Kristin, then smiled at me. "I'll look after Rowan and Tomoo. You go, darling."

"Okay, darling."

The feast was in the same *ger* I had been in earlier. Tulga and I sat in the place of honor. Michel, Justin, and Jeremy, I noticed, were suddenly in work mode, hiding firmly behind their cameras and sound equipment as a steaming dish of fresh-cooked organs was brought proudly to the low table. The patriarch and the three younger men who would guide us, plus their wives, all looked on expectantly as it was placed before me. I noticed a bottle of clear vodka on the table. That would help a little.

"All right," said Tulga, with what seemed a slight note of irony. "You will enjoy this, I think. This is the real Mongolian delicacy on this plate." He indicated the heaps of pungent, steaming flesh quivering before us. "This" — he pointed to two brownish lumps closest to us — "is lung. Very good, very tasty."

"Lung!" I said, holding out a little ceramic cup for the vodka that the older man now offered. "Fantastic!"

"And this, liver, heart, and kidneys, still with the fat." Indeed, they did still have fat, great half-cooked gelatinous globs of it clinging to the purplish globes. Tulga reached forward and turned the large metal plate slightly. "This is sausage made from blood . . ."

"Ah well," I thought, trying to reassure myself, "kind of like Yorkshire black pudding." Except it didn't look like Yorkshire black pudding, which resembles regular sausage enough to mask the fact that it's made out of blood and intestines. I went to university in York and ate enough of it while

I was there. This Mongolian version looked like guts and blood.

"And how about that?" I pointed to a large round brown bulbous thing, larger than the rest of the assembled organs, its membrane quivering ominously, straining to contain whatever horror was inside.

"Ah, yes." It was hard to tell whether Tulga was enjoying my barely concealed distress or whether he genuinely thought I was going to enjoy this. "This is stomach, and inside stuffed with intestine, some parts of the throat, and . . ." He searched for the right words but couldn't find them. "Some other parts."

"Other parts."

"Yes."

Perhaps it was better not to know. "I'll start with the lung," I said, taking another hit of vodka and passing Tulga the knife that had been placed in front of me. "Would you do the honors?"

I blanched slightly as Tulga cut into the steaming organ. It wasn't so much that it was lung that got me, it was that it *looked* so much like lung. If it had been chopped up, fried with garlic and onion, it would have been fine. Interesting, even. But *boiled,* for chrissakes, boiled and quivering — it was as if someone had thought, How can we present this dish in the most disgusting way possible? I know, let's boil it so that it's kind of only half cooked, looks pretty much exactly like it looks while we're gutting the animal, and serve it semi-raw and bleeding. Oh, and that way when you cut into it, all the interior tubes and valves will show up clearly, as if it were on a dissection table.

I meant no disrespect, and did my resolute best not to show what was in my head, tried to keep my face a mask, a polite smile covering my abject fear. I took the soft, barely cooked section of lung that Tulga proffered, popped it into my mouth, chewed heartily — rolling my eyes, smacking my lips, and trying my damnedest not to gag — and swallowed it.

"Right then," I said, taking another slug of vodka. "How about some heart?"

Tulga clapped me on the back as I swallowed. "Now you have tried some real Mongolian cuisine!"

I nodded weakly. I almost burst into tears when the older man's wife, beaming with the look of one who knows she's providing a special treat, passed me a bowl of fermented mare's milk. Jesus. I'd need counseling after this. I glugged it down like a good boy, fought down the nausea, and waited for the next bit of offal.

"What did I miss?" asked Kristin when, the ordeal over, I joined her back at the van. She turned pale when I told her. "I guess I had the easy option," she said. Then added, "I don't think he's going to get out of the van. It's like he knows this is it."

"Shall we ride a little?" I asked, poking my head into the leopard-skin interior, where Rowan and Tomoo were back at their play.

"No thank you!"

What to do? With the pressure of our near, or hopefully near, leave-taking rapidly mounting, I decided just to put him on the horse and have done with it. It wasn't quite as arbitrary a decision as it may sound. Back home in Texas I had learned early on that a sure way — in fact, the only sure way — to move Rowan abruptly from neurological tantrum to bubbly laughing happy boy was to throw him up on Betsy, clamber on behind, and just head off at a canter or gallop. The rhythm and speed always consoled and gladdened him. I decided to try it now, so I reached into the van, grabbed Rowan, and swung him up on board Blackie, just as I would do at home. His wail of protest died, replaced by a giggle, then a broad laugh, then by "Fast! Go fast!" as I kicked the little mare into a canter.

I spotted Jeremy walking back from the main *ger*. "Let's catch Jeremy! Shall we catch Jeremy?"

"Yes!"

I turned the mare at a run and rode straight at our friend, veering off only at the last minute, Rowan's laughter, the most welcome sound I'd heard all morning, pealing out like glad bells. From the corner of my vision I could see the rest of our group massing around the horses. I hoped to God they'd get done soon, for Rowan's new good mood would be tenuous at best. If only we could start *now*.

Then my girth snapped. Or rather the metal ring that fastened it to the main body of the saddle snapped off under the torque of Blackie's straining stomach muscles as she thundered around the wide circle to run at Jeremy once more. I pulled up right away, feeling the saddle begin to slip, careful.to keep my weight evenly down into each stirrup and then, as Blackie halted, kicking my feet free and swinging Rowan down onto the grass, leaping off myself immediately after. A poor workman blames his tools, but damn it, a saddle, especially a new one bought just a few weeks before, shouldn't have its vital parts break so soon. And for sure it was the only saddle in Mongolia that would comfortably take Rowan and me together. Amazingly, Rowan did not scream at having the fun cut short. I swung him up onto my shoulders and trotted back uphill, leading the long-suffering Blackie once more, to find one of the guides to help me do some saddle surgery in a hurry.

Up at the horse lines, all was confusion. Justin had brought large saddlebags to put his mixers in, but fastening them securely to his horse's saddle was proving to be a problem.

"Run! More run! Catch Justin!" demanded Rowan from my shoulders, his voice rising dangerously. Meanwhile Kristin was nervously asking Tulga from the back of her gray, "Are you *sure* this horse is quiet?"

Kristin is not a bad rider. What she lacks, though, by her own admission, is the particular kind of instinct that makes you want to tell a horse what to do, even when it wants to do something else. This instinct is important to horses, because they are herd animals, used to being bossed (not brutalized) by the herd leader. Dogs are the same. So you have to assert yourself, partly through learned techniques and partly through sheer will. Kristin wasn't interested, at some deep level, in asserting her will over another being (not counting husbands). This is not to say that she is any kind of pushover. Quite the opposite. I know few better self-advocates. She simply isn't interested in telling a horse what to do. Except that if you're going to be on its back, you have to, or you just aren't safe.

"Ru," she said weakly from atop the very quiet-looking horse she'd been assigned, "are you sure this guy's all right? I keep kicking at him and he doesn't want to move."

"That's just because he doesn't want to leave the others," I said offhandedly, trying to find the right knot to make a secure makeshift girth with the strip of rawhide that the one guide had managed to magic up from somewhere. "He'll go when the others go. You'll be fine, Kristin, seriously," I said, having no real idea if that was true. Rowan was starting to pull my hair and shout, "Run! Run! More run!" and the knot was proving difficult to tie and it was obviously going to take forever to get going. I got the knot secured, tested the pull on the saddle rings, swung Rowan back on board, climbed up behind, and set off in a wide circle once more, Rowan's rising laugh erasing his evident insecurity. But this time my own could not be denied. I couldn't run the poor little horse round and round forever, especially since we'd have many, many miles to cover before day's end.

I turned Blackie around and trotted back to where the crowd was still milling around. Justin was on horseback now, at least, his sound equipment finally secured in the saddlebags behind him, holding his sound boom like a strange, cylinder-headed lance — a nouveau horse warrior of the digital age. But Tulga, Michel, and Jeremy were still on the ground, arguing about something. Rowan stood up in the saddle, doing his Viking-standing-on-the-prow-of-a-ship routine, holding on to my hair for balance.

"Guys!" I shouted, trying to play the leader and cringing at the note of desperation in my voice. "We have to get Rowan moving. I don't know how long his good mood's going to last. He's been up and down all morning, and —"

"Go!" Rowan chimed in, confirming my anxiety. *"Go-o-o-o-o-o!"*

"Jesus!" I roared, as Rowan's back arched and he tore out a small handful of hair. I'd missed the moment.

"Vaaaaaan! *Vaaaaaan!* Let's go in the van! Down! Down! *WANT TO GET DOWN!"*

"Come on!" I tried a note of false jollity, kicking Blackie into a brisk trot up to a goat track that led, as far as I could see, toward the distant pass that I'd gathered we were aiming for.

Rowan screamed louder.

"Oh, don't be so silly!" I tried to keep the jollity going, resisting the urge to shout at him, desperately embarrassed because I knew that Justin was picking up my every word via my clip-on microphone. "Come on, little trot!"

"WAAAAAAAAAH! VAN! VAN!" Rowan began to hurl himself around. I looked back. The rest of the party, moving at last, was coming, the van crawling along behind them.

"VAAAAN! *VAAAAN!"*

Kristin came level. "I can't make this horse move, Ru! I'm having to kick him every step. I won't be able to do this! I'm exhausted already, I . . ."

I know when I'm beaten. I reined Blackie in, dismounted, and waited, Rowan thrashing in my arms, until the pimpmobile came level.

"Okay." I sighed. "Okay, Kristin, listen — why don't you get in the van, give the guide your horse. Take Rowan. He wants to be in the van anyway. Maybe later we can try again."

So Rowan, the Horse Boy, set off into the

wild interior of Mongolia in a diesel four-by-four van with leopard-skin interior and pink curtains.

10
A FATHER'S MISTAKE

It shouldn't matter, I kept telling myself as we rode along the muddy track, its red clay slippery under Blackie's hooves. *It shouldn't matter whether Rowan makes this trip in the saddle or in a vehicle. What matters is that he's here, doing it, however and in whatever way pans out. Right?* Sure. Except that it did matter. It mattered.

However, perhaps an hour after setting off, we had to stop yet again when one of the guides' girth broke. So we all reined in, out there in the middle of grass and hill and wind and silence, and just to see what his reaction would be, I stuck my head in the door of the pimpmobile and asked Rowan, "Want to try riding Blackie again?"

And he said, "Yes!"

"Do you want to ride with Daddy or just have Daddy lead you for now?"

"Just have Daddy lead you for now."

"Okay."

So up he went. Kristin came out of the van too and mounted a sorrel with a light blond mane and tail that one of the guides had been leading. The sun came out. The day grew warm. And then the next little drama hit. We'd only been walking along the track for a little while, out there in the great out-thereness, when I decided to peel off a couple of layers. I'd filled my coat, a kind of fisherman's vest, with every Rowan accoutrement I could think of — change of clothes, spare shoes, wet wipes, spare underwear, spare pants (two pairs of each), a tarp folded up neatly in case of a real rainstorm, everything but the kitchen sink. It was too hot, so I took advantage of the pimpmobile crawling along behind us to put the vest inside, thinking I could always gallop back to the van in the event of an emergency. Somewhere in that operation a quick movement caught my eye. Jeremy's horse, bucking.

It's amazing how quickly things can go wrong with a horse. It takes a mere split second — a flapping piece of black plastic in a hedge, a wasp sting, a rattlesnake rattle, a gust of cold wind at the wrong moment, a loud noise — for the laziest, oldest, most bumbling dobbin to suddenly become a bucking, bolting death machine. A horse weighs something around half a ton. All it has to do is get a sudden fright, leap sideways while you're leading it through a narrow gateway or sitting less than totally securely, and that, without a doubt, can be that.

In Jeremy's case, the stimulus was his removing his coat to tie it around his middle, the warm wind catching it, and suddenly his droop-headed old gray plodder — the same horse that Kristin had been complaining was too dead for her just an hour before — was doing a full-on bucking-bronco act. Head down, heels up, back almost vertical. Jeremy didn't stand a chance. I clamped an arm tightly around Rowan, ready to pull him off if the fun spread — for bucking fits can be contagious, especially when the other horses notice that one of their fellows has managed to ditch its rider. Horses are humorous that way. But fortunately Blackie stood rock solid, and though some of the other horses jumped around a bit, the herd was back under control by the time Jeremy, with only his pride bruised, thank God, got back to his feet, a nice dark muddy patch having stained the arse of his riding pants dark brown. The horse set off at a run back down the trail toward the home herd, two of the guides galloping in hot pursuit.

Would we be able to have even one hour without drama? I wondered, as we all started to move again across the tussocky grassland toward the rock-strewn slopes of a low mountain pass. I hoped so, for finally we seemed to be doing it. Here I was at last, leading my son on horseback across the wide, wide steppe, two eagles circling high overhead, the sun warm but not hot, the wind in the grass, and Rowan happy at last.

"Look," he said. "Bison!"

It was something he'd been doing more and more often when relaxed lately — pointing out imaginary creatures: "Look, a cougar. Look, an elephant."

"It does look like there should be bison here, doesn't it?" Indeed, it was kind of like Montana or Wyoming — the Wild West before the whiteys showed up to ruin it.

"Daddy to sing," he said suddenly, rocking gently back and forth with Blackie's rhythm as the little mare picked her way up the lower part of the long, rock-strewn slope.

"What shall we sing?"

"Overthehillsandfaraway." He said it in one big rush, so that it sounded like one word. "Over the Hills and Far Away," an old English or maybe Scottish folk song that

I sometimes used to comfort him down to sleep. So I sang it now.

Oh Tommy was a piper's son
He learned to play when he was young
But the only tune that he would play
Was . . .

"Over the hills and far away," sang Rowan, in perfect pitch.

O'er the hills and o'er the main
Through . . .

"Flanders, Portugal, and Spain," trilled Rowan.

King George commands, and we obey . . .

"Over the hills and far away," he replied.

And I would love you all the day . . .

"Every night would kiss and play," he responded, his diction clear, as it always was when singing.

If with me you'd gladly stray . . .

"Over the hills and far away."

"Over the hills and fa-ar a-way," we sang together.

And then it was impossible to sing, as the gradient of the slope began to steepen, to become more punishing. I started to sweat, pant, as Blackie picked her way delicately over the rocks and Kristin's sorrel followed close behind.

We crested the saddle of the pass, me still leading Blackie. I stopped and turned to look back at the wide valley behind us. Unbroken grassland as far as the eye could see. Distant mountains. Clouds. An ocean of grassland. Freedom. An ocean of freedom. Perhaps the freest place in the world. Despite the horrible food.

"Daddy to get up!"

"You want to ride with Daddy?"

"Yes please."

It was as if a five-ton weight had suddenly been lifted from me. "Scoot up, then," I said, moving him forward in the saddle to make room. I swung up behind him. "Which way?" I said to Tulga, just breasting the rise on his horse, the rest of the guys behind him. The van had disappeared, looking for an alternative way up the pass. It was just us, the horses, the wind, the endless space.

"Over there — follow the ridge. It leads down to a river after several miles. Just follow the track."

"Run!" shouted Rowan. I kicked Blackie forward, her hooves beating a three-time canter on the turf of the ridge, Kristin cantering beside me, the river in distant sight beyond. The wind in our hair. Happy.

But happiness, of course, can be fleeting.

We rode, joyful, as larks trilled high in the air above us, little dots up in the blue whose music came down to us on happy scales of liquid song. The sun shone gold on the grass, white-gold like the white grass that grows on the uplands of Britain, which also shines gold in the light of late afternoon. The slope fell away gradually before us until, little by little, trotting and running, Rowan laughing and twisting around in the saddle to slap at me and demand tickles, we reached the river.

"Down, get down and play," said Rowan, seeing the shallow water snaking its course between the treeless banks.

I looked at Tulga, trotting to catch up to us. "Do we have time?"

"Yes, sure," he said happily. "We have some time, I think. We went faster than I thought we would, even though we got a late start."

So I handed Rowan down to the ground, swung off Blackie, and gave her a hearty pat. Lord, but she had proved herself a good horse already, and this not even the end of our first day together. We all got off our horses, let them graze awhile after their long climb and run.

"We've done fifteen miles," said Tulga, having conferred with the guides. "We've only got another six to ten. We can take a break."

While we rested, Tulga decided to take the van and go up one of the nearby mountains to try to find a phone signal, there being some business back in UB he needed to attend to before the next day, when we'd be out of any possibility of range. Rowan was already happily fumbling about with the rocks and stones that lay along the riverbank. As Kristin and I scrambled down the bank to join him, our horses held by the guides, the rest of the party dismounted, stretched, went off to pee. Then Rowan went suddenly rigid, standing up on his tiptoes, flapping his arms, eyes fixed and scared-looking. I knew immediately what it was — he always did it standing. It was one of the reasons he'd been so resistant to toilet-training — he didn't like to sit down while doing his business. For some reason he had to be standing. When the fit came upon him, you could always tell. Body shaking, up on his toes, eyes popping.

But the wet wipes, the change of clothes, everything that we needed was in my vest, which was in the van, which was halfway up one of three possible mountains by now. Out of range. Okay, we could make a plan. I used the water from the river to wash him off by hand in the stream, buried the dirty underwear under a few stones, and pulled his pants back up. Yet somehow the experience, or rather the makeshift, unfamiliar way in which I had to deal with his accident — if that's the right word for a dysfunction that happened so regularly, so often — brought home to Rowan, I could see, just how far from home he was.

No matter — we didn't have more than a couple of hours to ride till the campsite, as far as I could remember Tulga saying. I lifted Rowan back up the bank and put him into the saddle, intent on getting him moving again. The guides were pointing to a gathering rain cloud, or rather rain clouds, plural, and tapping imaginary wristwatches, meaning that we should move on. So move on we did, crossing the river, riding up the other side, and away across the far side of the valley. And that's where it started to go wrong. Rowan must have been feeling disconcerted, and no doubt tired too; it had been an intense few days since we had left London. A lifetime, it seemed. Yet the trigger was something completely mundane. Perhaps ten or fifteen minutes after leaving the river, we met two herders on horseback driving a large flock of sheep and goats toward the river.

"Baby goats!" said Rowan, spotting two very cute black ones trotting along together. "Hold them! Get down and play with the baby goats."

But the guides, evidently wanting to make up time with evening coming on and rain threatening, were moving on at a fast trot.

"Baby goats! Baby go-o-o-oats . . ."

I tried to say comforting things, but his body had gone rigid. "Down, down. Off the horse! Off!"

"It's okay, we just have to ride to the camp and —"

"Van! Want the van. Van! *Vaaaaan!*"

We were moving fast over broken ground toward low hills. The guides were picking up on Rowan's distress. The tall young man, the one who had invited me into his father's *ger* earlier in the day, made a couple of gestures suggesting that the camp lay over two hills.

"Just two hills," I said to Rowan hopefully, praying that I was right. "Just two more hills and we can have a cuddle-cuddle in the tent."

But Rowan was screaming now. No, sobbing. Genuine distress. Too much adventure, too tired, too cold, too hungry, and I had let the van go, let the one point of comfort he had out here in the frightening new and empty steppe disappear. What an idiot.

Kristin was riding next to me, trying to offer words of consolation: "It's okay, darling, we'll be at camp soon."

But Rowan was having none of it. "Help!" He kept sobbing. "Help me!"

Michel rode up to our side, filming from the saddle.

"Put the damn camera away!" I snapped. Rowan's sobs grew keener, the kind that rend at the wall of any parent's heart. This was no put-on; I'd taken the poor little boy to his edge and now he was falling apart.

"Help!" He sobbed again. *"Help me."*

I looked around desperately for the van. Nothing. We were still moving at that fast, leggy trot, the most uncomfortable of all gaits on the back of a horse. Rowan had his eyes tightly shut now, as he retreated into himself. This is a very bad thing for an autistic kid to do, every autism parent's worst scenario: seeing his child retreat, withdraw, shut down, his nervous system overloaded.

I drew rein. Got off. Hugged Rowan to me. Sobs were racking his little body; the child was terrified. I'd overestimated what he could take, overestimated badly. I kept hugging him. Kristin appeared, holding her horse's lead rein, and hugged him from the other side to form a protective cocoon. We stood like that, trying to comfort him as he sobbed inconsolably, until we heard — thank God — the roar of an engine in low gear. I turned my head and saw that the van had caught up to us at last.

Later that evening Rowan got over his tears and began to play with Tomoo again while I, feeling ashamed of myself, sat down with Tulga and looked at the itinerary. I'd been a fool. I'd genuinely thought I'd designed the trip around Rowan's needs, making sure we had enough time each day for slow travel and for him to get out of the saddle and play or just hang out whenever the need or mood struck him. That just hadn't been realistic, not with so large a group, so complicated a camp, so much equipment. It meant we'd be lucky to get going much before noon each day and would have to ride at an adult's energy level to make the distance on horseback to the remote Lake Sharga in the eight or so days I'd allowed. So instead I asked Tulga where we might be able to find a road so we could make the rest of the journey by van.

Tulga showed me a place on his map, two days' ride away, where we could hit a road. "Not a good road," he warned. "But I think it could get us near the lake."

"Not a good road? You mean worse than the one we drove on to get here?"

"Oh yes, much worse." He gave the little nervous laugh that I was starting to recognize as meaning *severe discomfort ahead.*

"Well, Rowan doesn't seem to mind that," I mused, thinking with dread about how the rest of us might fare. Sitting on a horse was luxury by comparison to the cement-mixer of Mongolian road travel. Assuming that Rowan wanted to go farther. Assuming that there was anything at the lake to see, any real reason to put us through the ordeal of going there at all. Assuming I wasn't going to have to turn around and put him on a plane home the next day.

I spoke with Tulga. Would we lose much time if we took a break the next day, let Rowan rest? He assured me we could do it. One day of rest, then one more day of riding, and then we'd go back in the vehicle until we reached Siberia, where the only option was to go in on horseback again. But that was more than a week away.

Rowan came running over to where Tulga and I sat, consulting the map. "Ride on Daddy's shoulders!"

A surge of relief: he had forgiven me. I hoisted him up. "Where shall we walk to? Up the hill?" There was a steep rise just to the west of the camp. A better place from which to watch the sunset.

"Up the hill!" Rowan confirmed. So up we went, Rowan wiggling around until he perched sidesaddle on my right shoulder, as was his wont, me puffing and blowing under his weight and the steepness of the gradient. Once at the top we looked around us.

"I'm sorry I made you tired today," I said. He ignored me. "Do you like Mongolia?" I asked, not without trepidation.

"Yes, I do."

"Look at those mountains there." I pointed to the closer range to the east, the top of which was covered with aspen forest, from whose soft, foamy foliage jutted four great rock faces.

"Maybe there's an ibex there," mused Rowan. It was unusual for him to offer such a logical, abstract idea voluntarily.

"Maybe there is," I agreed. "Tomorrow

shall we go up there and see if we can see one?"

"Yes!"

"Shall we ride up there on Blackie?"

"No *thank you!*"

"Shall we try and go up in the van?"

"Yes!"

"All right then, we'll go."

11
ROWAN 1, FEAR 0

There were tiny wild strawberries growing up in the aspen woods that spread themselves over the upper slopes of the mountains. It was another world from the steppe below, a world of shimmering silver-gray leaves, gray-and-black trunks striped, as Rowan pointed out, "like a zebra's leg," the lush green undergrowth beneath them jeweled and glinting with wildflowers and butterflies. Color was everywhere, reds, purples, yellows, blues, all vivid against their main canvas of foaming green, swirling around the gray-and-black striped aspen trunks like the stilled waters of an emerald flood. Beautiful beyond compare. Rowan, refusing to come out of the van, ignored it all, playing steadfastly with his airport toys on the leopard-print seats and screaming *"VAN!"* whenever I suggested he come out and climb up to the ibex rocks, as he had dubbed them.

They reared up into the blue sky above us, great igneous ramparts hung with green and orange lichens, ferns and flowers peeping from their cracks and crevices.

"Come on, Rowan," I said from the open door of the van, flies buzzing lazily around my head. "Let's climb up to the rocks."

"VAN!"

"We're going to have to call this story *Van Boy*." Kristin laughed as she lay back among the flowers and tall grass, enjoying the warmth of the sun, chatting with Tulga and the boys of the crew. I laughed too — outwardly, at least. The horses, which the guides had ridden up the mountain behind the van (it was incredible, a testament to the Russian engineering of the van, that it had reached this far up the rugged slopes), snorted happily at the end of their lead ropes, grazing on the lush growth and swishing their tails at the flies. I had Blackie at the end of a lead line too.

"We're not going to ride," I assured Rowan. "We're just taking Blackie to carry our stuff in case the slope gets too steep." The remaining hundred or so paces between the van and the foot of the rocks was almost vertical, and I'd rather Blackie did the carrying than I did. "Oh, who am I kidding?" I admitted to Rowan's back as he arranged his planes and toy traffic cones on the van's leopard-skin seat. "Of course I want you to ride. But whether you do or not is up to you, I promise. Now, come on, let's go climb the rocks."

"VAN!"

"Oh, come on!" I reached in, took him around the waist, and, ignoring the protest that didn't seem to a practiced ear to register on the real-distress scale, hoisted him back onto my shoulders.

"Let's go see an ibex!" said Rowan, as if he hadn't just refused to come out of the van.

"Let's do it!" I said, relieved. Tugging at the rope of the reluctant Blackie, I started to climb the steep slope, picking my way to the side of the great outcropping of rock so that the horse could follow. Ibex, or some kind of mountain creature, had indeed been making tracks up here, zigzagging close to the hill. Slow work, and breathless, but at least Rowan was out of the bloody van.

Once at the top of the ridge I put Rowan down and tied Blackie to the trunk of a gnarled, wind-sculpted pine, its stunted, twisted shape a reminder that winter in this lush and gentle upland must present a different picture indeed. Then we stepped out onto the wide granite platform that formed the strangely flat top of the rocky bluff.

"Look!" said Rowan, pointing. "An eagle's nest."

"Sure," I said, panting, assuming it was one of his change-of-mood imaginary pointings.

"Actually, Ru," said Kristin, stepping onto the rock behind us as Tulga hung tactfully back, "I think that *is* an eagle's nest."

In a grove of small pines just below eye level was a great shaggy mass of twigs, almost more a platform than a nest, adrift with stray downy feathers.

"You're right!" I said, surprised.

Rowan trotted to the edge. "Eagle?"

"Careful!" Kristin and I lunged after him, but we need not have worried. Rowan, dexterous as ever, had got down on his belly to look over the edge. We followed suit. The view from the eagle's nest, which was empty but strewn with feathers and bones, was like something out of the imagination of a god. Down below us were the horses, the crew, and the guides, half hidden by the shimmering aspen canopy; below that, the narrow cleft in the mountainside where aspen gave way to flower-strewn meadow; and below that, a green, blue, and finally violet vastness, an immensity that dizzied the mind, caught at the stomach, almost too much to look at. As if you might, like an eagle, or a person flying in a dream, go soaring involuntarily out, Icarus-like, over the great rolling emptiness below, only to find yourself suddenly falling, falling. Next to me I could hear my son's breathing.

"Do you like Mongolia?" asked Kristin from his other side.

"Yes I do!"

"Is it beautiful?" I asked.

"Yes!"

"I love you, Rowan," I said.

He didn't look at me, kept squinting at the meeting of heaven and earth below, but said matter-of-factly, "I love you too, Daddy."

Such a rare pronouncement, rare like a jewel. I sat up, swept him into my arms, and hugged him to me. This enigmatic, impossible, unknowable boy.

Then, from below, one of the horses gave a loud, shrieking whinny, and Blackie, close at hand, answered with earsplitting force.

"Arrrrrgh!" screamed Rowan, flinching at the sound and twisting in my arms. "Go home! *Go home!* VAN! *V-AAAAAAAAAN!*"

"Guess we won't be seeing any ibex, then," I quipped sourly a few minutes later as I loaded Rowan into his beloved van. "I wonder if we *should* just take him home."

"Don't worry, love." Kristin put a hand on my arm. "It'll work out. He's just making the adjustment, that's all."

"I don't know. I think I might have really messed up. He won't even look at the horse."

"I know, love, I know." Kristin looked down, as if lacking anything more to say, as Rowan piled busily into his toys and the driver fired up the engine.

"Let's go back to the camp and see Tomoo," said Rowan.

"Mind if I ride down on horseback?" I asked. "I kind of need to —"

"Sure," said Kristin, leaning out to give me a little kiss. "It'll be okay, really."

I wasn't so hopeful. What if Rowan refused to get on a horse again? What if I really had blown the one thing that provided the link between his world and ours? Or did he only need a chance to get over himself, his anxieties? Back home, the best way to do that was always just to swing him up into the saddle. Maybe this evening I should try.

I kicked Blackie forward, urging her to catch up with Tulga and the others, who had galloped on ahead, hooves flying. The summer wind was warm in my hair.

That afternoon it rained hard again. We

crouched in our tents, waiting it out, Rowan alternately playing with his toys, being read to by Kristin, and playing tickle games with me. After an hour or so of this I heard shouting, laughing, whooping, and looked out the tent flap to see Michel and Jeremy running naked in the rain, private parts flopping, while Tulga, the drivers, and the guides, coaxed from their own tents and shelters by the noise, fell about laughing. I laughed too, then read to Rowan until the rain let up, while Kristin took an afternoon nap on her side of the tent. When she at last woke up, I left her and Rowan playing a singing game together and went down to where the horses were tethered.

One of the guides came running over immediately, caught Blackie for me, and, seeming to know what I intended, put her saddle on. High above us two eagles — they often seemed to go in twos — rode a thermal, circling slowly upward, keening to each other with high, clear cries. The light was shifting now toward evening. Gold, pink, and intense blue notes began to dot the hitherto gray skies. A large gap of blue hung over the place where the sun would set, but what looked like another dark front of rain threatened to blanket it all again soon. The grass began to take on a golden sheen, the light to rarefy, rendering exquisite the land, the mountains, the shiny flanks of the grazing horses, the faces of those around me.

The other two guides joined me, walking alongside as I led Blackie up to our tent, wondering if I was about to win the crappiest-dad-of-the-year award. Though we'd barely had a chance to connect, what with the events of the past day or so, it was clear that there was a tact, a grace to these people, as if maintaining a supportive presence yet allowing personal space was something so familiar as to be instinctual. Maybe I was projecting, but the oldest of the three smiled at me and patted my arm, suggesting both moral support and sympathy if things went wrong.

"Hey," I whispered to the horse. "Help me out here, okay?" I led her over to the tent, where Kristin was still singing the Carpenters song, over and over, to Rowan, a slight note of desperation in her voice.

"Hey, Rowan," I said, unzipping the tent. "Come on, let's go for a little ride on Blackie."

"Noooooo thankyou! Tent! Tent! *Sing with Mommy!*"

"Oh, come on, Rowan," said Kristin, torn between relief at being able to stop with the song and distress at his distress. "Just a short one!"

"Row-*an!*" Tomoo appeared at my side, peeping in. "Ro-*waan!*" he sang. Rowan ceased yelling a moment to offer a throaty, bubbly giggle to his new friend, then yelled again as I reached in, put my arm round his middle, and swept him up and into the waiting Blackie's saddle, Tulga doing the same with Tomoo. "Ro-*wan!*" sang Tomoo again, clasping my son around the middle from behind as I led Blackie off at a walk, the setting sun descending like a disk of red burnished gold behind us.

The yells turned to wails. "Down! Get *down! Tent! Teeeeeent! TEEEENT!*"

It wasn't working. He needed to run. I swung Tomoo down, got up behind Rowan myself, turned Blackie with my legs, and kicked her into a gallop. The wails went up a notch, echoing off the hills around us. Rowan had his eyes tightly shut. What was I doing? Yet again that inner voice, irrational as ever, said, *Give it one more try.*

I ran the horse full tilt toward the far hillside, then swung my weight back, bringing Blackie onto her haunches, wheeling her around, and setting her at a hard run back toward the tents once more. Rowan's wails stopped, replaced by a giggle.

"You little faker!" I yelled.

"Fakerrr!" said Rowan, and giggled again.

"You little Scubby Boy," I said, using his pet name. "Jesus, you had me worried. Want to go for a run?"

Rowan opened his eyes, gave me a look of pure devilment, and said, *"Run!"*

I clapped heels to Blackie's sides, suddenly wildly, deliriously happy that Rowan was happy, seemed happy, on a horse once more. We reached the end of the short plain again, stopped, turned. I couldn't lose this moment. What to do to reinforce it? "Want to stand?" I asked.

It was what Rowan always did when at his happiest on a horse, scrambling to stand upright, feet on the saddle horn, one hand firmly holding on to my hair for support, the other free, balancing there with my arm around him. Usually I was careful to let this happen only when at a walk. But now was no time to observe the safety rules. Anyway, Blackie had accepted him the same way Betsy had — that much had been clear yesterday. "Go on, you little Scubby Boy!" I yelled, turning Blackie at the canter to ride for the tents once more. "Stand if you want to!"

Laughing, Rowan brought his knees up, scrabbled his feet on the saddle, on my thighs, gaining purchase, grabbed a hank of hair, and pushed himself upright. "Don't do anything bad, Blackie," I said, a little pointlessly, and tightened my arm around Rowan's middle as the mare thundered back toward the tents, Rowan's laughter dancing on the gilded air, the sunset pouring over us like a spiderweb of pink and gold. Blackie, more sensible than I, slowed to a walk of her own accord.

"Yay!" I shouted. "You did it! *Yay, Rowan!*"

My son turned and looked at me, and I saw a kind of light bulb go on behind his eyes as he realized that for the first time he had overcome his usually paralyzing, neurologically driven anxiety and fear. That he had, perhaps for the first time in his short life, managed to conquer it, rise above it, cast it aside instead of letting it rule him. *"Yay, Rowan!"* he echoed, squinting his eyes at me in his autistic way and bonking his forehead against mine, raw life force, sheer joy, just throbbing in him.

"Arms up!" I shouted, raising my arms on either side of him, so that he had to lean back against my chest and neck for support. "Yay, Rowan!"

"Arms *up!*" he shouted too, and raised his little fists proudly to the heavens. *"Yay, Rowan!"*

A round of cheering and clapping erupted from the onlookers — Kristin, Tomoo, Tulga, the guides, Michel, Jeremy, even the usually taciturn Justin and Naara, the two drivers, the grumpy cook. All of them were clapping, cheering him. Blackie slowed to a halt in front of them all. *"Yay, Rowan!"* shouted his supporters, echoed by Rowan himself, his arms punching the air one last time.

And I handed him, giggling joyously, down into his mother's waiting arms, as the last of the great red disk disappeared behind the shoulder of the mountain.

"Where's the vodka?" I asked, everyone laughing and cheering around us. Tomoo came running, arms outstretched. Kristin put Rowan down and he ran to meet his friend. His *friend.* Clasping each other in a great bear hug, they fell to the ground, rolled around a moment, then Tomoo clambered to his feet and started doing the slow, swaggering victory dance, hips swinging, arms in the air, that Mongolian wrestlers perform after a victorious bout. He helped Rowan to his feet, tried to get Rowan to follow his movements. "He wants to show Rowan he's won!" Tulga said, laughing. But Rowan tore past Tomoo, past all of us, shouting, "I'm a horse! I'm a horse! *Gallop!*

Gallop!"

And away over the steppe he went, half running, half galloping in imitation of a horse.

Jeremy appeared with a bottle of crystal-clear Genghis Khan vodka — "Mongolia's best," Tulga assured us, unscrewing the top and raising it in the twilight. "To Rowan!"

"You know, Ru," said Jeremy, after he had taken his second swig, "I think you just had your prayer answered."

"For sure," I said, reaching for the bottle, taking a slug, then handing it off to the guides, who had come up to drink to Rowan's health too.

"No," said Jeremy, "I mean specifically. I've heard you say that you'd open a bottle of champagne the first time Rowan lied to you, because it'd show he'd made a kind of leap in cognition. Well, I think you just got your first lie."

It was true. I had said that in the past, because when a child lies, it means a certain cognitive leap, the ability to take another's perspective, has occurred. It's part of the development of the intellect. I wasn't sure this quite applied now, but I could see what Jeremy meant. Rowan had been faking his fear, after his initial, very real distress. But then his mood had suddenly shifted, as if he had realized for the first time that he didn't need to be so completely caught up in his own feelings anymore. It wasn't quite the same as a lie, but it did mean he had taken a leap of the mind, the imagination, and freed himself from unnecessary trauma.

I took the vodka bottle as it was passed over to me. "Here's to Rowan's being free of his own shit."

"That's worth drinking to for any of us," said Kristin.

"No kidding."

So around the bottle went again, while Rowan and Tomoo tore after each other on the steppe in the gathering dusk and the stars came out above the mountains.

"To freedom!"

Tulga translated for the guides, who roared approval and toasted it too. I looked up at the darkening sky, more elated than I had been in months. A sickle moon was beginning to rise. A new moon. A new beginning?

That night we made a fire and sat around it eating delicious deep-fried meat and veggie pastries, while Rowan, as if on amphetamines with the euphoria of his achievement, ran around and around the camp with Tomoo, playing at being a horse, at being an eagle, flying, wrestling, laughing. This is the beauty of the steppe — out here there are no hazards: no cars, no precipices or pits to fall into, no poisonous snakes, no predators, just a vastness of open space in which a child's spirit can soar. At first I'd been worried that Rowan might run among the hooves of the tethered horses, but he seemed to avoid them instinctively. So we sat and ate and drank and sang, the guides offering long, beautiful herding songs about their love of their land, we answering with folk songs gleaned from memory, then descending into pop tunes — Abba, Village People (Jeremy, Justin, and Michel jumping up for a spontaneous "YMCA"), anything silly we could think of as the vodka made the rounds.

Suddenly Rowan crashed into my lap, laughing, just as we were finishing a song. I'm not sure whose idea it was, but somehow we started singing the theme from *Madagascar,* one of Rowan's favorites before he had suddenly decided to go cold turkey on all videos a few months before. "I like to move it move it, I like to move it move it, I like to move it move it, I like to —"

"Move it!" yelled Rowan.

So I started with the techno beat, making a noise in my throat to imitate the *ootz ootz*

ootz sound of drum, bass, and high-hat (the vodka helped, but give it a try and you'll see that you *can* make techno in the human throat). Then Kristin started the synth melody, *Na-na-nana-na-na-na-na-na-nana-na,* and I, from memory, managed to find the words to the half-rap, half-reggae, Jamaican-style verse, stumbling through it in a fumbling white-boy fashion.

Then Michel sang, as we kept the beat going: "Go, Rowan, go, Rowan, go, Rowan, go, Rowan . . ."

We all took it up: Go, Rowan, go, Rowan, go, Rowan, go, Rowan . . .

And incredibly, Rowan took it, starting, to our utter amazement, to freestyle rap. In perfect time. Just gibberish at first: "Heb-e-beb-e-blah, heb-e-beb-e-blah, hebeb-ebba, hebeb-ebba, hebebe-ebba — blah," then morphing into real, if Rowan-centric, lyrics: "Buster's coming, Buster's coming, Buster, Buster, Buster's coming" and "It's a Gobi, it's a Gobi, it's a Gobi, it's a Gobi."

Where had he got that from? Tulga, on the long drive out, had told us that his family was from the Gobi region and that he considered the desert the most beautiful part of Mongolia. Had Rowan taken that information in? Who knew? Who cared? He was freestyling, for crying out loud. Amazing. Incredible. Hilarious. Strange. A complete mystery, as always.

We went to bed laughing, even as we performed the rituals with the vodka, water, and burning grasses that the shamans had prescribed. As we fell asleep, with just a sheepskin and the tent's fabric between us and the steppe, I heard the rumble of hooves as a herd of horses — ours? a different herd? — came cantering by under the thin new moon.

The next day Rowan refused to get on Blackie.

"All right," I said, trying to mask my disappointment and not doing a very good job of it. "No problem. You can ride in the van if you want to."

So we rode uphill out of the campsite to a low pass below the ibex rocks, where we had seen no ibex, the van trailing us at a snail's pace, Rowan looking steadfastly at a catalogue of animal toys he'd brought with him from the U.K., Kristin and Tomoo riding with him.

"How d'you feel?" asked Michel, riding next to me and leveling the camera. I tried not to snap at him. It was one thing to have the camera vaguely in the background, another thing to have it up close when things weren't going well. But it was part of the deal, and what was the point if we weren't going to be honest? Even though it meant being shown warts and all.

I felt terrible, I told Michel. And worried. Worried that if Rowan wouldn't get back on a horse when we got to Siberia, where the reindeer people were, and where we'd have no van support, we would not be able to reach the next shamans and complete the healing that my gut told me waited for Rowan, for us, up there in that distant wilderness. "What else can I say?" I trailed off lamely, as Michel continued to focus the camera from atop his horse. "Listen, Michel, can you shut that bloody thing off, please?"

Why was Rowan resisting being on the horse now, after his triumph of the previous night? Was it because he didn't want to continue? But he had said he wanted to go see the reindeer people. Was it simply a way of asserting himself, his wants, his needs, during a journey that for him was part wonderful, part confusing and strange? Up on top of the pass we stopped the van and tried a new tack. Kristin got out, mounted Blackie, and took Rowan in the saddle in front of her while I led them. Rowan didn't tantrum, but he wasn't exactly cooperating either. As we walked down the long green track of the pass, down toward a lush valley of verdant pasture below, Rowan refused to open his eyes, insisting, after a few hundred yards, on sitting facing away from the landscape, burying his face in Kristin's chest, eyes shut, making strange grunting sounds. *Ugh ugh ugh.*

So Kristin started singing him a song in time with Blackie's walk:

I'm tired and I want to go home
Just had a drink about an hour ago
And I'm feeling . . .

She fished for a lyric.

. . . like a garden gnome.

"Tired and I want to go see the *giraffe!*" shouted Rowan, his voice muffled by her coat. We looked at each other. She shrugged.

I'm tired and I want to see the giraffe
Just had a drink about an hour ago

And it's really quite a laugh

Blackie snorted and tossed her head on the end of the lead rope, as if protesting the bad rhyme.

I'm tired and I want to see the . . .

"Ibex!" shouted Rowan.

Just had a drink about an hour ago
And I'm feeling . . .

Kristin looked at me for help.
"Um . . . like I've just roasted some chicken in a dish made of Pyrex?"

Rowan giggled.

"You little faker!" said Kristin.

"Fak-*errr!*" echoed Rowan. Did he understand what the word meant? *Was* he faking? Or was it something else, something much more complex and unfathomable?

We weren't far from the floor of the valley now. Below us was a group of *gers* crouched next to a big circular wooden corral similar to the one in the valley we'd started from, full of bleating, baaing sheep and goats.

"Look!" I said, knowing this would catch his interest. "Baby goats!"

For that, Rowan was prepared to tear his face away from Kristin's breasts and open his eyes. Which lit up. A few minutes later we were walking toward the *gers* and the corral, Tulga shouting *No-khoi, ko-rio,* "Hold the dogs," while a little girl, no more than six or seven, trotted out of one of the *gers* and did in fact launch herself bodily onto one of the clan's great shaggy sheepdogs, which had been baring its teeth at us. The beast could easily have shaken her featherweight off, but it lay submissively beneath her, her little hand closed firmly around its muzzle, while her parents came out of the interior, smiling. Tulga trotted up with Tomoo, explaining what was what. As soon as we caught up, Rowan was off Blackie and blissfully holding a little tan baby goat, hugging it close, talking to it: "Look, it's got eyes. And a little nose. And ears. And a little butt butt."

I thought for a moment about offering to buy it to take with us, then pictured the impossibility of holding a baby goat and Rowan in the saddle at the same time — not to mention having it in the van. The drivers would strike.

I tried riding with Rowan one last time. It was perfect riding country; the valley floor was good turf, following a river, its sward dotted with starlike little white flowers and the aspen and pine forest gray-green and dark green on the slopes above us. We set off at a run, making up time, cantering past carved standing stones — markers made by soldiers who left these valleys, said Tulga, to fight with Genghis Khan's armies hundreds of years before. We cantered up to a huge eagle tearing at the carcass of a fawn. It flapped away as we approached. We thundered past the little disemboweled, spotted creature, its eyes still glossy with death. The eagle must have caught it on the heights and brought it down here to gorge, for no deer frequented these lower elevations, where the nomads rode with rifles in scabbards on the saddles. Through all this Rowan alternately cried, asked to run faster, asked to get off, then asked me to make the horse run again. Was he happy? Sad? Both? I couldn't tell. Finally he struggled upright in the saddle as we loped along, performing one of his feats of equine acrobatics, yelling some song of his own invention in time with Blackie's smooth, rocking gallop, then turning round and burying his face in my chest as if afraid, while I held him in place with one hand, held the reins in the other, and trusted the horse to read the ground and not trip — which, off-balance as we were, would have fired us both pointblank into the green blur of turf below.

When we finally pulled up in the meadow, the horses breathing hard and dipping their heads immediately to graze, Rowan would not open his eyes until the van had caught up with us. Then he struggled down to the ground, ran to the vehicle, hopped in, and busied himself with his animal catalogue. Hopeless. Even when a herd of local milk cows came out of the forest to investigate us as we lazed about on the grass, eating, and the guides caught one of the calves and held it so Tomoo and Rowan could ride, Rowan ignored them.

It was time to let go. As we lunched on noodle soup with gobbets of meat and fat, the cloud cover parted and the sun came out. There was a sudden heavy, oppressive rise in temperature that made my eyelids want to close. I stretched out on the daisy-studded greensward, folded my arms under my head, and before I knew it I was asleep.

Kristin and me traveling in Coorg, India, just after meeting. *Ranjan Abraham*

The new arrival. *Kristin Neff*

Rowan seems to have a direct line to all animals, not just to horses.
Kristin Neff

Rowan's grandmothers could not understand the strange distantness of their infant grandchild. Here he squirms in the arms of Kristin's mother, Teri. *Kristin Neff*

Even chickens.
Kristin Neff

Obsessively lining up toys into patterns, rather than playing with them as other kids do, can be part of autism. *Kristin Neff*

One of the first few days on Betsy.
Rowan gives me his first verbal command: "Run!" *Kristin Neff*

Exhaustion — and this is only the start of the trip. *Justin Jin*

The first day on horseback in Mongolia.
What were we thinking? *Justin Jin*

Praying to the Lords of the Mountain — the first shaman ceremony. *Justin Hennard*

Where the shaman
world and the autism
world connect.
Justin Jin

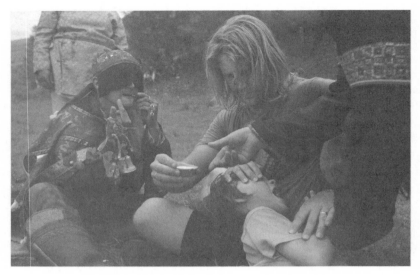

Here—drink this offering of sacred mare's milk (easier said than done). The first shamans' ritual, day two of the journey. To say this day was stressful would be an understatement. Yet halfway through the ritual, Rowan made his first friend. *Justin Jin*

Can you forgive your crazy husband?
Justin Jin

"Mongolian brother!"
Rowan's first friend. *Justin Jin*

Just three days before, Rowan would never have allowed
this kind of closeness from another child. *Justin Jin*

Mongolian mommy!
Justin Hennard

Rowan 1, Fear 0.
Justin Jin

Rowan and Tomoo playing,
just after Rowan conquered his fear. *Justin Jin*

Rowan stops to make a new friend. *Justin Jin*

See the top of those mountains there? That's where we are headed. *Justin Hennard*

Central Mongolia, day three of the journey. *Justin Jin*

Watching the landscape drift
by from the pimpmobile.
What goes on in that mind?
Justin Hennard

At the top of the mountain pass, deep in southern Siberia,
after nine hours of ascent. Where are the reindeer people? *Justin Hennard*

Hoping to God that Blue doesn't put his foot in a hole . . . *Michel Scott*

By the shores of Lake Sharga—a remote *ger*.
Note the milk curd drying on the roof. *Justin Hennard*

Rowan and Abracadabra—gratuitous cuteness overload. *Justin Hennard*

The tepees of the Dukha people. Ghoste's is on the left. *Michel Scott*

The Dukha people still ride as well as herd reindeer. Rowan switches from horse to deer.
Justin Hennard

Rowan on the third day with Ghoste—will this be the healing we came for?
Justin Hennard

After Mongolia, Rowan—previously isolated from his peers— soon had a whole circle of friends. *Michel Scott*

Teaching the kids at the New Trails Farm—where autistic and neurotypical kids can come together for learning and therapies, with the horse as the meeting place. If Rowan had not shown me the way with Betsy, this would never have happened. *Kristin Neff*

Ten months after—Rowan can handle Betsy on his own.
No words can express the joy. *Michel Scott*

12
THE VAN BOY

So we left him in the van, and — by way of an experiment, now that he had made his first friend — left Tomoo and Michel in there with him while Kristin and I rode on. Together. For the first time in a long, long while. With the exception of when one of the grandmothers came to visit, Rowan was never away from one or the other of us. Not that we hadn't tried babysitters, tried to have a life. But Rowan had screamed, beat himself, drummed his head on the floor, hurt himself, driven every potential baby-sitter we had tried away with the distress, the tyranny of his bowels, the sheer impos-sibility of his misery, the inconsolability of it, the *autisticness* of it. To get around it, we took it in turns to go out once a week with friends. But dinner together? Dinner and a movie and dancing? We'd given that up long ago.

But now, as we rode out across the gradually widening valley, our horses taking the central path across the green while the van followed the rough track along the far mountain wall, Rowan, amazingly, seemed content to let us go. We took a walkie-talkie with us in case he suddenly had an anxiety attack and needed his mommy. Every now and then I flipped the switch on it, just to check in, but each time, as our horses walked over the short-cropped green grass, Michel assured me, voice fuzzy with static, "No, he's fine. He and Tomoo are just playing in the van. No problem, really."

I looked at my beautiful wife riding along beside me, long-legged and elegant in the saddle, as she always was. A light breeze got up, ruffling her long brown hair and bringing the temperature down to a perfect seventy degrees. She looked at me.

"Can you believe he's actually letting us go?" she asked.

"No, I can't. I keep thinking Michel's going to call at any moment and one of us'll have to run back to him."

"You don't get much time together?" Tulga, riding next to us, had been listening. "Well," he said, gesturing around, "this is a good place to enjoy it."

Indeed it was. The mountains hereabouts were taller, sharper, more defined in their peaks and ridges, their forested upper slopes luxurious with evergreen and aspen. There was no settlement in sight, no *ger,* not even a herd of animals, just wide-open space, the air like wine.

"Do you think this could be the start of something?" asked Kristin. "Like —"

"Babysitters." I finished the sentence for her.

Then the walkie-talkie beeped.

"Hello?" I flipped the switch. "Hello, Michel? Everything okay? Over . . ."

From the other end, silence. Then Rowan's voice: *"Ootz, ootz, ootz, ootz."*

I burst out laughing and turned up the volume so Kristin, Tulga, and the others riding nearby could hear.

"Scubby?" I said into the receiver. *"Ootz, ootz, ootz, ootz,"* came the reply. I could hear Michel and Tomoo laughing in the background.

So I started to sing, first the tune, then the rap lyrics, from the *Madagascar* song, and as before, Rowan started to rap back to me, Michel doing the *ootz, ootz* in the background to keep him going. "Buster's coming, Buster's coming, Buster's coming, Buster's coming . . . It's a Gobi, it's a Gobi, it's a Gobi, it's a Gobi . . ." Back and forth, trying to contain my laughter, purring with delight, as we rode gently across the green valley.

A pair of lanner falcons flapped noisily overhead, their cries high-pitched, intense, their flight rapid, purposeful. A faint blur of blue-gray up ahead revealed itself as we drew closer to be a small flock of cranes, elegant as a group of fashion models clustered by some wilderness runway. Serried ranks of white cloud hung motionless in a sky of liquid blue. It was good just to be out on horseback. Just to *be.*

Then the walkie-talkie buzzed once more. It was Michel. "Umm, Rowan's not smelling too good. I think he just had an accident. I asked him if he wanted me to try and change him, but he just said, 'Mommy, Daddy.' Over."

"This one's yours," said Kristin from behind me. It was true — we always divided the more noisome chores fifty-fifty.

"Okay," I said into the walkie-talkie. "I think you must be up ahead of us a couple of miles. I'll be right there! Over."

And so, having made sure that I had wipes, new underwear, and a change of pants in my jacket pocket, I clapped heels to Blackie's sides and took off up the trail at a gallop, urging her on by whacking her sides with the plastic pack of wet wipes, her hooves shaking the ground as we thundered poo-ward.

"Code Brown!" I shouted with mock urgency as I pulled up by the van, waving the wipes above my head. *"Code Brown!"*

Rowan, standing outside the parked vehicle, giggled. Tomoo stood next to him, holding his nose, watched over by the monolithic driver and a small girl and her whip-thin dad, who sat atop a pile of hay loaded onto a yak cart and had stopped to take in the spectacle.

"Code Brown!" I yelled again, waving the wet wipes in the air theatrically and leaping off Blackie into a dead run, stuntman style, just for the hell of it.

"Stinky," said Rowan matter-of-factly. "Stinky, yucky."

We camped by a stream nearby. In the gorgeous golden light, Tomoo and Rowan stripped off and played with his animals, setting them up in the fast-flowing, tinkling water. I knew he'd likely lose one or two but didn't have the heart to interfere, so involved were they in their play.

I left them alone. Asked Jeremy and Kristin to keep an eye on the boys and, there still being at least an hour of daylight left, took Blackie for a ride up the mountainside to the forest margin to sit and think. Justin rode with me, intent on capturing some "wild sound" — it made me think of some invisible gorilla made of ether — of the birds, the wind. I offered to watch the horses while he walked off with his strange-looking equipment of mixer bag and hand-held boom mike wrapped in what looked like a huge fluffy sock, a kind of dirty gray Pekingese impaled on a stick. I selected two birch saplings to tether the horses to, sufficiently far apart so they wouldn't get tied up in each other's lead ropes or fall to fighting and kicking, as some horses do. I sat down on a stump. The light up here was brilliant — sharp, clear, filtered through leaves. There was birdsong everywhere, distant sounds of voices and whinnying horses from the camp below. I took out my notebook, clicked the pen to begin writing. The changes were coming so thick and fast. Since the shamans, Rowan had made his first friend, had temporarily gotten over his fears and anxieties, had consciously misled us (or so it seemed, anyway), had spontaneously rapped, had allowed Kristin and me to leave him without protest, and was becoming more verbal by the day.

And this day of firsts still had one last surprise left in it. That night, after we'd eaten our usual noodle, meat, and fat soup — should one of us take over the cooking? I wondered — the temperature fell so rapidly that we all retired early to our tents. But Rowan just wasn't tired. From my side of the tent I heard him talking to himself, some of it gibberish, some of it words I could understand, mostly about animals, the usual stuff. Kristin sang to him, tried to gentle him down to sleep, but he seemed to have an unusual energy tonight. As I drifted in and out of consciousness, I heard him asking her to sing over and over, and her "Time to sleep now" became gradually more desperate. On a sudden impulse I wriggled out of my sleeping bag, got up, and unzipped their side of the tent.

"Hey, Rowan," I said. "Want to go for a walk with Daddy and see the stars?"

"Walk with Daddy!"

"Great," said Kristin with well-earned relief as Rowan struggled out of her embrace and I felt in the dark for his feet so I could put his Crocs on. Then I took his little hand, and out into the cold starlight we went.

We trudged up the gradual slope behind the tents, hand in hand, crossing the narrow dirt track that served as the local highway, heading in roughly the same direction that I had ridden earlier on Blackie. It's strange how gradients, when walked in the dark, seem to surprise your legs, as if the hill has come alive and decided to shock your knees by suddenly rising underneath them, the way moguls do when you ski. Rowan was full of beans, trotting along beside me, talking to himself in his singsong voice: "Look at the stars! Look at the beautiful moon. How d'you spell *moon?* M-O-O-N. It's a hill. We're walking. It's a big hill."

"Want to go up to the forest?" I asked, somewhat rhetorically — it was pretty far, after all, and the darkness, but for the sickle moon and stars, was almost total.

"Yes, I do!"

"Good yessing, Rowan."

"Good yessing, Rowan," he echoed. "It's a *goo-oo-ood* yes."

"Indeed it is."

We walked on in silence awhile, the hillside growing steeper, our breath making steam in the cold air. There would be frost later. We must be at a very high elevation here, I thought, as our pace slowed. Strange how hot this place was, yet how cold. How amazing to be here at all, with my son. Out walking in the Mongolian night together, his small hand in mine, surrounded by stars and silence. We stopped, the hill too steep now for comfort, to breathe it all in.

"There was a very small boy," said Rowan suddenly, his voice disembodied in the dark.

"A small boy?"

"A very small boy. He went on an adventure."

I began to say something, to make some comment, as Kristin and I, the therapists and teachers, all of us always did, always trying to encourage imagination, speech. Then some instinct told me to shut my mouth.

"A very small boy on adventure. He went on adventure. And . . ." Here something unintelligible, followed by the word *shamans*.

"Shamans," Rowan continued, his little voice like music in the dark. *"Whack, whack, whack* on the back. And then Tomoo . . ." Again something I couldn't follow, then the word *friend.*

"A friend," Rowan resumed, talking to whom? To the stars, to the night, to himself, to me, to God? "And the van and horses," he went on. "And Rowan was quite upset. And mountains and eagles."

My son was telling a story. The story of his own experience. I was stunned. He fell silent awhile.

"Is Buster in the adventure?" I hazarded at last, wanting him to continue.

"Yes, Buster and Rowan and Tomoo. Once upon a time there was a little boy called Rowan, and he went to Mongolia and saw some shamans."

He began to walk again, pulling me with him, back down the hillside now, back toward the snorts of the tethered horses and the faint moonlit glow of the stream, alternating between babble and tangible, relevant words: Tomoo, friend, pirate, play, horse, mountain, eagles, shamans.

"You're telling me about your adventure, Rowan. That's amazing."

He giggled. I could feel his smile in the dark, hear it in his voice. "Rowan's adventure," he said, leading me downhill by the hand. "Rowan's adventure."

We took leave of our guides by the banks of the stream in the sunny, rapidly warming morning. A number of herdsmen had ridden in, no doubt having heard through the local equivalent of the bush telegraph that foreigners were camped out here in the middle of . . . well, not exactly nowhere. This was their home, after all — to them it was local, familiar. To us, utterly exotic and foreign. Suffice to say that we were entertainment. Despite the early hour, as we packed up the tents and backpacks, ready

282

to say goodbye to the horses and to the guides who'd taken such good care of us, and to load everything into the van, bottles of vodka began to appear. Another man showed up, not on horseback but on a motorbike, with a large plastic jug of *airag*. We were all a little tipsy by the time the first thermos of tea appeared on the little camp table, along with the inevitable Mongolian butter cookies (aptly, and hilariously, named *Rain Man* cookies). Rowan and Tomoo splashed in the stream, looking for — and finding, thankfully — a number of the toy animals that had been left there in the mud the previous evening.

"Time to say goodbye to Blackie," I said to Rowan. "Come on, let's give her a kiss and say thank you for carrying us."

"Goodbye to Blackie," echoed Rowan automatically, not that interested, then yelling loudly as I lifted him up to make the goodbye a reality.

"All done horses!" he yelled, kicking his legs.

"Yes, all done horses," I confirmed. "We're just giving her a kiss goodbye!"

He relaxed, allowed himself to be taken over to the grazing Blackie, and dutifully gave her a hug around the neck and a kiss on her soft black nose, then ran back to the riverbank and Tomoo. I watched him go, feeling sad, despite the magic of the night before. And worried, again, that when the time came to head off into Siberia to find the reindeer people, he would not get back on a horse. Which was the only way to get there. Not to mention the nagging worry that I had actually put him off horses for good, out of my desire for him to be some kind of horse wonder boy. When I'm heavily stressed, I sometimes manifest it physically with cold sores on the lip. I could feel the tingle of one coming now, and sent up a prayer that it wouldn't be a big one.

There was a tap on my shoulder. The youngest and tallest of the guides was trying to say something to me, pointing to Rowan and pointing to Blackie. With no Mongolian, I couldn't understand, but I did make out the words *kuni* and *boli,* horse and boy. Kristin wandered over, as did the other guides and the locals who had gathered. A vodka bottle was proffered from somewhere. I took a breakfast swig.

"Is he calling Rowan a horse boy?" I asked, trying to make sense of what was evidently a fairly important message. "We need Tulga. *Tulga!*"

I had to shout it a few times before Tulga emerged from the toilet tent, waving a hand

284

as if to say, *I'm coming, I'm coming.* Couldn't get even a few minutes' peace, poor man.

He came over, listened to what the young guide had to say, then smiled from ear to ear. "Oh, listen, Rupert, this is a great honor. They are giving Rowan the horse."

"Giving him Blackie?"

"Yes. Rupert, Kristin, you must sit down. There is a . . . a sort of ceremony to this. It's very . . ." He fished for the right word. ". . . Unusual, no, *rare,* to be given a horse like this. This is something very special. Sit, sit. I'll translate. Wow, I have to say I'm very surprised by this." He laughed, looking pleased, surprised.

So we sat there on the warm, close-cropped turf, side by side, the sound of Rowan's and Tomoo's happy chatter floating up from the stream bank. Two blue silk scarves were brought forward, the same kind we had seen hanging from the larch trees at the shamans' site outside Ulaanbaatar and had subsequently seen at various *ovoos* along the road. Each scarf represented a horse, for they were giving Rowan not just Blackie but also a younger, sorrel horse that was, they said, a racehorse that had already won many of the medals I'd seen hanging in the grandfather's *ger* on the morning we'd set off.

"They say," Tulga translated, "that they are sure that Rowan will be healed. And that the next time he comes to Mongolia he will be riding by himself, and riding well enough to ride in races like the Mongolian boys do. So they are saying that Blackie and the racehorse there will be kept for him, as his horses, for his return. They say not to worry, that everything will be okay with Rowan. They have been watching him, and they see how he is with the animals, with the nature, and that you and Kristin have done the right thing to bring him here. He will be healed, and he will come back to Mongolia. And when he does, he will ride by himself, like a child of the steppe."

I felt tears starting. I should say something. I began to stumble clumsily through my thanks, to say how honored I felt, wondering what thing of consequence I could possibly give in return. I thought of Betsy, waiting for Rowan back in Texas, the horse that had carried us here, to this point, both physically, to a large extent, and morally. Then an idea occurred to me. "Please tell them that I would like to give a horse too. When I go back to America, would they like it if I was to find a good stallion there, the same breed that Rowan's horse is back home, and send them some semen from him for one of their best mares? Would that be a good thing?"

Tulga translated. There was a roar of assent. The vodka came round again. Kristin hissed: "You sure you can do that, Ru?"

"Yes, I think so. My granddad in Zimbabwe used to import bull semen from Texas for his Brangus ranch. They travel it in frozen nitrogen. Tulga, do people ever do this here?"

"Yes, I think so. I've heard about the veterinary department at the university in Ulaanbaatar doing things like this. I think it can be arranged."

So we drank to it, brought Rowan over for some reluctant Polaroids (fortunately, the guides didn't seem to mind his lack of social graces), then had more vodka and hugs all round. God, but they were strong — solid muscle, all of them. No wonder they'd conquered the world on their tough little horses. And then given up the warrior path for Buddhism. You had to admire these people — how many nations have gone from death-dealing to enlightenment like that?

Then the oldest of the locals who'd shown up to help see us off said something to Tulga, something that made Tulga's eyebrows fly up in genuine surprise. There was a spring, he said — a healing spring, close to Lake Sharga — that was known to be good for the brain. More than that, on the way to the lake there lived a man, a traditional healer, who specialized in healing through channeling *qi,* or *chi,* the Eastern term for energy. Did we want to see him? asked Tulga. I looked at Kristin. It involved merely the laying on of hands, Tulga went on, and the man's house was along our route. I nodded. It couldn't hurt, I reasoned. And the spring, I asked, as we bumped along the rough, rough road — would that be easy to find?

"The old guy said we'll find it no problem." Tulga turned around in the front seat, Tomoo sitting relaxed and easy on his lap. "It's maybe twelve miles from the lake, but easy to find. Maybe less, even. Just ask anyone around there, he says. It's famous."

"So famous you've never heard of it?"

Tulga grinned. "Well, I am a city boy."

The healer lived in a small town of log cabins huddled incongruously on the steppe like the afterthought of civilization that it was. "The Soviets built these towns to try to make us easier to control," said Tulga as we bump-bumped a couple of hours down the appallingly potholed dirt road toward the place. And indeed we'd passed areas of steppe where Tulga had pointed out that the grass grew in straight lines with little dips separating them. "That's where they tried to plow. One tractor per community. It didn't work — the grass has grown over it now, but they wanted the steppe to be one big wheat field. This town even has a railway. *Had* a railway. To take the grain away."

It did — an old grain depot falling to pieces by a short remaining piece of track that went from nowhere to nowhere: a monument to the failure of the Soviet dream and the triumph of the free life of the steppe. Yet towns are strange things — build them and people will continue to live in them, no matter how dirty, rubbish-strewn, and decaying, even when there is virgin country just outside. So with this town, as we drove through it, dodging dogs, yaks, cows, sheep, goats, and straying horses. There was no shortage of people inhabiting the log cabins, faces peering from doors and windows. "What do they do for work here?" asked Jeremy. Tulga just shrugged.

We'd been prepping Rowan for the encounter with the healer, worried that he might be anxious after the high drama of the shaman ceremony back in UB. But no sooner had we stopped by the great green-painted wooden doors of the yard that Tulga and the driver thought was the right one than Rowan was out of the van, saying, "Let's go see the old man healer." And off he went down the concrete pathway over the yard, where a few sheep and goats grazed, and into the house, all by himself.

We followed, Tulga a little embarrassed, to find Rowan staring at the old man and his wife, who sat at a battered table under a big wall hanging depicting running horses, irrelevantly saying, "Elephants come from Africa and India," and giving them his broadest, most charming smile.

"Indeed they do," I said, grabbing him and plonking both of us down on the seventies-era sofa that the smiling couple — who seemed amused rather than irritated by Rowan — indicated for us to sit on, while Tulga explained our sudden arrival. The old man had a huge face, with massive cheekbones and the rest of it rough-hewn as if from a log in a forest somewhere, a face blunt-cut from wood, then animated by some forest sorcerer, two intelligent black eyes deep-set below the jutting brow.

If the man, who looked to be in his midsixties or so, was in any way disturbed by our appearing out of the blue like this, he hid it well, instead listening to Tulga's description of Rowan's condition and asking questions as if this were a consultation booked weeks in advance. To my alarm, his wife went off and then reappeared a few moments later with a dish piled high with dried sheep's-milk curd. I took one and tried to nibble at it convincingly, as did Kristin, who had just joined us. Fortunately the old man chose that very moment to ask me, through Tulga, about Rowan's history.

I explained as best I could, then, at the old man's request, gave some facts about Rowan's birth — that he had been breech, had come a month early, had had to be delivered by C-section. The healer nodded, taking in the information. Then he explained, again through Tulga, what he intended to do.

"He says he needs to feel Rowan's skull, see if there is any blocked energy there. Do you think Rowan will let him?"

I fully expected Rowan to scream, resist, when the old man put his hands on his head, and partly to reassure my son, partly to check that it indeed was not going to be painful, I asked if the healer could put his fingers on my cranium first.

Rowan looked on curiously as I sat on the floor before the healer and let his strong, experienced fingers quest their way over my head. Not only was it not at all painful, it was downright pleasurable, something between a head massage and . . . well, healing, I suppose. The feeling of well-being that started to suffuse me from the head down was undeniable. I closed my eyes, trying to pay attention and not just let myself be taken by the good feeling while the old man talked and Tulga translated.

"He says you have blocked energy there at the bottom right corner of your skull. He wants to know if you ever get headaches there."

I did. The old man's fingers traveled up the right side of my skull, spreading little smiles over my head as he did so. I didn't want it to stop.

"He says these things run in families. Rowan may have the same problem," translated Tulga as the hands stopped. I sighed, then leaned forward to scoop up Rowan, who had watched the whole process with some interest.

He did not scream. To my amazement, Rowan sat quietly, contented, and let the old man's fingers travel over his scalp. The healer confirmed, through Tulga, that Rowan did indeed have the same energy blockage as I did.

"He says you need to massage him like

this, up along the vein that runs along the side of the skull here," said Tulga. I watched. "Head scrobble," said Rowan. He should have been twisting out of the man's grasp by now — he hated being messed with by anyone, especially a total stranger.

He *did* yell when the old man's fingers began to touch more strongly, as he tried, he said, to unblock the energy. But only for a moment, for the old man let Rowan go at the point of crisis and told us that if we noticed a difference — less tantrumming, more even-temperedness — over the next day or so, then we might think about trying something like this back home. If not . . . He shrugged modestly — he couldn't always heal everyone. But he felt that the energy was flowing better now. When we asked, gathering up our things, whether he recommended we visit the spring we'd just heard about, and the sacred lake, he merely shrugged. "That is outside my ability to know," he said honestly. "But it certainly can't harm him."

With that, a young couple holding a baby with a strangely bulbous head came shyly into the room. It was time for him to see this patient, said the old man apologetically, gesturing that we should go. He bowed, as we conveyed our thanks through Tulga.

Behind him, on the wall, I noticed a picture of him, years younger, wearing a Communist-looking uniform hung with medals. Was he older than he looked? A veteran, perhaps, of World War II's Mongolian front, when the Russians had fought the Chinese, using these soldiers of the steppe as cannon fodder? Or had he been drafted into some later war? The gentleness in his eyes belied any past ferocity. But the picture was a reminder of the Soviet tyranny that had once held sway over these lands, these people.

As we drove out of the town, along the terrible road, all sudden, spine-juddering brakes and swerves, I asked Tulga, "Was he in the Soviet army, do you think?"

"Oh, yes." Tulga smiled. "Everyone was. Had to be, for a while anyway. Whether they liked it or not. It was communism."

"And what about shamanism? Was that allowed under communism?"

"Absolutely not! If they found a shaman's drum or robes in someone's *ger* or house, that person went to jail. Same with his kind of healing. If someone said to the authorities, 'That one, he's a healer or a shaman,' they'd arrest him. Even you guys — ten years ago we'd have had the KGB trailing us, interrogating me afterward. We probably would not have been able to do this. Certainly not go to see shamans."

"So how did the tradition survive?"

"Father to child. And in the remote places, like Siberia, where we're going, there wasn't so much control. It's coming back now."

We passed two standing stones carved with representations of great, swirling-horned reindeer, a testament to the colder climates of thousands of years ago. Back then, closer to the last ice age, there had been reindeer herders in Spain even. People had tamed the reindeer before they'd tamed the cow, the horse, the ass. And as the ice sheets had retreated north, the herdsmen had gone with them. Now Mongolia was the farthest south you found reindeer cultures.

The land hereabouts was dry, more arid than the green highlands we'd camped in the night before. We must have dropped to a much lower elevation. The day grew hot — uncomfortably hot. An hour or so beyond the little town, Tulga called a halt for lunch in a grove of elms by a broad river, the Orkhon, shallow and fast-flowing, perhaps fifty yards across. A few hours on from here, he said as the pimpmobile shuddered to a merciful halt and we piled out, stretching and groaning, there was another, larger town, called Bulgan. There we could decide once and for all whether to go on to Lake Sharga as planned or just start heading north to the reindeer people. Kristin still wasn't convinced we should go to the lake at all, knowing it meant something of a hell-ish drive for probably no tangible result.

It was a beautiful spot on this elm-grown riverbank. Or at least it would have been had the place not been strewn with broken vodka and beer bottles, plastic bags, candy wrappers, diapers, tampons, and condoms. We'd noticed as we'd neared the town and the road had widened that the amount of litter had gone from nothing, to a lot, to piles of the stuff, here in what should have been a local beauty spot.

"Be careful of Rowan if he wants to go in the water," warned Tulga. Rowan, along with Tomoo, was already stripping off in the heavy heat and heading for the sparkling shallows. "People throw vodka bottles in there when they get drunk. Best if he keeps his shoes on." He shouted something to the same effect in Mongolian to Tomoo, who nodded and promptly stopped Rowan from kicking off his Crocs. To my amazement, Rowan, instead of yelling, as he would have done if Kristin or I had stopped him, complied without a murmur.

"Jeremy, can you keep an eye on his toys?" I asked. "He's bound to want to play with them in the water." Sure enough, Rowan was already heading back to the van, saying, "Where's Simba?"

I decided to go for a short walk along the riverbank, to try to check in with my gut. Should we sign up for a drive from hell toward a lake that even the local healer had seemed pretty equivocal about? Or should we save ourselves time and effort and just head straight north, which would give us more time to find the reindeer people, more time to spend with them if we did manage to locate their camps, and more time to look for a shaman if we needed to? It seemed a pretty obvious choice. Why, then, this compulsion to go on a wild goose chase to a place that I had found just once on the Internet three years ago? There was no rational reason for going at all. Just this odd instinctive feeling, along with the thought that I'd always wonder . . .

A big gray heron flapped up from the reeds. A few yards farther on I stepped delicately around a neat pile of dried human turds, the toilet paper stiff in the semi-desert air. A flock of wild ducks — some kind of teal, judging by the blue-green stripes on their wings — chattered and swam on the water. A tern, thousands of miles from the sea, winged overhead, keening like a gull. Was it nesting here or just passing through en route to the far-off Arctic Ocean, where — incredible though it seemed — this river must eventually drain? I walked back to the vans, where a table had been set up under the elms' shade. Tulga was unfolding the map.

"It *is* really far," I could hear Kristin saying doubtfully.

"Yes," agreed Tulga quietly, looking at the map. "Yes, it is."

So we batted the pros and cons back and forth across the makeshift camp table once more. Good sense said skip the lake, head north. The irrational, or rather nonrational, voice said go, find out what was at the lake. In the middle of our deliberations, Rowan came up from the riverbank to fetch his bacon.

"Okay," I said on a sudden whim. "Why don't we let Rowan decide?"

There was a general murmur of assent. So I gave it a try. "Hey, Rowan! What d'you think? Shall we go to the lake first, then go to the reindeer people, or shall we —"

He had already trotted off, completely ignoring me. If I wanted an answer, I had to get down to his level. I got up, followed him, and bent over to where he had set up his animals in the sand.

"Dad! Dad!" he said, not to me, but speaking for the animals. He was enacting a scene from *The Lion King.* The most dramatic scene, in which the father lion is hanging on the cliff, and the lion cub, Simba, his son, is trying to reach him, to stop him from falling down among the hooves of the stampeding wildebeest in the gorge below. "Dad! Dad!" is what the cub screams when his father falls among the hooves to die.

"What have you done?" This was Scar, the evil uncle, talking — the lion who manipulates the young cub into thinking he has accidentally killed his father. I noticed that a toy tiger was standing in for the lion Rowan usually used for Scar. Funny — I hadn't heard him screaming about the loss of one of his toys. It was somewhere back in the stream under the starlit mountain, no doubt.

"Hey, Rowan, do you want to go see the reindeer people?"

"Yes I do."

"No, hold on. Do you want to go straight to the reindeer people? Or do you want to go to the lake first, then the reindeer people?"

"Go to the lake first, then the reindeer

people," he said, without looking up.

"All right, then, we will. Hey, everyone —
we have a decision. He says lake first, then
reindeer people."

13
REPAIRING
THE WIND HORSE

That evening we made camp in a high green meadow at the edge of the forest, looking out over a long, wide valley perhaps thirty miles or more in extent — a view of unbroken green rising to distant snowcaps that seemed almost impossibly beautiful. Like something not quite real, a painted backdrop for some Hollywood epic. We'd climbed slowly, over hours, back into the highlands, leaving the hot semiarid country behind us after the town of Bulgan — which, unlike the forgotten Soviet settlement that the healer lived in, was possessed of some charm. It had a main street with some old Russian-style public buildings with shuttered windows and green-painted roofs and porches, now dilapidated but still whimsical in their way. There was a sort of supermarket, sparsely stocked, but it had bacon, which, along with white bread and potato chips, seemed to be all Rowan would consent to eat now that he'd landed on Mongolian soil. It also had wet wipes and, to our collective gratification, four bottles of astonishingly fine Bordeaux red wine for sale, priced at next to nothing. We bought the lot, then took a leg-stretch up and down the dusty main street, dodging the usual interested livestock and returning the polite greetings of the townsfolk, who, with typical Mongolian tact, treated the arrival of our ragged band on their dusty main street as if it were nothing out of the ordinary. There was a light feeling to the place. The corrugated iron roofs of the ubiquitous log cabins were painted festive colors — reds, blues, greens, yellows, all reflecting the afternoon sun. People smiled, nodded as we passed. As we drove out, two young boys raced their horses alongside our van for a hundred paces or so, grinning from ear to ear.

Even the road improved, the litter dwindling and eventually disappearing as we climbed steadily up through higher steppe toward the forested slopes of low but jagged mountains, their clearings carpeted with vibrant purple willow herb. We stopped at two *ovoos,* stone cairns dedicated to the lords of the two low mountain passes we crested on our steadily rising drive, and walked once around each *ovoo* after Haada and Darga, the two drivers, to offer thanks for safe passage. We bought wild strawberries in glass jam jars from a group of women sitting by a bridge, where we stopped to let Rowan take a wade in the fast-flowing mountain water. When we finally stopped to camp in the high mountain pasture at the forest's edge, with the incredible view out over the green infinity of the surrounding highlands, it felt as though we had arrived somewhere close to heaven.

We gathered dead wood in the open, park-like glades of the forest margin. The pines were small, slender, perhaps fifteen or so feet high, feminine-looking, like dancing maidens with their rich greenswards strewn with flowers. Rowan began to gather one particular type that looked, as he put it, like a "red raspberry flower." When he began to stuff one in his mouth, I shouted to Tulga for advice.

"Don't worry," he replied, laughing. "We use that one for . . ." He fished in his vocabulary for a moment. "For our immune systems. We dry it and eat it in the winter, with honey. Rowan can eat it, no problem. Tomoo should too. Hey, Tomoo!" he called to his son, who was busily gathering kindling while the rest of us dragged the large fallen limbs and boles out toward the open hillside where we'd parked. Tulga's suggestion, given in Mongolian, resulted in only a grimace and the universal tongue-out *yuck* expression that kids everywhere know how to give. Rowan, however, usually so picky about food, picked handfuls of the flowers and wolfed them down as if they were candy.

These landscapes: all the world is beautiful, except where humankind has deliberately worked to destroy that beauty. To me, farming landscapes are as beautiful as wildernesses. But to see a landscape that has changed not one whit from the way it looked when it came out of God's hands, that is a rare thing. Stopping a moment to get a better grip on the log I was dragging, I happened to look up and see a spiderweb hanging from the lower needles of the tree that stood between me and the steppe. The evening sun had caught the silk, respun it in gold, gilding the spider too, so that it hung motionless, like a masterpiece from a master goldsmith's workshop — which in a way, I suppose it was, the trees, the web, and the golden spider within that web all marking the transitional point where forest ended and green, green steppe began. A window on eternity.

Rowan ran past me. The whiff from his

pants obliterated the moment's grace. Or perhaps that was eternity too. I certainly hoped not.

That evening, though, as the light faded and died and our fire caught and flickered into dancing, orange warmth, Rowan and Tomoo ran and ran — farther, in Rowan's case, than I had ever let him go before. He ran until he was no more than a distant speck down in a fold of the hill below. I stood to call his name, and as I did so, he stopped, turned, and went on with his game, acknowledging me, not ignoring. There had been a time when we'd despaired that he would ever know his own name, much less stop and look around when called.

Tulga was talking more about the shamans and how it had been under communism. "You know, I went to see a shaman myself, maybe three years ago. I was also whipped." He grinned. "But seriously, just a couple of years before that, anyone going to consult a shaman would be arrested. The shaman too. But after some years, the police, even the secret service, they became afraid to arrest shamans. There were stories about police-men dying or falling ill. Also about prison wardens going into the cells and finding that the shamans had disappeared. No one could explain. So after a while, toward the end of communism, it became a bit less harsh. People started returning to the traditions. As long as you didn't make a big noise about it."

"And the Buddhists?" Kristin wanted to know. "What about them?"

"The same. When the communists first came, they destroyed temples. Many temples. Monks were killed, libraries destroyed. At first it was just like in Tibet. But then not as bad. After a time, I think, the leaders didn't want to do it anymore. It was bad luck. So they tolerated the monks, as long as they stayed out of politics. In fact, some of the leaders used to go consult with the monks for readings for their luck, to get advice. In China too, I think. Officially it was frowned on, but by the end they were all doing it."

"What do you mean, 'readings for luck'?"

Tulga, dressed this evening in a traditional *deel* to keep out the rapidly rising cold, was looking more and more the traditional Mongolian nomad, less and less the semi-Westernized scion of the new Mongolian tourism boom. His beard was beginning to grow ("I grow it when Naara's not around to see," he'd confided earlier, grinning).

"You can ask the monks for a reading

from the . . ." Again he fished for the right word. "Scriptures. No . . ."

"Sutras?" offered Kristin.

"Yes, the sacred texts. You can ask for a reading to help you with your Wind Horse, your luck —"

"I thought the Wind Horse was the sha-man's drum," I interrupted, having read this somewhere. "Or at least the drumming the shaman does to go to the spirit world."

"That too. It's complicated."

"How *does* it work, exactly?" I pressed. "I mean, the Lord of the Mountain idea and all that — what is it? Are there other spirits? Ancestors?" I was thinking of the Bushmen and their idea that God lives in a village populated by the spirits of the ancestors, to which place a healer climbs while in his or her trance, to bargain directly with God for the soul of the sick person or the soul of the community. Used to such generalities — the Bushmen tend to keep things a little vague, a little malleable — I was surprised by the precision of Tulga's answer.

"Each shaman prays to the Lord of the Mountain or River where he comes from. We all do it too — when we go over a mountain pass or make a river crossing, we give thanks at an *ovoo*. You've seen them. But in addition," he said, "each shaman has other gods that he works with. There are ninety-nine of them — ninety-nine golden pillars that hold up heaven, each of which has its own god. I mean, there is one god, Tenger, but under him there are fifty-five white *tengers,* or gods, and forty-four black ones —"

"Subgods?" I interrupted.

Tulga thought a moment. "Maybe. Kind of. More like aspects of the same god. Or of humans. Of the different ways humans can be, good and bad, black and white."

"I see," I said, trying to bend my brain around it. Archetypes, I supposed. But so many.

"Each of these *tengers* governs a part of human life. Each shaman works with his own *tengers,* some black, some white, to try to help human beings. So they talk with them, as well as with the local gods or the gods of their own places, the Lords of the Mountains and Rivers, when they are doing the rituals."

"Are all the gods male, then?" asked Kristin.

"No. Many different. It's hard to explain . . ."

How did one explain God in any language? A memory flashed into my mind. I had asked Temple Grandin, the adult autist and professor of animal sciences who thought in pictures, what came into her mind when I said the word *God.* She'd replied that she saw an image of the universe — galaxy after galaxy, unending, infinite. Beyond understanding.

"Look." Rowan burst suddenly into the firelight, holding up a toy baby elephant and a toy baby rhino. "It's Lee Lee and Asha, from Whipsnade Wild Animal Park!"

Before coming out to Mongolia, while we'd been in England, we had taken Rowan to Whipsnade, Britain's largest zoo, and there he'd fallen in love with a baby Indian elephant called Lee Lee and a baby Indian rhino called Asha. "Lee Lee and Asha!" he repeated, with passion. "They're friends! Buster's going to give them some food!"

And he dashed back to his game in the half-dark, muttering to himself about Lee Lee and Asha and Buster. I noticed he was placing the animal figures at the wide entrance of a marmot hole. (Marmots are the large, ground-burrowing rodents whose flesh provides a ready source of extra sustenance for the nomads of the steppe and whose fleas, in certain very hot summers, occasionally produce bubonic plague; the storied Black Death of Europe's calamitous fourteenth century began out here on the

Mongolian steppe, an unseen kind of death-dealing horde different from the ones that usually exploded out of Mongolia and into the rest of medieval Eurasia.) I made a mental note to check the whole area for toys before we left next morning, to get the others to help quarter the ground. For where there was one marmot hole there was sure to be a dozen others, and if we started losing too many toys now, we'd have nothing to keep Rowan going. Not to mention the tantrums that would ensue when he wanted them again and found them lost. It never ceased to amaze me how the boy could have such a steel-trap memory in so many ways, yet so routinely — and with such disruptive results for us — mislay his much-beloved animal toys.

"Tomorrow, perhaps halfway to Sharga Lake, there is a Buddhist monastery," said Tulga. "Maybe we can stop there."

"I'd like that," said Kristin, the only practicing Buddhist among us. "I'd like that very much."

Next day, though we searched the campground and looked down all the marmot holes, both the baby elephant and the baby rhino were well and truly lost. Rowan uttered not a peep.

The long hours in the van slipped by,

eased by storytelling games. "What's your most embarrassing moment ever?" suggested Jeremy as a way to pass the time. Kristin won, having the boys in stitches with tales of her attempts as a young girl in California to be cool: "I wanted to be a death rocker. Big hair, white face makeup, and black clothes, in all that L.A. heat. But I never had much luck with the boys. The day I finally plucked up courage to talk to the boy all the girls had a crush on, this weird thing happened. As I was talking to him, and it was kind of going well, I . . ." Her face creased up at the memory, half cringing, half laughing. "I blew this huge snot bubble. Right there in front of the coolest boy in the school. *Nice snot bubble,* he said, then got up and walked away. I wanted to die. I didn't have Rowan's lack of ego, that's for sure."

The stories ended, and silence, except for the ever-present grind of the engine, took over once more. We drove through empty steppe. Green like Ireland — seas and oceans of grass; gentle hills covered in grass, mountains on each horizon. We glimpsed yellow marmots diving into their holes at the vans' approach. Miles and hours seemed to melt into nothingness. You could see how you could just get on your horse, as the medieval Mongols had, and think, "Why not just keep riding until the sea of grass runs out and conquer as we go?" A great bloody wheel, rolling and rolling down through the centuries, leaving a wake of carnage and suffering too enormous to contemplate.

And then, after hundreds of years of doing that once a generation, the Mongols had just given it all up, realized — somehow collectively — that no matter how far and fast you rode, you're still right where you are. A cliché, but true. So they had embraced Buddhism, which had been brought into Mongolia in the seventeenth century by an itinerant monk who had wandered a thousand miles or so from Tibet. And by so doing they kept their freedom, their manly sports of wrestling, horsemanship, and archery, gave freedom and autonomy to their women, and then learned to survive gracefully by playing off two power-mad supernations, Russia and China, over whom they had once held sway and who now wanted to hold sway over them. All this, even during the industrialization and Sovietization of the twentieth century, while somehow keeping both the steppe's ecosystem and their own culture more or less intact. No mean feat.

Perhaps it wasn't that simple. Before coming out here, I had run a quick search on mining concessions in Mongolia and downloaded a map of the country. It was pretty alarming: almost the whole country was colored in, denoting mining rights of foreign companies. Would this great emptiness, so full of life and the human freedom that went with it, still be here in a decade?

We passed a flock of gray-blue cranes, the only vertical things in this landscape of grass and sky. Sometime later we came upon a herd of camels, great shaggy two-humped beasts who looked as surprised as we were at the sudden meeting. "Look!" said Kristin. "A baby camel." But Rowan would not look. Nor would he get out of the van.

It was time for a leg-stretch, however, so everyone else climbed out to get a closer look. Jeremy, stripped to the waist in the rising heat, stalked up to the mother camel — perhaps less than wisely — and almost touched noses. Everyone was laughing, joking. Still Rowan refused to get out of the van. Refused even to look in the direction of the animals. I felt the growing sore on my lower lip with my tongue. It was starting to hurt more, gathering its strength. Being in the present moment was all very well, but what if Rowan wouldn't ride?

I was becoming like a broken record. No

good Buddhist, I. Perhaps it was a good thing we were going to pass a temple, if only as a reminder not to get too attached. As if such a thing were possible. We climbed back into the vans, the mounting heat beginning to pound the lightness out of the air, and began the long, long miles up and into the forest zone again, back down into the lower steppe once more, floating through a landscape that seemed to shimmer, as the temperature steadily rose, in some strange middle place between earth and sky.

The monastery was a simple affair — a rude wooden cabin surrounded by several other wooden cabins in the middle of another of the far-flung log-built towns huddled on the steppe. The temple itself, marked out from the dormitories and refectory buildings by its sculpted eaves and the large prayer drum sitting out front, sat next to a big, rundown concrete school. Nomad children now attend boarding school nine months out of the year, but the building was empty of students for the summer, the kids having gone back to their family *gers* to help with the herding, leaving the playground to be overrun by a troop of six pink piglets.

"Baby pigs!" Rowan was out of the van and over the fence as soon as we had parked. I

followed, climbing over the fence after him as the piglets ran squealing in several different directions, Rowan laughing with delight. Trying to shadow him, I blundered immediately into a stand of stinging nettles of a viciousness that, dressed inadequately as I was in shorts and sandals, had me hopping, wincing, and cursing as Rowan, in long trousers and Crocs, rushed blithely in pursuit of his little pink prey. "So *cute!*" he shouted, trotting in their squealing wake.

Rowan was no match for the piglets, but that did not prevent him from trying to catch them as they darted in and around the school building, ripe-smelling outhouses, more stands of nettles, and the usual detritus of broken glass, old planks with nails sticking out of them, and pieces of jagged metal that seemed to permeate every public space in Mongolia, especially playgrounds. It was all I could do to keep him safe — or go through the motions of it, for truth be told, both he and the pigs were moving too fast for me to be of any real use. My legs were smarting and streaked with red by the time I heard Jeremy call, "Hey, Ru, they've invited you and Rowan into the temple."

I'd assumed we wouldn't go in. Rowan in a hallowed place where silence and reverence were expected? Hardly. The stop had been more for Kristin than for him.

"I don't think he's going to want to stop chasing the pigs," I said, as Jeremy climbed over the fence into the overgrown schoolyard. But Rowan, to my surprise, left off his chase as soon as I asked — or rather shouted across the playground — if he wanted to go see the temple.

Once inside, though, he behaved predictably enough, entering at a smart gallop, with a joyful yell of "Hey, look, candles!"; barreling past the row of chanting, golden-robed monks, past Kristin where she knelt before them, hands held together in prayer, head reverently bowed, to the back wall of the temple, where rows of candles glowed and guttered in brass bowls set before icons of the twin Tibetan goddesses of compassion — White Tara, the lady of serenity and grace, Green Tara, the lady of virtuous activity; vigorously blowing the candles out, shouting, "Yay! Birthday cake! Good job, Rowan!"

I expected the row of seated monks, with their abbot on the dais, to leap up, gesticulate, throw us out. They didn't. Rowan's shenanigans, if anything, seemed to gently amuse them. I saw the abbot beckon for me to bring Rowan to sit next to Kristin on the richly patterned carpet in front of him and his monks, all reading from the sutras in their hypnotic bass monotone. Tulga emerged from the shadows and conducted me to the spot, pushing the now protesting Rowan in front of me *("Candles, candles!")* while Tulga whispered, "They asked why we're here and I told them, and they want to do a reading for Rowan, and for you guys, for the journey. You and Rowan have to sit here —"

"You did explain to them that Rowan can't sit still in one place and —"

But to my astonishment, he did sit there, while the monks switched imperceptibly from the sutra they had been chanting to one chosen specifically for Rowan. He sat unnaturally quiet in my lap, while Kristin, her head still bowed, her hands still pressed together, prayed next to us in the lotus position, which she had perfected over years of meditation retreats. I, trying hard to look reverent, kept a loose arm around Rowan, waiting for him to lunge forward and try to grab the little bell that the abbot picked up and rang after every couple of verses. But he didn't. He sat there like a normal, well-behaved little boy. And the monks did their part perfectly, timing the end of the reading to almost the exact moment when, after a few brief but unusual minutes, Rowan began to twitch.

"He can go now," whispered Tulga from where he had seated himself behind me. I bowed as best I could with Rowan in front of me — so did Kristin — and we got up, the monks smiling at us and nodding as they chanted on fluidly into the next passage of the sutras. As we walked toward the open door, a young woman, one of the devotees who had been seated along the back wall when we came in, headed us off, smiling, and indicated that Rowan should turn the wheel of a large cylindrical drumlike thing, a sort of prayer barrel with handles to crank it round.

"It brings good luck, turns the prayers inside the wheel, brings us closer to enlightenment," explained Tulga.

"As individuals or as a species?" I quipped. But Rowan, quicker on the uptake, had already grabbed one of the yellow-painted handles of the trundle-wheel and started to rotate the drum clockwise, to the evident delight of the young woman, who had clearly wanted him to do just that. I did the same, each of us giving the prayer wheel one full revolution, then Rowan going round and round with it — not in his usual hyperactive, semimaniacal way, but with a measured cadence that made the young woman beam from ear to ear. She bowed to him. He grinned and gave her a spontaneous hug. From her pocket she drew a small packet of little wafers with a picture of a Bambi-like deer on them, and two hard candies.

"Little deer cookies," said Rowan, happy with the gift.

"Say thank you," I said, ever anxious to teach him the social scripts.

"Say thank you!" he chirruped, already out the door, heading for the pigs.

We never had time to find out exactly what sutra had been read for him. But Rowan's mood, as we floated across, bumped across, seemed sometimes almost to dream across the hours and hours of hill, steppe, valley, hill, steppe, valley, all covered in green, green grass, remained unnaturally calm. The day, as always, grew almost stiflingly hot. Michel and Jeremy, both proud of their lean bodies, stripped down to their shorts, Jeremy adding a touch of high comedy by donning an orthopedic neck brace, which, with its off-white color and a big old brown stain from coffee, food, or drool on its front, detracted somewhat from the male-model effect.

"I find it really useful!" he said defensively, against the hoots of laughter that followed his putting it on. "I use it on long flights and stuff."

"So, er, do you get to talk to many women when you wear that thing?" said Michel.

"Or is it a way to keep them off?" quipped Justin from the very back seat, where he sat crammed against his equipment, the dust from the road flying into his face through the narrow open window.

"Kind of like gaydar, to help them know where they stand."

"More like geekdar."

"Mock if you will." Jeremy closed his eyes and smiled. "But I'm going to ride in comfort."

So of course we all had to try it on, each of us looking ridiculous in a different way. "It's not comfortable at all!" I said when it was my turn.

"Well, if you don't like it, you can give it back."

"Gladly."

We drove on, literally over hill and dale, the pimpmobile baking in the heat. Rowan looked out the window, through the pink curtains that fluttered in the wind created by our movement, taking in the green emptiness, the herds of livestock, the occasional *gers* or lone horsemen. Then it dawned on me, what the old man, the healer, had said the previous day: "Watch him for the next twenty-four hours. If he's noticeably quieter . . ."

He had been. The lost animals at the marmot holes. His willingness to leave the piglets, to sit in front of the monks like that. And now, quietly taking in the landscape, his green-blue eyes marking the passage of the great grasslands.

We'd stopped, before leaving the little wooden town where the monastery was, to buy some more water and other supplies at a rundown store that also stocked a few cheap plastic toys from China. Rowan had pointed to a small orange duck on a bicycle, whose legs went round on the pedals. He stopped looking at the landscape and reached for the new toy.

"What's the duck's name?" asked Kristin, eager, as we always were, to engage him in speech about his toys, project his imagination, for just a year before we'd wondered if he'd ever do imaginative play at all. "Is it Daniel Duck? Or Davy Duck?"

"Or Doodle Bug Duck?" I offered flippantly.

"Doodle Bug Duck!" confirmed Rowan with intense satisfaction, and went back to looking out the window.

We had been on the road almost ten hours by the time we went over a rise and saw, breaking the green monotony of the grasslands, a wide, rapid river set in a shallow gorge. "Ah, good," said Tulga. "I heard that there would be this river. Sharga Lake can't be far away."

We ground down the side of the gorge in low gear, splashed through the ford, and went up the other side on a road now composed of hard black volcanic rock that jolted the van terribly, throwing us around and into each other. Rowan and Tomoo were delighted, the rest of us resigned. At ten and a half hours of road time we breasted another rise and there, to our front, shining in the sunlight, lay a vast body of silver water, flanked on three sides by steep, flat-topped mountains.

14
THE HEAVEN
HORSE LAKE

I'd half expected Lake Sharga to be a total
disappointment, perhaps no more than a
large, muddy puddle set into the fold of
some low hill, its banks churned to a stink-
ing welter of black mud and dung by wal-
lowing livestock. We'd passed a few such
places en route, joking each time that this
must be it. But Sharga Lake, as Tulga called
it, was eerily beautiful, a volcanic leftover
from an earlier geological age, so ancient
that the surrounding walls of the crater had
disintegrated, leaving three lone basalt
mountains, now grass-covered, with a small
fringe of forest at their tops, black rock jutting out from their time-eroded shoulders,
to stand like sentinels above the flat, shining
waters. Grass grew down to the water's
edge. It was a lake of horses — hundreds of
them, divided into their various herds, each
with its own thick-necked stallion nosing
about the fringes of his harem. Some of the

herds — small, wiry horses of every color imaginable, brown-and-white, black-and-white, sorrel, dark bay, bright bay, buckskin, every possible shade of gray, white, black, palomino — grazed the banks, tails swishing against the flies and mosquitoes. Some stood out in the shallows, dark from basalt silt, knee deep, keeping cool. Out in midwater, wild swans sailed like sedate white schooners. The air was thick with insects, a quaking haze of them.

One of the benefits of living in central Texas, where the heat and humidity of summer produce a breeding paradise for biting and stinging creepy-crawlies of every possible variety (and a few impossible ones), is that you are never without repellent and anti-itch cream. Everyone had come armed. Yet no sooner had we stepped out into the mosquito hell, our cans of repellent at the ready, than we realized that an essential element of these insects was missing.

The mosquitoes of Lake Sharga didn't bite. Nor did the flies.

Unheard of. Mosquitoes that don't bite? "Catch one," suggested Michel as one landed on his bare forearm (he and Jeremy had both wisely donned shirts again as we'd arrived, and Jeremy had ditched the brown-stained neck brace), but it evaded his attempt to catch it. Rowan was already happily setting up his animals on the green, Tomoo helping the drivers, Tulga's nephew Bodo, and the cook pitch the tents. I let one of the insects land on my wrist and looked at it. Yep, a mosquito in every detail but one.

"What can they live on?" I asked Kristin as the benign creature flew off, leaving my arm unscathed. "Let one land on you and see if it doesn't bite as well."

"I don't know." Kristin let one land. "No, nothing," she said as it flew away again. "Weird."

The lakeshore had a narrow beach of black stone and sand, much churned by horses' hooves but smooth in stretches. The water, warm from the summer sun, lapped cool and dark at our ankles. Should we wash Rowan in this apparently sacred water? Should we try to make some kind of ceremony, even though we had no idea what the lake was sacred for?

There was a silence here, broken only by the soft snorts of the wading horses, the occasional slap of a large fish jumping for flies out on the otherwise smooth surface of the lake. The insect drone of the shore died as soon as we were standing in the shallows, which seemed to go some way out, for after fifty wading steps the water still came up no further than our knees. Out farther the white swans drifted, distant and elusive as clouds.

"Rowan may not want to come into the water," Kristin pointed out. True enough — he went up and down with his relationship to water. As a very small toddler he'd been afraid to splash and wade. Then he'd really gotten into it, almost dangerously so, having to be watched around friends' swimming pools. The previous summer we'd started teaching him to swim in the above-ground pool at Greenbriar — an excellent thing to do in the hot Texas summer. Yet halfway through that summer, for no apparent reason — certainly there had been no trauma or incident — his fear had suddenly come back and he'd violently rejected any further attempts to make him amphibious. He enjoyed splashing in the shallows of a stream, but larger bodies of water were out. Would he consent to our washing him down in these strange, calm black waters?

We turned, hearing the sound of splashing, to find that Rowan had answered the question for us. He'd brought a toy hippo down to the water, entered of his own accord, already stripped himself naked, and was not just wading but lying down in the basalt-colored water, squinting at the hippo as he made it dip and dive under the rippling surface. "Just like a lake in Africa," he said, looking up as Kristin and I splashed over to him.

"Yes, that's right. Just like a lake in Africa." The water lapped over his lean, prone body, washing him more effectively than I could ever have done, as he splashed and played in the sunlight, the horse herds standing out in the water like twin headlands jutting out from the shore two hundred yards on either side of him. "Just like in Africa," he repeated, his imagination working away, stimulated by the warm water. Overhead, a flight of cranes flew, croaking their harsh cry, toward the far-off northern mountains.

At last, with dusk approaching, we trekked back along the road a ways to find the healing spring. It hadn't been hard to locate. While crossing the river on the way to the lake, Tulga had noted a road that forked off to the left and guessed that it must lead to the spring, a suspicion confirmed when we stopped, on the way back there that afternoon, to ask an old man sitting in front of a *ger* pitched by the side of the road (if you could call this scar left by truck wheels and yak carts a road).

"*Ger! Ger!*" Rowan shouted, but time being short, we drove on, especially as the old man had said that after we followed the fork in the road till it dead-ended at the cliffs over the river, it was a fair hike to the spring. "Actually, he says it's many springs," reported Tulga as Haada cranked the pimpmobile back into gear. "Maybe twenty of them, all coming out of the rock. Each one good for a different part of the body. He says people have been coming here from all over Mongolia since before the time of Genghis Khan."

"Yet no one had heard of it in UB?" I asked.

Tulga shrugged. "Big country, not so many people."

In fact, it was a resort. Or had been once. The track did indeed dead-end at the cliffs, but on the cliffs was a small complex of wooden chalets, left over from the Soviet era again, Tulga told us. The Soviets had apparently tried to develop this impossibly remote place, fully two days' drive on the roughest of rough roads from anywhere, four days' travel on horseback from anywhere, into a Soviet-style health spa. The chalets, now derelict and dilapidated, were as far as the building work had gotten, but scores of people were camped out around them, some in tents next to battered old vehicles of various kinds, some with horses. The ground was strewn with sharp rocks and rubbish. People looked up at us, families sitting around fires, young men drinking beer, kids running about, young women walking together hand in hand, here and there people riding. Yet most were on foot, heading down to or up from the cliffside trail to the river and the springs in a constantly moving two-way stream. It was bizarre, as so many things were here in this most extraordinary of countries — fifty yards back down the track, you'd never have known this was here.

"Where have they all come from?" asked Justin, getting his equipment together, voicing what we all wondered.

"Oh, Moron, Bulgan, other places . . ." Tulga answered, helping Michel shoulder the camera bag. "They must be very powerful springs, I think."

"House!" shouted Rowan, sighting one of the derelict chalets, surrounded by startled campers who looked up at his sudden outburst. "Wanna go in the house? *House!"*

"We can't go in the house, Rowan. Let's go down to the river instead. Come on —"

"House! *House! HOUSE!"* Rowan arched his back. "Gi-*RAFFFFFE!"* The shriek was loud enough, high enough, to shave the scalp right off your head. Everyone within fifty feet of the epicenter stopped dead, transfixed by the small Western child screaming his lungs out in his father's arms. So much for the healer's cure. Earlier in the day I'd remembered the healer saying, "Watch him to see if he's quieter, calmer — then you'll know it's working." Well, that was out the window now. I swung Rowan up onto my shoulders, since the ground was too hazardous for him in his tantrumming state. He squirmed onto my right shoulder, dug his chin hard into the top of my skull, grabbed hair, pulled out an agonizing chunk, and moved his fingers down to gouge at my eyes. I steadied him, trying to twist my face away from his angry fingers, ignoring his kicking legs, his screams.

Down the steep track we went, weaving in and out of the bemused campers, me trying to keep my balance, Rowan thrashing about on my head like a toddler, an autistic toddler.

"Rowan, don't hit yourself!" I heard Kristin say from behind me. I felt the telltale jerking of his body and pulled him down so I could carry him like an infant. "Put your arms round my neck," I said, trying to keep my cool as he shrieked and struggled. He'd gone to another place completely. I held him to me as I was used to, clasping his wrists together and pressing him to my chest to stop him from doing himself harm. He head-butted me hard between the eyes. I reeled. Someone — Jeremy, perhaps — steadied me from behind. Rowan went rigid in my arms, horizontal, legs straight out, as if he were made of hard wood. By the time we had reached the bottom of the hill, where a grove of elms led to the lush riverbank, I was punch-drunk, confused, thrown back to a place I'd thought, hoped, prayed, was long behind us.

The screaming, thrashing, and attempts to hit me and himself ceased when we got to the river. I put Rowan down on the ground as we began to walk along the well-worn trail on the bank. The sun was so low now that our side was deep in shade, but the rocks and small cliff of the opposite bank were lit up in late-afternoon golden-hour light. A man on horseback was driving cows along that sunlit bank. Our side, wider, made a kind of meadow, full of wildflowers. A family was coming toward us, a little girl of perhaps three or four trotting gaily along out front. Rowan saw her, sprinted forward, grabbed her around the waist, and threw her to the ground. We were on him in an instant, the distressed, outraged family grabbing their precious girl back, Tulga apologizing as we dragged our raging son away.

"GIRL! GIRL! FRAY-ENCH-FRY-YI-YI-YI-YIES!"

His back arched again as Rowan hit his head once, twice, hard on the ground. What was going on? I picked him up again, let him pull my hair, gouge my eyes, drum the point of his chin into my cranium, anything to keep him moving. We passed several springs, Tulga reading the Cyrillic script scrawled on the boulders: "This one is for the eyes," then, a hundred yards farther on, "This one for the stomach." And then farther, "This one for the nervous system." At each spring a family would be pouring water over their heads or drinking from little plastic cups that they carried. You could see how a family might come here by truck or horse or cart and camp out for a week, giving themselves treatments every day, drinking and dancing at night with their fellow campers in a kind of unofficial summer festival. Ordinary families, that is. Not freak families like us.

Rowan calmed down for a quarter mile or so, then lost it again, inexplicably, at the sight of a calf that came meandering down the trail on its own, lowing for its mother.

Raging, screaming, thrashing, completely out of control. So what had gone wrong now? What neurological switch had been thrown? Was this the kind of regression we'd been warned about by other autism parents? For they *had* warned us — never to get too attached to any kind of progress, because one day we might see that progress slip away like a sandcastle before the waves. I let Kristin walk on ahead. Neither of us could speak. It was like being kicked in the heart.

We'd covered something over a mile by the time we reached the brain-healing spring, the last in the series of natural springs spread out along this lengthy stretch of river. The spring flowed out of the ground a short distance from an exposed boulder with a kind of natural drain-hole on its riverward side. Two middle-aged couples, the paunchy but muscled men shirtless, their wives overflowing out of swimsuits with towels wrapped around their waists, had got there before us and were taking turns lying on their stomachs across the boulder, their heads hanging down over the drain-hole, while their spouses poured the healing spring water over their heads.

Yelling *"Water! Water!"* Rowan clambered down my body like a monkey, rushed to the couple washing at the boulder, grabbed their plastic cup, and poured the water out on the ground. I retrieved him instantly and gave the cup back to the ambushed people, Tulga explaining, apologizing in Mongolian, and getting a justifiably huffy response as Rowan promptly, publicly, and perniciously shat himself, emitting a stench that had Tomoo holding his nose and falling on the ground with laughter.

"Well," said Kristin, "at least that got us the spring to ourselves." She turned to me, where I was struggling to change the horrid mess, Rowan screaming and thrashing so that I got it all over me. "Think he'll consent to being washed?"

I let Rowan go naked and held out my own hands to be washed. It took a bottle and a half to get clean. Meanwhile there was more shouting. Rowan was at the drainhole in front of the boulder, bending his head to drink. The shouts were from the two couples we had so rudely displaced, who had turned back to see him doing this. "They say he mustn't drink that!" said Tulga worriedly. "That's the bad water that takes the brain problems away. He mustn't drink it."

So once more I had to scoop him up, contain him while he fought, tried to hit himself, shrieked so loudly his voice rebounded off the walls of the riverside cliffs. It was as if all the fast-forward gains of the past few months, and the faster development since we'd come to Mongolia, had suddenly crumbled away. I remembered how Rowan had been at the gathering of shamans in California three years before, right after his diagnosis. How he'd shot forward, begun to lose his autism symptoms, started to speak, point, and communicate with people, only to regress again a few days after coming home. It was what I had feared.

"Oh, well," I said, trying to keep my voice level as I held him. "He's at the rock now. We might as well do it."

So Kristin took a plastic cup from one of the thermoses that Tulga had thought to bring along from camp, filled it with ice-cold water from the stream, and, as I half pushed, half fought Rowan onto the boulder, poured it over his head. With predictable results. I looked up from where I stood, trying to hold my son's thrashing arms, preventing him from hurting me, from hurting himself. He grabbed another hank of my hair in his fist and pulled. Out of the corner of my eye I caught a glimpse of Michel's camera pointed at me and snarled my irritation at him to take it off us. Just then the camera battery died.

"Blast," said Michel, lowering it.

That same moment Rowan suddenly relaxed in my arms and looked up at me, smiling. He was back.

Not one minute later he and Tomoo had joined forces to fill the cups of both thermoses from the spring and throw the water all over everyone, soaking us all, roaring with laughter, chasing Jeremy around and making him perform a silly dance in his efforts to escape their cold water time and again. We all took turns having the water, which was so cold that for a few seconds it erased thought, poured over us, then filled cups to drink it straight from the spring.

Rowan allowed cup after cup to be poured over him, as if there had never been any problem at all. We filled the thermoses up to take back to camp. When another family showed up to take their turn at the spring, Rowan and Tomoo abandoned their game without protest. Rowan walked back along the half mile or more of riverbank, holding my hand, sometimes running on, sometimes stopping to eat the red wildflowers he liked or to check out a butterfly dancing in the last of the dying light. Like any normal child. When we reached the van once more, he ignored the dilapidated chalets that had set him off on his weird regression, turned to me, and said, "That was fun. The spring was fun. I like the water."

It was long after dark by the time we reached the camp on the shores of Lake Sharga. Food, long gone cold, was waiting for us, but Kristin and Rowan were too tired to eat and retired to the tent to snuggle together. Tomoo went to the tent he shared with his dad to burrow deep into his own sleeping bag, against the rapidly falling temperature of the Mongolian summer night. Stars blazed overhead. The moon, half full now, shone on the water. Horses snorted and whinnied out in the darkness. I sat up, exhausted by the ups and downs of the day, listening to the guides talk. We heard hoofbeats. A horseman rode up out of the dark. Tulga greeted him and called to the cook, who was still up, to bring a thermos of hot tea and give the man a cup.

"Can you ask him if this lake really does have any healing power, any story?" I asked as Tulga handed the man the cup brimming with warm milky, salty tea.

Tulga waited until the man had drained the cup, then asked the question. No response. He asked again. No response. Tulga looked at us uncertainly in the moonlight, laughed nervously, then repeated the question a third time. Still no response.

"Think he might be deaf?" suggested Jeremy.

"Maybe," said Tulga, and, cupping his hand around his mouth, he yelled directly, comically, into the man's ear. This produced a grunt, and the man pointed somewhere out over the lake. Then he got up, mounted his horse, and rode away into the dark.

"What did he say?" we all wanted to know.

Tulga was shaking his head. "He just said, 'Yes. Over there.' That's all. I think maybe he is simple or something."

"Not too simple to ride a horse in the dark," pointed out Justin. "That takes skill."

"Autistic, maybe?" I thought as I bid the crew good night and headed for my tent. Would that be Rowan if he grew up here, in this far place?

I crawled into my sleeping bag and was asleep in seconds. I dreamed of a young bull calf walking through wildflowers, and of swans gliding way, way out on black water, of Rowan looking at me with water for eyes — dark spring water in which danced the bright reflection of stars.

Next day we washed once more in the basalt-stained waters, watching as the rival horse herds came drifting down from the higher ground, the foals and young stock skipping and bucking around the plodding broodmares, to wade in hock-deep and drink. Every now and then there would be a scream and a snort as the stallions challenged each other. As they grew louder, Rowan looked up from his splashing game with Tomoo, alarm in his eyes.

"It's just horses saying hello," said Kristin in a bright, deliberately cheery tone.

"Hello! Hello!" I played the part of the horse. Rowan, reassured, went back to his game.

This had been the first morning he'd woken up and not said, "Let's go home." Instead he'd woken up and said, "Let's go see the reindeer people. First the water, then we'll go see the reindeer people."

What did he picture in his mind's eye when he said *the reindeer people?* People with horns and hooves, walking on two legs — some kind of Mongolian race of fauns and satyrs?

Something in his body language, his demeanor, was softer. As if, on some fundamental level, he had ceased to resist the journey. Or was I just projecting, once again, into the great mystery that was my son?

Kristin and I felt we should make some

kind of ritual. So while Rowan splashed and the horses snorted and drank, we stood hand in hand in the water and prayed. Prayed for our son. Prayed for ourselves. Prayed to be allowed to complete this journey. Prayed that it would help him.

We still wanted, before we left this strange, slightly eerie place, with its lonely beauty, to know if the lake really was sacred, if any story of significance to Rowan, or to ourselves, was attached to it. Perhaps I simply wanted vindication. It wasn't enough just to *be* here, somehow. So when we came upon a group of four *gers* a little farther on around the lakeshore, I asked Tulga to stop so we could ask the people there more about the lake.

A young man in his twenties, busy working on the engine of a tough-looking Russian motorcycle while his naked kids tumbled around him, directed us to the middle *ger.* The old man there was the person we needed to speak to, he said, a cigarette hanging from his mouth. On the felt roof of his *ger,* trays of curd were drying in the sun. Goats and sheep nosed around the edges of the camp, where horses, saddled for whatever they might be required for, stood tethered to poles. Two teenage girls held the usual growling guard dogs at bay, hands clasped tight over their muzzles.

The old man that the youth had referred us to welcomed us into the shade of his *ger.* He smiled as Rowan ran in ahead of us, giggling deliciously, and dived, clothes and all, straight under the covers of the nearest of the brightly painted truckle beds set along the sides of the *ger* — much to the delight of the family's children, and those of the other *gers,* all of whom crowded inside to check out the strange visitors.

Seen from closer to, our host wasn't really an old man at all, simply middle-aged, graying, lean and tough, as most nomads were, with a handsome, weatherbeaten face whose lines bespoke years working outside on the steppe, summer and winter. In fact, he said, once the introductions had been made and the reasons for our being here had been given, he spent more of the year riding from place to place than others in the region did, as in addition to working his own herds, he worked for the government as an environmental supervisor, making sure the number of livestock in the district did not exceed what the land could hold.

Airag was brought — this time a clear liquid, fermented to almost pure alcohol, a kind of mare's-milk vodka, the inevitable essence-of-throw-up aftertaste almost, but not quite, masked by the liquor's warming bite.

"There is a story about the lake, yes," confirmed the man once we had drained the first cup. Rowan got up from the bed and went dashing outside, pursued by Kristin. "Both a mythological story and a real one. The waters are known for curing thyroid problems. People usually come up here once they've spent time at the springs, or if they have . . ." Tulga, translating, fished for the right word, made a gesture at the spot where his neck and jaw met. "Goiter?" I offered. "Maybe," said Tulga. "I think so. Anyway, he's saying that the lake is known for this, has been known for this for hundreds, maybe thousands of years."

"Baby goat! Look at the baby goat!" Rowan came running back inside, a wooly-coated, big-eyed, tan-colored kid in his arms, followed by the same laughing children and an embarrassed-looking, shrugging Kristin. Holding the goat in his arms, Rowan managed to climb back onto the bed.

"Time for a cuddle-cuddle! Cuddle-cuddle with the baby goat. Look, he's so cute!"

The man laughed. "Let him do it," he said, Tulga translating. "Baby goats are good for children." I thought about Rowan's goats back home. The man was right: kids were good for kids.

"But there is an older story too," the man went on, as Rowan lay, absolutely in love with the little goat, between my back and the wall of the *ger,* cooing softly: "Look, he's got little eyes, and little ears, and a little nose, and a little butt butt . . ."

"An old story, or legend really. It concerns horses. This area, all around Sharga Lake, is famous for breeding good horses. Many of the horses that win at the big Naadam races in UB are bred around here. Something in the soil makes the bones strong, the horses faster. Even in the days of Genghis Khan, they used to get the fastest horses from around Sharga Lake. You know what *sharga* means? It means shining, when a horse's coat is really shining."

I looked at Tulga as he translated this, surprised that he hadn't known the word. Picking up on my expression, he shrugged slightly, as if to say, *City boy, sorry,* and continued. "There is a legend to explain why the good horses come from here. They say that in that mountain, over there on the other side, the south side, of the lake — where that simple man you met last night pointed to — the first two horses came

343

down from heaven and entered a little lake that's up there on the mountaintop and that drains, underground, down into the main lake here. These two first horses, made by the gods, went down into this underground river and emerged in Lake Sharga. Then they came out of the lake and bred together and created the first horse herd, here. And it was from here that horses went out into the rest of Mongolia and the rest of the world, because everyone knows the horse began here in Mongolia. Even in the schools they teach that. So it is good you brought your son here for healing, seeing that he has this connection with horses anyway . . ."

Assuming he still had that, I thought. Assuming he'd get back on when the time came to go into the deeper wilderness, where the reindeer people lived. I pushed the thought away, trying to concentrate instead on the man's words.

"You were right to bring him here," the man said in conclusion. "I think it will help him a lot."

"He's got a little butt, little feet, little eyes . . ." chanted Rowan from behind me, still loving the baby goat.

It was time to go.

"Time to say goodbye to the baby goat, Rowan," I said, standing up a little unsteadily, for we'd drunk cup after cup of the clear-colored, vodka-strength *airag.* I expected the usual tantrum.

"Okay, it's okay," said Rowan, as if to comfort himself. "We'll come back and see the baby goat next time." And with that he hopped off the bed, the docile creature still in his arms, deposited it outside the door, and ran to the van, saying, "Let's go see the reindeer people!"

15
GUINEA PIGS
OF MORON

We drove north, out of the high country, back down into the hotter realms once more. It was incredible to think, as we shuddered and juddered through the mounting heat, that the first frost was a matter of mere weeks away, that in three months this whole sandy, increasingly arid grassland would be covered by its first snowfall. Snow that would stay for months and months. We sweated in the back of the pimpmobile, hour melting into stifling hour, the wheels of the hardworking van fighting for purchase in the sand.

We stopped every so often, in shady spots along the road, to stretch our legs, have a snack, listen to the wind and the birdsong — the high liquid trilling of larks, the more piercing cries of the hawks and the ever-present steppe eagles, at least two of which always seemed to be hanging way up in the blue whenever you turned your gaze skyward. "Just like an African desert," said Rowan, getting out, toy animals in hand, to set them up in the roadside sand.

We crossed the broad Selenge River, gateway to the north, by means of an old-style pontoon powered by rope cables, onto whose boatlike platform we drove the two vans. The ferrymen who lived in this isolated spot winched us slowly across the deep torrent. More hours floated by. We came into the foothills of more mountains, started looking for a place to camp. But the ground hereabouts was stony, not the smooth-turfed steppe we'd gotten used to. Finally, after some searching, we came upon a cleared area in a narrow valley through which a hot wind blew, a wide circle of ground devoid of vegetation, where recently a *ger* and a livestock corral must have stood. The stones had largely been cleared too, so we stopped, put up tents in the gusting wind, and went to gather piles of dung, desiccated by the dry, dry air, to ready a fire for the evening's inevitable chill.

I wandered off some distance, taking advantage of the search for dung piles to snatch some solitude, gathering the dried dung cakes into plastic bags, looking at the wildflowers and animal tracks scuffed in the dusty ground. A couple of times I put up startled coveys of grouse, which went flapping away, the wind behind them. The forest on the high tops of these mountains was part dead, I noticed, as if a disease had killed off half the trees. Or drought. I had read that Mongolia had suffered several severe droughts and harder-than-usual winters in recent years, a phenomenon that had caused catastrophic die-off of livestock. The Mongolians had a deceptively simple word for these drought/hard-winter years: *zud*. Even out here, I had read, people were wondering if the rash of recent *zuds* was a result of global warming. Was the landscape of this most natural of countries being harmed by manmade weather patterns, with hotter summers and colder winters? I walked, my mind wandering ahead of my feet. I thought of Rowan, his condition, this new epidemic of autism, which scientists increasingly were saying might stem from heavy metal poisoning, plastics and pharmaceuticals in the water table and the soil. We seemed to be pushing our planet, ourselves, further and further into ill health, unable to stop whether we wanted to or not.

When I finally went back to camp and dumped my dung cakes on the pile that marked where the fire would be, I noticed that Rowan was walking a little ways off by himself too, and went to catch up with him. He ignored me, intent on some inner dialogue.

"Buster and Blackie and Lily go to Whipsnade Wild Animal Park and ride the train and give Lee Lee the baby elephant and Asha the baby rhino some food."

I stopped dead. How many words was that? The most words I'd ever heard Rowan string together in a sentence was maybe eight or nine. This was . . . I counted them off on my fingers. Twenty-nine.

"Hey, Rowan!" I trotted to catch up, for he had sauntered on, talking to himself all the while. "Who're Blackie and Lily? Is Lily another friend of Buster's?"

"Blackie the hippopotamus and Lily the little girl rabbit."

"So Buster has two friends — Blackie and Lily?"

"They go on an adventure."

This was almost conversation. Not just back and forth, affirmatives and negatives.

"An adventure in Mongolia?"

"In Mongolia, with mountains and eagles and horses and *whack, whack, whack* on your back like a shaman."

"And after Mongolia, what will Buster and Blackie and Lily do then?"

Rowan walked on a moment, as if considering. "Back to London and go to London Zoo, and then to Whipsnade Zoo and ride the train. Oh no! Come on, guys! Let's give Lee Lee the baby elephant and Asha the baby rhino a cuddle-cuddle! Quick! Run! Run to the zoo!"

And he set off up the road at a trot, talking to his imaginary friends, the words just spilling out of him. I stopped, watched him go, instinct telling me to intrude no further, marveling at . . . well, just plain marveling. Were these three imaginary friends running through the landscape with him? I had been allowed that rarest of rare things — a glimpse of Rowan's reflection on his own experience, a peep through the window into the inner life of an autistic child. And how rich that life, that world, was.

Later, under the pale light of a half moon, I took Rowan for a walk, carrying him on my shoulders, where he dug the point of his chin painfully into the top of my cranium as usual. I didn't care. A herd of horses came ambling around the side of the hill that separated this narrow valley from the wide one where our road ran northward. The stallion whinnied, high and loud. Rowan froze. "Just horses saying hello!" I reassured him. "Saying hello to Buster and Blackie and Lily."

He relaxed. "Hello, Buster, Blackie, and Lily, said the daddy horse."

"That's right!"

"He's saying hello to Buster and Blackie and Lily."

"And Asha and Lee Lee?"

"No!"

"Why not?"

"Asha and Lee Lee live in Whipsnade Wild Animal Park!"

Rowan had just answered his first "why" question.

Later still, we sat around the glowing fire, its dense cakes of processed, digested grass throwing out far more heat than a wood fire would. Tomoo and Rowan lay snuggled together in a blanket. Tulga was talking, trying to answer a question posed by Kristin under the influence of red wine and euphoria at what I'd told her about Rowan's language that afternoon. How was it that a nation as peaceful as Mongolia could so revere a guy like Genghis Khan? It had come up because Rowan had gone into the pimpmobile and taken down a little card depicting a mounted medieval Mongol warlord that Haada, the driver, kept as a kind of talisman on the visor above the windscreen. "Genghis Khan!" he'd explained, grinning, as Rowan peered intently at it. *"Genghis Khan!"* Tomoo had shouted, and run for his toy sword, and then he and Rowan had fallen to wrestling and tumbling in the dust under the dusk of evening. So now Kristin — and the rest of us — wanted to know how it could be that a nation could go from Genghis Khan (and Kublai Khan, and Tamerlane, and the other mass murderers of the medieval age) to its present Buddhist state.

"But Genghis Khan was a great man!" protested Tulga, accepting a refill of the good Bordeaux we had bought back in Bulgan. "He was a uniter! Until he came along, all Mongolia was split into many clans, always fighting with each other. He united them and —"

"Took them off to murder everyone else in Asia," I interrupted.

"But he united those countries too, the Khazaks, the Russians, giving them law, order —"

"By cutting them to pieces, raping their women, and enslaving their children."

"I know that for the West, Genghis Khan is seen as a kind of a devil. But for us . . ." You could see nostalgia for the warrior past competing with the contentment of the modern, Buddhist Mongolia on Tulga's wine-flushed face. "Even the Russians," he said, changing the subject slightly. "When they came here, they made us rewrite all the history books in school, because they didn't want to admit that the Mongols had once ruled them. If anyone said this, they went to prison."

"Is Russia still the enemy?" asked Justin from his chair by the hot, glowing fire.

"No — China is. We are caught between — how do you say it? — two evils. But China is the worst. We have to keep them out of Mongolia or they'll destroy everything. For the Russians, we are too far away."

"Outer Mongolia," I said.

"Yes." Tulga chuckled. "When I was in London, everyone would always ask me where I was from. And when I told them, they'd go, 'Ooooh, Outer Mongolia,' like it was the moon or something."

"For the West, Outer Mongolia *is* the moon," Jeremy said. "Or might as well be."

"Yes," I put in. "You can say 'Outer Mongolia' to mean the farthest place you can think of."

"The ends of the earth," said Tulga.

"Yes, the ends of the earth."

"But for us, you know, it's home."

"The home of Genghis Khan."

"Yes! You know, he also invented many

things. He was a very clever man."

"Like what?"

"Like the sandwich, for instance."

"The *sandwich?*" we all chorused incredulously. "Come on . . ."

"No! It's true. He wanted to have a way his troops could eat fast, on the move."

"But you guys don't even farm! How would Genghis Khan have gotten the flour to make bread?"

"From the Chinese. China was the breadbasket of Mongolia."

"We have our own myth about the sandwich," I said. "The English claim that it was the earl of Sandwich, who was a famous gambler, who invented it, as a way to eat without having to leave the gaming table. But that has to be rubbish too. I can't believe that the first person to think of putting a slice of meat and a slice of cheese between two slices of bread was an eighteenth-century English aristocrat. He might have popularized it, though."

"I don't know," Michel said. "I kind of prefer the Genghis Khan story. A convenient snack that you can eat in the saddle, leaving one hand free to cut off the heads of your enemy."

"Yes!" Tulga was laughing now. "Our horses can go without reins, you know — a good rider can direct them just with the legs. So, one hand to eat, one hand to cut. Like I said, Genghis Khan was a great man."

Long after we had retired to our tents, I lay in that half-conscious state between sleeping and waking and heard muffled hoofbeats from across the valley. A lone horseman was riding there in the dark, going from where to where? Spotting the glow from our dung fire, he hailed us, but in song, some kind of folk song that must be universally known, for suddenly Tulga sang back to him from his tent, projecting his voice through the nighttime air to reach the traveling horseman. Song to song, heart to heart, two countrymen conversing by music here at the outer ends of the earth. Or home. For are not all places at once both the ends of the earth and home?

Moron, which we tried to discipline ourselves into pronouncing *murren,* as Tulga did, and not as the Western sense of humor dictated, was gearing up for its own Naadam. I had thought before coming to Mongolia that there was only one big cultural festival, one Naadam, *the* Naadam, as it were. The one we had not attended on our first day in the country, when every other tourist and half the population of the capital had been hovering in and around the great wrestling stadium and the horse-racing area close to UB. In fact, every region has a summer Naadam of wrestling, archery, horse racing, and music, and in a few days, Tulga told us, Moron would host the largest in the Mongolian north. Sure enough, as we drove closer and closer to the town, which would be the first settlement of any real size we'd seen since leaving UB, we began to see riders leading strings of leggy horses — animals with a more athletic look than the usual workhorses of the steppe — northward on tracks parallel to the road. A few times we passed homemade horse vans bumping along with horses, swaddled in rugs and leg bandages, standing in their flat-beds. Haada began to sing as he drove, and Tulga teased him, because he knew he was excited at the prospect of seeing some of the preliminary wrestling bouts that would undoubtedly be taking place near the *ger* camp, just outside the town, where we would be staying.

A *ger* camp — for us, that was the excite-ment. We were going to spend only one night in Moron before heading north to Si-beria and the reindeer people. But Tulga had told us that in addition to having our own *gers,* with real beds and pillows, the

356

camp would give us showers. Hot showers. We could do laundry too. Relax, drink a few beers, maybe even eat some palatable food — for our cook, who we now realized was Tulga's sister-in-law, had settled into a rut of noodle-and-meat-fat soup delivered grumpily, and later and later, each and every night. The *ger* camp had a restaurant, Tulga promised. We shivered with pleasure at the thought. Most important, we had arranged to pick up a load of bacon flown into Moron from the capital by Tulga's wife, Naara, because we were close to running out, and without that Rowan would never make the trip into and out of Siberia.

Siberia. We were really going, then.

If only I could feel good about it. But all I could feel was anxiety. For the taiga, the great forest, in whose southern mountains the reindeer people lived, lay two full days' drive from Moron. Plus another day to get within three days' ride of the reindeer people's summer camps. Assuming they were at those camps. And if Rowan still refused to get on a horse, then what? Carry him on my shoulders through the bogs and up and over the mountains?

In perfect response to the rising anxiety, I'd woken in the small hours racked with pain, not just in my lip but in my whole face, as if an electric current were being pulsed through my lip, chin, mouth, nose, even up to the eyes. I'd never let a cold sore go this far without antiviral drugs before. Now the virus, loosed to its full potential for the first time, was making a playground of my face. I finally dozed off somewhere toward dawn, but woke with my lips stuck together. My whole lower lip had cracked open, all the way, in one big red sore.

It was a morning of strange humor. Halfway to the outskirts of Moron we passed another van, stopped beside the road, a group of Westerners standing about disconsolately while their guide and driver squatted in the shade of the vehicle (it was hot again), smoking cigarettes. They'd run out of fuel. We gave them some from our reserve and chatted a little with the travelers as Haada tipped the jerry can and their driver held the funnel. The travelers were mostly teenagers from England, young adventurers on a sort of Outward Bound course, who'd helped build a school somewhere in the south and were now, like us, heading north, hoping to find the reindeer people. When they learned why we were traveling, the kids and the two teachers accompanying them wanted to meet Rowan. So we opened the van door, to find Rowan busily playing with himself.

"Penis," he said, pointing it at them with a benevolent smile.

But when we got to Moron we found the joke was well and truly on us, for the three young women who ran the camp had no record of our booking. We could not stay. We could only pay to use the facilities — get our laundry done, take showers (well, at least we could still have those), buy some more supplies, and wait for the flight from UB with Rowan's bacon to come in, before heading out to camp on the steppe once more. Not that this was so bad in and of itself, but — from an autism parent's point of view, at least — Moron and even the *ger* camp itself turned out to be a place of absolute torment.

For a start, there were the *gers* themselves, all occupied by other travelers, both Western and Mongolian. Rowan could not understand why he couldn't just run in and out of them at will and began to tantrum dangerously. Outside the *ger* camp was a main road, complete with passing trucks, horsemen, large dogs, broken glass, lumps of jagged metal from wrecked cars — not a place Rowan could run. The showers turned out to be either scalding hot or ice cold. Finally he broke into a *ger* in which a huge wrestler and his family were staying for the Naadam, along with two pet guinea pigs in a cage. Guinea pigs? In a Mongolian *ger* camp? Rowan fixated on them immediately, spotting them the moment he kicked open the door. He rushed into the room, under the astonished gaze of the vast, dangerous-looking man and his relatives, opened the cage, and had the little animals in his hands before, apologizing profusely, I too invaded their space, tore the rodents from his grasp, and dragged him out.

"GUINEA PIG! GUINEA PIG!" The screams were loud enough to cause a party of horse-men riding past the front gates of the camp to rein in and stare. Rowan was rolling in the dust, hitting himself, having to be restrained. Tulga was nowhere to be found, having gone with both vehicles to get more fuel, more supplies, and to take Michel, Jeremy, and Justin to a Chinese restaurant while they waited for the plane to come in with Rowan's bacon.

Despairing, Kristin and I tried to take Rowan into town, letting him ride on my shoulders to keep him out of the way of dogs, glass, vehicles, and other hazards. But the town, larger and slummier than any we'd seen since UB, was not entirely friendly. A pair of drunk, solidly built men came wandering over and hassled us in Mongolian, some mixture of threats and demands for money. They did not pursue us as we walked away, but it didn't make exploring the town in greater depth seem that attractive. There were broken-down tenement buildings as well as log cabins and *gers* behind palisades. Whenever Rowan saw one with a gate standing open, he'd try to climb down my body, screaming *"Ger! Ger!"* and hitting me and yanking out hair.

We went back to the *ger* camp. He quieted down when he discovered, in the room next to the showers, a chess set that had obviously been made in India and had carved wooden elephants for pawns. He played with them awhile as Kristin and I tried to snatch some down time. I dozed off a moment in my chair, only to start awake a few seconds later and find Rowan gone. Heart racing, I rushed outside, just in time to see him making his escape from the wrestler's *ger* with the guinea pigs in his arms. Once again I returned the little animals to their rightful owners. Then I hoisted Rowan, now yelling his head off and thrashing to and fro with anger, back onto my shoulders, walked out the camp gate, and headed north toward the open steppe and the mountains beyond. Anything to get him away from the object of obsession. I spat at the flies that, attracted by the open sore that was now my lip, came buzzing close, looking to feed. Some rest stop this had turned out to be.

The vans came and picked us up after half an hour or so. Exhausted, I climbed into the pimpmobile and glared dully at the passing steppe as we climbed out of the wide bowl in which Moron lay and up into hill country once more, first stony, then increasingly covered in rich, smooth turf. Two hours out of the town, back in country so open you could see for miles with no sign of humankind upon the landscape, we made camp in a high, shallow valley as the last light moved toward the west and the moon came up over the highest point of the ridge.

As we cooked and gathered dung for the evening's fire, a young boy, maybe eleven or twelve, came riding bareback over the ridge on his pony, no doubt having spotted the smoke from wherever his own family had their camp. As he sat playing with Tomoo in the grass, eating cookies, and joking with the drivers, I looked enviously at him. Envious of what? Of his parents, for having such an independent, self-sufficient child, able to handle himself alone on horseback out in this great vastness. Would Rowan ever be able to fend for himself like that? Would he ever be able to look after himself at all? I saw him playing a few hundred yards away, by himself, with his toy animals. He had run off, shouting "No thank you!" as soon as the pony had appeared in our camp, and was now entirely engrossed in his game, back turned to us. He sat bare-arsed on the turf, having already soiled two sets of pants and underwear since leaving Moron. Would he ever be continent in his body? His emotions? Would there ever be healing, true healing for him, for us?

The moon rose as the sun sank below the ridge line and dusk turned to night. Trusting to his horse's sense of direction, the boy who had come to visit us swung himself onto the animal's strong back and rode off into the gathering dark.

■ ■ ■ ■

PART THREE

■ ■ ■ ■

16
INTO SIBERIA

I woke to see a devil's shadow looming on the tent wall, pressing in at me where I lay. I started, still caught between sleep and consciousness, then realized it was a yak, licking the dew off the flysheet. Yaks were munching all around the tent. I heard Rowan waking up, giggling. "Look at all the yaks!" he said, sticking his head out and causing the beast licking the tent on my side to jump away with an alarmed fart. "Stinky!" said Rowan, climbing out into the sunlight.

Rowan chased off the remaining yaks, sending them, tails up, floundering for the ridge, shy despite their long horns. As they ran, their shaggy coats flapped like the fringes on a Western jacket. I'd have laughed if the cold sore hadn't made it so painful. Rowan, pulsating with energy, ran up to the two drivers and crashed headfirst into them, holding his arms up and shouting, "Hoo-wah!" They caught on quickly, tossing him up in the air and shouting "Hoo-wah" while I stumbled over to the kitchen tent to look for hot water to make tea.

Kristin, hair mussed up and eyes still bleary, came out of the tent. I handed her a steaming mug of morning brew. As she stood sipping it, she said, "You know, I usually don't remember my dreams. But last night I dreamed about my grandmother — my mother's mother, the one who went mad. You know, my mom used to take me to see her in the home — the nuthouse. She never really knew us, so it was weird — sad. She was only committed after her husband died, but my mom told me that the cycle really began after her son, my mom's brother, got killed by a car when he was only eight. You know how the shamans back in UB said there was a female ancestor on my side being 'unhelpful'? Anyway, I had this dream about her last night."

Kristin looked out at the steppe, where Rowan and Tomoo were now chasing after the yaks, again shouting and laughing. Then she went on. "In the dream I had this sense that she was clinging to Rowan somehow, to make up for the loss of her own son. I know it sounds crazy. But I woke up with the feeling so vivid. I think — maybe this is nonsense, but I think we should pray for her to release him, to be happy. I think we should pray for her peace, her happiness, so she can let Rowan go."

That day we drove and drove. Up into higher ranges than we had yet crossed, on roads so rough it sometimes seemed we'd make better progress on foot. After the first few hours — amazing how hours in a vehicle can slip by when you don't fight them — we decided to stretch our legs while Haada negotiated a particularly nasty section of mountain track. Away from the road, the high, wide valley was carpeted with edelweiss, literally carpeted with it. Flocks of shelducks, which look half duck, half goose, flew overhead. Rowan and Tomoo ran for a while, then demanded shoulder rides. When Rowan started to press his chin into my skull as usual, I said, not expecting a response, "You know, Rowan, the chin on my head is ouchy. But a hand would be nice."

To my astonishment, Rowan immediately placed his hand under his chin, cushioning my head.

I must have said this to him a hundred times in the past few years. Suddenly he was understanding, complying.

"Thank you, Rowan!" I could barely contain my delight. Kristin just stared.

"Thank you. That really helps Daddy."

"Rowan and Buster and Lily and Blackie were a bit upset," he said, ignoring me. Or was he? "Then they went to see shamans and after the shamans they went to Whipsnade Wild Animal Park and gave Lee Lee the baby elephant and Asha the baby rhino some food."

His hand stayed in place. "Thank you, Rowan," I said again. "Thank you for helping Daddy."

So quietly it was almost a whisper, his voice came, just above my ear: "You're welcome."

We forded a river so wide, so twisted back around itself, that we had to cross and recross through the gravel shoals, splashing great gouts of water into the air, Rowan and Tomoo cheering as the pimpmobile dipped, swayed, and bucked, gears grinding, wheels spinning as they fought for purchase.

We crested a high pass — the highest yet — and stopped awhile there, not just to stretch our legs (necessary after so many hours in the van) but because the view required more than mere looking at. Homage had to be given, for here was where one great ecosystem ended and another began. At this mountaintop the great grasslands of the steppe gave way to the beginning of the taiga, the great Siberian forest, the largest forest in the world, which stretches all the way from the Pacific Ocean in the east clear across Russia to Scandinavia in the west. I stood in the last of the great, continent-sized meadow that is the steppe and gazed at the forest wall. It was like facing an army. An ancient army. Its charge, its presence, was palpable. The sound of the wind in the trees was like the sighing of God's breath.

A great *ovoo,* so large that it comprised not one but several cairns, had been built on top of the mountain, facing the forest wall. All festooned with blue silk scarves, animal skulls, and the usual vodka bottles, cigarettes, and money, the cairns looked more like strange silken haystacks than heaps of stone. "This is the end of things," said Tulga as the drivers went to leave their offerings. "Beyond here, well — for us, *that* is the real ends of the earth."

Slowly, as if entering a cathedral, we went down into the great forest, the hush closing in immediately around the van. Was it mere fantasy, or was there indeed a real charge, an emotional presence, to this great immensity of trees, this absolute negation of civilization? The feeling was there, irrational but impossible to ignore, seeming to whisper from the dark spaces between the crowding,

371

ancient trunks. A world where the force of nature was still undiminished, unfenced, unfettered. Where shamans still practiced their craft.

And what was this thing, or this non-thing, that people called shamanism, anyway? This thing that defied all rational explanation, could not be justified or defended by logic? Was it fantasy? Was making this journey a mere indulgence of fantasy? Certainly it defied all my Western conditioning, yet here I was. And why, I wondered as the van bumped down the steep forest track, do we in the West make such a cult of rationality, applying the same fundamentalist, obsessive approach to rationality, or science, that we previously applied to religion? All that cannot be explained by the rational is cast out as heresy. Yet so much of our lives is governed by things we cannot hope to quantify in rational or scientific terms. Like love, for instance. Everybody experiences it, craves it, requires it for his or her very existence, knows it's there. But no one can explain it, break it down into physics and chemistry.

Then again, if we aren't skeptical, we become the prey of charlatans and snake-oil salesmen, priests and dictators. We know from bitter experience that if something is outside our knowledge base, we are right to mistrust it, or at least withhold our judgment until experience has shown us whether we can trust it. We are left stumbling through a gray fog, knowing only that while some things can be readily explained, some things cannot. That is how life is.

"Look at all the trees," said Rowan, the awe in his voice palpable. "The trees are happy."

After perhaps two hours we came out into a great clearing, in the middle of which sat a little town straight out of a fairy tale, all log cabins with turf roofs and turf streets in between them, grazed into greensward by goats, sheep, and yaks. Ulaan-Uul marked the official end of civilization. Beyond was only forest, all the way north to the Arctic Ocean, fifteen hundred or more miles away. We refueled, Rowan chasing the bleating lambs and kids that grazed next to their mothers between the low wooden buildings, and then we drove off once more across a vast floodplain between two sets of high, rocky mountains. Here and there were *gers*, herds, last bastions of the steppe herders before the forest took over once and for all. We made camp at the edge of the trees, staring back across the valley at the moon rising over vast, rocky peaks dusted with late-summer snow. Behind us rose more ranges, somewhere in which were the summer camps of the reindeer folk.

Rowan ran straight into the forest, shouting, "Let's go see a wolf, a moose, a maral! Let's go see a red fox, a lynx, and a wolverine! Let's go see a wild boar and a raccoon dog!"

These had been among the forest animals displayed in the Museum of Natural History back in UB, where he'd spent that first mad day rushing from room to room. He'd taken it all in, then. He climbed up on a fallen log, mosquitoes dancing around him (biting ones this time), and shouted, "Let's go see the reindeer people!"

"We have to take horses to see the reindeer people, Rowan — you know that. Are you ready to ride again?"

"No thank you!"

That night, as Kristin and I did the nightly ritual of burning herbs and washing with holy water that the shamans back in UB had prescribed, we prayed for her grandmother, if she was holding on to Rowan in some way, to let him go. To let him be. To release herself and him from any suffering she might be clinging to.

In the pale light of morning, a group of

horsemen rode up from the valley to ask us our business here. Led by a large, older man in a *deel* and pointed wrestler's hat, the riders dismounted, greeted us, and squatted down to talk. Tulga called me over, as protocol dictated. In another time, another era, such a visit would have struck fear into the heart of any human being from Kazakhstan to Vienna. But these men wore broad smiles instead of weapons. They were simply curious to know what we were doing in this far-off place. Tulga told them why we had come, about Rowan and our search for a shaman, adding that we intended to drive a further day north to a place where he had contacts for finding horses, in the hope that the summer camps of the reindeer people would be within a day or so's ride of there. And that we would find a shaman in one of those camps.

"Actually," said the old man, stretching his stiff, short, but hugely muscled legs out on the turf and rubbing at an arthritic knee, "you don't have to go that far." The two men chatted for a minute. Then, "We're in luck," said Tulga. "This old man says the most powerful shaman in the area is only a hard day's ride from here — two days' ride if you take it steady. Or so he says. He can get horses for us, take us there."

I raised an eyebrow, and safely assuming that none of the muscle-bound nomads seated in front of us had any English, I asked, "Do you think he's straight up?"

"I think so," said Tulga, keeping his voice level. "I mean, in Mongolia it is very unusual for someone to lie. Especially about anything to do with a shaman. He says this shaman is very powerful, and also a friend of his, and he goes to him if he ever has any big problem. Then again, if we hire him and his sons and nephews here to take us, well, that is a nice bit of money for them. I don't know these guys. I do know the guys to the north. But if these guys are honest, then it would be better to go with them, as my contacts don't know the shamans personally, and it's farther, which gives us less time once we do get to the reindeer people."

"My gut says to trust them," I said, almost surprised to hear the words coming out of my mouth. I had nothing to base them on. But it was true; my gut did say to trust them.

"I think so too," said Tulga. He switched to Mongolian and told the old man okay — we wanted him to find horses for us, guide us, and agree on a price.

"One thing, though," I put in. "He needs to know how slowly we'll be traveling. I mean, we have so much equipment. And then there's Rowan, who might or might not decide to ride. If he decides he has to get down every half-hour and play in the dirt, then I'm going to have to let him. Bottom line, if Rowan refuses to ride at all and I end up having to carry him on my shoulders, is that possible?"

The old man listened gravely while Tulga translated this, scratching at his cropped head under the jauntily tilted wrestler's cap. "If we have to ride at the slowest possible pace, it will take three days," he answered finally. "If we have to carry Rowan, there are many shoulders here." He grinned, indicating the younger men around him. "So it shouldn't take much longer than that either way."

Three days in and three days out. Would that give us enough time with the shaman?

To that, the old man could only shrug. Who could say how long or how short a healing could be?

What about hazards, obstacles — how difficult of a ride or hike would it be?

Again the old man shrugged. "Not much. Just one big river. And some bogs. And a pass. Actually, two passes, a small one and a big one. Nothing too bad." Except one of the bogs was pretty bad. You had to be careful not to lose a horse in there. And, of course, the farther up into the taiga you went, the more things there were that could eat your horse — more wolves, bears, and so on. The men would bring a gun. But it was possible the horses could stray if wolves came by in the night. That could slow us down if we had to round them up again. No, all in all, it wasn't too bad a trip.

"Sounds bloody impossible," I confided to Tulga once his translation was done. "Do you think we can do this?"

Now it was Tulga's turn to shrug. "Once we're in the taiga, we're on our own. No vehicles. If anything goes wrong . . . But then, this is why we came, yes?"

"I guess so." I looked at the ground, thinking about it all, listening to the horses as they chomped the grass nearby. "What's the name of the shaman?" I asked as an afterthought. Maybe it would be one of the ones I'd read about in my research before coming.

"Ghoste," said the old man as soon as Tulga had relayed the question.

My heart jumped. It *was* one of the shamans I'd read about. Unless there were others in the region with the same name?

"No," Tulga assured me on behalf of the old man. "Only one with that name. He's the most powerful. But he doesn't agree to help everyone. No one can guarantee that. The old man says he knows him, though, and he's pretty sure he'll accept."

Two days' ride, over a river, into the Siberian forest, through bogs, one or more of them downright dangerous, up and over two mountain passes.

"We must be mad," I said to Tulga, who grinned.

"Maybe just a little."

We took the two vans as far as they could go — another few miles over the rough turf of the valley, then back up the hillside to the forest's edge once more, where a trail led into the trees via a swampy, boggy meadow on whose shallow pools cruised large shelducks, and through which a large maral hind went bounding away as we cut the engines and got out. End of the line for the internal combustion engine. The old man had told us it would take him and his men the better part of the day to round up the sixteen horses necessary to transport all of us plus our equipment to the reindeer people. He had told us to wait until then at this rendezvous point, where the drivers would camp out with the vans to await our return, successful or otherwise, from the taiga.

So we sat in the shade of a grove of great

pines, packing our saddlebags with the minimum of clothing, sorting the equipment, figuring out what to take and what to leave in the vans. It could be cold up where we were going, Tulga warned; the large pass we had to go over was something around 11,000 feet. So we had to be prepared. It was hard to imagine real cold this afternoon, for the temperature steadily rose, and it was humid. Mosquitoes bit us but buzzed away once we had lit two or three little dung fires around the rocks on which we laid out our equipment and clothes, sorting and resorting.

For Rowan alone we had to have several changes of clothes, bottles for water to wash his soiled trousers and underwear, the little blue plastic bucket, which would hang from my saddle. Not to mention a tarp, in case we got caught in the rain, wipes, waterproof pants in case he wanted to go wandering off into the bogs on a cold day. Oh, and the bottles and boxes of medicine that the shamans back in UB had prescribed for the nightly rituals we were still performing as Rowan went to bed. His stuff alone filled two saddlebags. We counted up the packets of bacon, too. Up in the mountains it would keep longer, but we had enough for six days total, maybe seven if Rowan would consent to eat some other things. Two days up to the reindeer camp, two days there, two days back — that was virtually a week in and of itself. Not counting the two days it would take us to reach Moron once more — the nearest place we could replenish his supplies. We'd better hope nothing went wrong.

And, of course, all this was assuming that Rowan would even agree to begin the trip. He watched us warily, playing with his dwindling supply of toy animals and hanging out in the stationary pimpmobile, obsessively catching flies as they buzzed around the windows and dumping them out the open door. Making it clear that the van was where he wanted to be. Kristin and I had made a point over the last few days of reminding him that in order to reach the reindeer people, which he said he wanted to do, getting back on a horse would be unavoidable. He had remained resolutely silent on that point.

There was a sudden wail from the van. We turned, in time to see Rowan, in tears, without pants on, diarrhea running down his bare legs in two chestnut brown streams, come running out, shouting, "Code Brown!" At once heartbreaking and funny. And also — the autism parent in me could not help but notice this — he had taken in the Code Brown jokes of the week before and applied them in the correct context. Distressed as he was, he had made an appropriate connection. We cleaned up both him and the van (Haada stared aghast at the brown pool on the floor of his beloved vehicle), and I scrubbed the pants clean, then stretched them out to dry on a rock. When I looked up, I saw movement down below us, through the trees. Horses. Lots of horses. The old man and his sons and nephews were coming. Five horsemen, each leading a clutch of other horses by long ropes. The moment of truth had come.

Or rather, the torturous, drawn-out buildup to the moment of truth, for the arrival of the sixteen horses in our shady pine grove was really just another part of the preparations. Without the possibility of vehicle backup, much of the camera equipment had to be experimentally tied onto the pack saddles to see whether it could be balanced enough for the horses to carry it easily across rough terrain, or whether we might need extra horses. These preparations took a good two hours, while the horses stamped and fussed and snorted and the old man and his lads tied and untied, loaded and unloaded our odd collection of equipment several times, until fully satisfied that they had the right formula.

Rowan watched from the van, catching the large horseflies. I checked on him periodically. Each time he held a fistful of the buzzing insects, none of which bit him, though they harassed the horses — and us — under the trees.

"That one out there," I said, pointing at a brown-and-white-spotted horse that the old man had said was especially good with kids. "That's the one we'll be riding to the reindeer people. We'll be leaving soon. Are you ready?"

"Sixteen," said Rowan, and flung the fistful of flies he'd gathered out the open door of the van. "And now get sixteen more." He went back to the window, where a small legion of flies buzzed against the pane, and began picking them off one by one with his right hand and putting them into his left.

We gradually mounted, getting the feel of the horses the nomads had brought us. They were good ones, responsive but quiet. The brown-and-white creature reserved for Rowan and me had a kind eye, which I always look for in a horse, and a forehead whorl placed exactly midway between the eyes, which in old English horsemen's lore denotes intelligence without rancorousness. A gelding, it also had a long mouth, another good sign: short mouths almost always seem to go with a sour, sulky disposition. This horse, if Rowan would only get up on it, looked like the right one for the difficult ride ahead.

The main obstacle seemed to be finding the best horse for Justin — one solidly built enough to take the two mixing boxes in saddlebags across its hindquarters, tall enough for the precious equipment not to get wet on a river crossing or in the bogs, and quiet enough not to shy at the long boom mike with its fluffy oversock. It took two or three changes of mount to find the right one. I stole nervous glances at Rowan as the first two horses spun in circles and snorted at the approach of the strange cargo. I knew he'd be watching everything, missing nothing. Tiring of the flies in the van, he had now ventured out onto the highest of the rocks under the tree. He was playing *Lion King* with his animals but in reality taking in everything that was going on. Trying to contain my anxiety, I waited until everyone was mounted before interrupting his game. I didn't want to make the same mistake I'd made the first day, when I'd gotten Rowan into the saddle long before everyone else was ready and then lost the good mood. Not that I could read his mood at all today.

One thing I did know: we were starting so late that we'd be able to get only an hour, at most, under our belts before making camp. But that would be perfect — just enough to get him going again, not so much that he'd get sick of it. If he'd only consent to start.

At last there was no time left to procrastinate. The whole group was on board, studiously looking off in different directions so as not to spook Rowan. Tomoo sat happily in front of Tulga; they also had a brown-and-white horse. Kristin was riding a pale chestnut in small circles, getting the feel of it. At my suggestion, the old man and his son had already started off down the trail across the swampy meadow with the pack-horses in tow. I took the lead rope of our horse from one of the old man's nephews and approached the rock where Rowan played, deliberately ignoring all the activity around him.

"Okay, Rowan, time to go see the reindeer people."

Kristin, at my prompting, was already riding off after the guides.

"See? Mommy's on her way. Let's follow her."

"Rock! Want to play on the rock!"

"Come on, Rowan, don't you want to go see the reindeer people? You said you did."

"Want to play with the animals!"

"We can bring them. You can hold them while we ride. Come on."

He ignored me. My horse twitched its ears, looking off after the others.

"Come on, Rowan, please?"

"Stay on the rock!"

"Then we'll be left here all alone."

"Stay on the rock!"

I took a deep breath, circled his waist, and lifted him down, the toy lion and lion cub still grasped tightly in his little hands.

"Rooooooooooooock!" he wailed as I swung him into the saddle and climbed up behind. *"Roooooooock!"* he kept wailing as I put heels to the horse's sides to close the distance to the others. "Off! Get off! *No thankyou riding horses!*"

Okay, I thought. Just give it a few minutes, see if he calms down, see if we can do this.

And then the worst of all possible things happened. Out of the forest came charging a great herd of semiwild horses, perhaps eighty strong, led by a pugnacious-looking dark bay stallion, who came trotting over to us, screaming his challenge at our horses. Rowan went rigid, shutting his eyes tight as two of our guides broke away from the main group and rode at the stallion, whose territory we were probably invading, cracking whips and shouting to drive him away. One by one each of our horses, Rowan and mine included, let go an earsplitting whinny, to which a number of the free herd responded. Rowan burrowed into my chest, hands over his ears, eyes screwed shut, emitting small noises of distress. With my gut tying itself in knots, I said in my most reassuring (but sadly fake-sounding) voice, "Hello! Hello! said the horses. Just the horses saying hello."

I saw Kristin looking back, worried. The herd was past us now, but Rowan was saying, "Down, get down!" and we were in the middle of the boggy meadow, where getting off would mean sinking calf-deep in sphagnum moss and mud. The horses had to put on some engine to get through the slop and jolted into a ragged trot. A great gout of mud slapped up on us, landing *splop* on my leg and on Rowan's, drenching his pants. He yelled. This was going from bad to worse. I fished for inspiration.

"Yuck!" I said. "Wet and sloppy. Just like a Code Brown." I wiped my fingers in the glop of mud that had drenched his thigh. "What's that?" I said, as if to an imaginary audience. "It's a Code Brown. Yuck! Poopy everywhere."

And then the miracle happened. Rowan giggled.

I pushed the joke a little further. "Poopy everywhere! Yucky! Disgusting!"

The gods of toilet humor must have heard us, for Rowan suddenly became a different child.

"What's *that?*" he said, sitting up and pointing at the trees of the forest wall.

"I don't know — what is that?" I didn't know where he was going with this, but wherever it was, I wanted to follow.

"It's a . . ." he said, grinning at me.

I gave him a sharp intake of breath, kind of denoting a question mark.

"Code Brown!"

And so it went, Rowan squealing and laughing, causing Tomoo and Tulga to turn around and laugh with him, the guides smiling despite not understanding what was going on. Kristin and the crew looked around hopefully, knowing how much quite literally rode on this. My heart was in my mouth as we kept the game going, Rowan now as natural and relaxed in the saddle as he was back home on Betsy. The horse also relaxed under our twistings and gigglings and jerkings and shoutings, and the great Siberian forest opened its arms to receive us.

After the near-disaster of the screaming

horse herd, this laughing, joking delight was more, far, far more, than I could have hoped for. Deeper into the forest we went, then once more the trail came to a wide, boggy meadow. A snipe winged across our pathway, whistling as it flew. Our horse — all the horses — began to sink and struggled to keep going, the suck of their hooves pulling free of the clinging glop almost loud enough to drown Rowan's laughter. Then, quite suddenly, the horse disappeared from underneath us.

It's potentially one of the worst kinds of falls you can take. The horse founders underneath you, rolling sideways with you stuck half on, half off, ready to be crushed as the horse lurches desperately to get up out of the mire or trampled as it strikes out with its hooves to try to find purchase to right itself. Horses panic when they go down — it's a situation where, in the wild, they would immediately be prey. Loss of balance and a fall unhinges even the best-trained animal. Down we went.

I hurled Rowan to the side. He landed with a wail and a thud in the soft turf, screaming but clear of the rolling half-ton and thrashing hooves. I wriggled to the side, kicking my right foot, which was still stuck in the stirrup, to try to free it before I got dragged. The horse rolled toward me. I kicked at it, hard. It rolled back. My foot came free. I could hear Rowan crying, people shouting. The horse struggled up out of the bog, black mud dripping from its legs, its belly. A rear hoof kicked out, flying just over my head, as the horse tried to fling the clinging glop from its skin. Another kick and it was free. One of the guides rode to head it off, lead it to firmer ground, while I rolled up and onto my feet and grabbed Rowan in a huge hug. It had all happened so fast that no one had even reached us yet. He was sobbing. Christ, I'd blown it after all. And we'd been so close.

And then once more a miracle happened. A baby snipe, or rather an almost full-grown snipe, but one whose wings had not yet fully fledged, got up from the reeds right in front of us and went running for the forest.

"Look! A snipe!" I said in my most upbeat voice. "Let's catch it!"

And to my surprise — whether because of the adrenaline, the timing, the fact that Rowan could rarely resist having any cute baby animal almost within his clutches, or maybe all three — the tears and the fear lifted and Rowan's smile broke through. "Let's get it!" he echoed, and off we went, splashing in its whistling wake, as the guides caught our horse and Kristin and the rest of the party dismounted and ran to intercept us.

17
THE WHITE IBEX

Next morning, under a light, cool drizzle, Rowan bounced from foot to foot as the guides took their time making sure all the equipment was tied properly in place. The horses stamped and whinnied as they were loaded. "Ride!" whined Rowan, impatient to be off. "Ride!"

"Thank God," I thought, "he still wants to ride." And so we did, Code Browning our way along the forest paths (what a monster I'd created there). But once we had the first hour under our belt, Rowan decided he wanted to get down and play in the dirt with his animals. Unwilling to do anything to upset him, I called a halt, and as the shout went along our long, drawn-out convoy of riders and packhorses, I dismounted, lifted Rowan down, and stood in the middle of the trail. A wide clearing was all around us, with a great shoulder of mountain marching from the west. The horses grazed, the old man and the guides smoked, Tomoo wandered off to throw stones, and the rest of us just sat in the shade of our horses (how quickly the days got hot here) while Rowan played *Lion King* in the dust. Half an hour went by. Forty minutes.

Tulga eventually rode up, the old man at his side. "Rupert, we have to try to make some time. Do you think Rowan could be okay to ride again now?"

"We can see," I said, and asked Rowan, "More play or ride a little more?"

"Ride a little more."

Well, we were getting somewhere. But as we rounded the corner of the mountain and came out to a wide vista of marshland, at whose center lay a round, shallow lake, the guides shouted something, and Tulga, relaying the message, said, "Ah . . . okay . . . they're telling me that — see that peak over there?"

I followed where he pointed, Rowan leaning back into me and drumming his head rhythmically against my sternum. "Those mountains?" They seemed impossibly far. A faint, pale blue massif way off to the north. "That's where we have to go? By tomorrow?"

"Yes." Tulga's voice was a little nervous.

"Maybe they underestimated the distance." From where he sat in front of his father, Tomoo reached out and tickled Rowan's side. Rowan giggled.

"At this pace? You really think we can make it?"

Tulga gave the uncomfortable laugh that I had learned meant trouble. "Maybe. If we're lucky."

"We're going to have to put on the pace a bit."

"Little bit, yes."

"The last time you said 'Little bit' like that, I ended up getting whipped."

Tulga laughed again, but without mirth.

"Down!" said Rowan, suddenly twisting and trying to scramble out of the saddle. "Get down and play!"

"Halt, everyone!"

Back down the line went the cry. Rowan was already on his belly in the trail dust, squinting at Simba and Scar as he put them through their paces: "What have you done? Dad! Dad!"

Half an hour later, the day by now having grown really hot, I managed to coax him back into the saddle. As we reentered the forest, I asked him, "Do you like this horse? Yes or no?"

"Yes, I do."

"Really?" I asked, unsure if he was just responding to cues or if he was really saying what he thought. "In that case, have you got a name for him?"

"Yes."

"What is it, then?"

"Blue."

Perhaps half an hour after that, Rowan decided he'd had enough of being in the saddle for good. "Ride on Daddy's shoulders!"

Wanting to keep us moving, I climbed down, took him up on my shoulders, and led Blue, as Rowan scrambled around to his usual sidesaddle position on my right shoulder, chin pressing hard into the top of my skull.

"The chin is ouchy . . ." I began.

"But the hand is nice," Rowan finished the sentence for me and immediately placed his hand between my head bone and his chin.

"Thanks," I said.

"You're welcome."

On we walked, the day growing ever hotter. Thank God for long hair — his and mine — which saves the back of the neck from sunburn. The forest had retreated far to either side of us, leaving us exposed to the full glare. With every step, Rowan's weight seemed to bear down harder on my right shoulder, the heat to grow more intense. Blue, whom I was leading along by his tether-rope, had to be dragged ever so slightly, and pulled back ever so slightly in that half-cooperative, half-reluctant way that horses have. I found myself swearing under my breath, trying to blow away the flies attracted by my pulpy lip, pulling Blue along with one hand and steadying Rowan's leg with the other. A wave of anger at Rowan — his difficultness, his sheer bloody high maintenanceness — pulsed through me. I breathed hard, blew at the flies.

Then a voice inside my head laughed. And spoke. Perhaps it was the sun. Perhaps it was the sheer intensity of this situation. This journey. This dream. But clear as day I heard my inner voice say, *What are you complaining about, Rupert? Just what are you complaining about? You're walking across Mongolia with your little boy on your shoulders! What in God's name are you whining for? Where do you want to be? Pushing him round a supermarket in a trolley? Sitting in traffic on the way to some therapy appointment or other? Are you really going to waste this incredible experience, this incredible adventure you're sharing with your son, complaining that it's uncomfortable? Don't be an idiot. Savor this. You'll never be here again.*

Clear. And so, spontaneously, I began to sing.

"Daddy sing!" encouraged Rowan, pulling at my hair.

The song that came flowing out was one I hadn't sung in years, an old Irish one from the childhood memory bank, though it wasn't one my mother had sung. No, it was another: "The Girl I Left Behind Me," no doubt remembered from some impromptu pub ceilidh in London in the eighties, twenty years ago or more, when my liver was younger and stronger. Out the old tune came, spilling from my lips like water:

O the dames of France are fond and free,
And Flemish lips are willing;

"You wish," said Kristin, riding up next to us.

And soft the maids of Italy,
And Spanish eyes are thrilling;
Still, though I bask beneath their smile,
Their charms still fail to bind me.
And my heart goes back to Erin's Isle,
To the girl I left behind me.

"Daddy to sing!" shouted Rowan delightedly.

397

So I gave voice to the rest, notwithstanding my utter and complete lack of any Irish blood, stepping out along the trail, Blue behind me, my son on my shoulders, the sun on my shoulders, my wife riding beside.

I'd be lying if I said I remembered every word. There was a fair amount of *hum-pum-pum* and *zum-tum-mmm* filling in the gaps. But we swung along in fair style, the singing keeping the flies away at least, for a good few miles until the heat and weight finally began to take their full toll and my tongue began to grow dry.

Fortunately, that was the exact moment at which we rounded a bend and saw a stream trickling down along the gradually narrowing valley, with several great tall pines shading it right there on the trail and the cool forest margin creeping closer on the northern bank. "We'll stop there for a break," I heard Tulga say from somewhere behind me. I fixed my eye on the spot and, with Rowan yanking my hair in time to the music, tried to keep up the pace, thinking of the shade and rest.

I handed Blue off to the young son of the old man, watched as they splashed across the cool brook so the horse could be picketed in the shade of the forest on the other side, and saw Rowan tear off his clothes and splash blissfully into the water. And down under the shade of the pine I dropped.

"Jeremy," I asked — he happened to be standing nearby — "could you possibly watch him for a moment while I . . ."

And a moment later both Kristin and I were asleep, nestled together in the shade, the pine needles a mattress between us and the warm, life-giving earth.

There were ants in it, though. Biting ones.

"Arrrhgh!" Kristin sat up suddenly, the siesta abruptly over, smacking at her bare arms where the buggers had bitten her.

"Just like Texas, huh?" said Michel, appearing with two bowls of soup — noodles and mutton with globs of fat for me, and noodles with noodles for vegetarian Kristin. Again. Rowan, tucking into a fistful of bacon, waded naked under Jeremy's benevolent eye. Tomoo and the others were all a hundred yards away on the far bank, with the horses and the fires that had been lit to cook by, despite the day's heavy heat.

"Good idea." I looked at Michel. "Think we could get one going this side to keep the flies off?" I licked my raw lip.

Michel made a fire from dried pine sap and tinder. We lay awhile in the shade, letting the smoke play over us, enjoying the way it freed us from the flies. When Rowan, inevitably, had another Code Brown, I got up, sighing, filled an empty bottle from the river, and cleaned him. Then, as Rowan splashed into the water once more, I heard Michel say, "Oh no!"

He stood, bottle in hand, looking aghast and spitting.

"Did you just . . . ?" I asked.

He nodded, the hurried, alarmed nod of someone who's just . . .

"Drunk a bottle of the river water I filled to clean Rowan's . . . ?"

Michel nodded, wincing. I had separated the bottles — usually carried in my fisherman's vest pockets — out on the pine needles, the left-hand two for cleaning, the right-hand two, having been put through our ultraviolet water-filter thingie, for drinking. Michel had confused them.

"Well," I said, trying to be positive, "Rowan's drunk from the streams here and there when I couldn't stop him. And Tomoo. They're okay. So far. You'll be fine."

As the first cool breeze of late afternoon came soughing in over the stream, we mounted once more and set off at a brisk trot, Rowan demanding an increase in speed over the final miles of the broad, broad clearing, through further belts of forest to the banks of a wide river. I'd been secretly dreading this. I'd crossed enough rivers on horseback in my time: the loose stones underfoot, sudden deep holes in which the horses could flounder, weird currents, even the horses panicking — all could result in a drowning if anything went wrong. So we went slowly, picking out where the shallowest shoals ran, avoiding the deeper pools and eddies, making sure of the route before we attempted a crossing with the boys and the gear.

It took us a good hour to cross, going in relays back and forth with the equipment, using both the packhorses and the saddle horses to make sure that no one horse was too heavily laden, which meant unpacking and repacking several times over. There were sections where the water came up over the horses' bellies, and a couple of spots where they had to swim. Before sending the riders across, the old man, his son, and his nephews rode a longer route, following the shoals, looking for the shallowest way, where the water never came higher than the girth. Having found it, we went across with Rowan, me praying to the Lord of the River, to God, to the universe, to see us safely over without the horse falling, without accident.

My prayers were heard. Rowan laughed and giggled the whole way across, then

401

demanded to get off immediately afterward and go wading in the shallows while the equipment was loaded once more onto just the pack animals, and away we went, riding westward with the river, squinting against the sun.

God, but it was beautiful. Violets, meadow pinks, yellow cowslips, blue columbines, and purple lupins dotted the riverside meadows. The forest, deep green, somber, marched along the opposite bank. On our side the mountains came tumbling down to the river's edge, making a narrow way for us to ride at the fast, leggy trot that Rowan was now demanding, saying, "Trot! Trot! Shall we have a little trot?" whenever the pace slackened.

The valley broadened out into wild pasture and marsh dotted here and there with little oxbow lakes, old meanders of the river that had gradually, over millennia, become cut off from the main flow and now stood by themselves, still, reflecting the Siberian sky. Swans cruised on their mirrorlike surface. Flocks of widgeon and teal went whizzing overhead like arrows, to land, cackling, on the river. Large fish — trout and taimen (a kind of giant landlocked Siberian salmon) — jumped for flies, falling back into the river's golden surface with a loud splash.

We came to the foot of a particularly beautiful mountain, its rocky slopes terraced as if by hand, with granite ledges topped with grass, almost like a giant staircase, decorated here and there with little fir trees, ascending in a steep cone to the sky. "Perhaps we should start thinking about a place to camp," I shouted to Tulga, who was trotting with Tomoo just ahead of us, Rowan being taken up in a strange, husky-voiced monologue about Buster, Lily, Blackie, and Lee Lee the baby elephant and Asha the baby rhino from Whipsnade Wild Animal Park.

"They know a place," Tulga called back over his shoulder. "It's a mile or two farther. There's a spring. We can camp there."

To camp by a spring in the lee of a Siberian mountain — it sounded magical. That was when Kristin said, "Where's Michel? And the others?"

We'd been hustling along at such a good pace that our group had gotten strung out. I looked around. It was just the old man, his son, and his two nephews with the packhorses up ahead, Tulga and Tomoo on their spotted horse, me and Rowan on ours, Kristin on her chestnut, and Justin with his mixers strung over his horse's loins and the

403

boom mike in his hand like an *urga* or a lance.

"Jeremy!" we called. "Michel! Bodo!" The cook's son and helper was missing too. And his mom, the cook.

A few moments later Jeremy and the cook came jogging over the rise.

"Are Michel and Bodo close behind?" we asked. They didn't know. Hadn't been looking since we had started our faster pace.

"Go! Go!" Rowan was starting to whine.

"Listen, I think we'd better not lose the mood," I said to Tulga. "Maybe send one of the guides back down the trail to check that Michel and Bodo are okay while we go make camp?"

"Bodo's with him. It'll be okay. Let's get to the camp, and if they don't show up we can send someone back. We should get set up while we still have daylight."

So on we went, sometimes trotting, sometimes running the horses the last couple of miles into the setting sun, Rowan laughing with delight just like he used to. We followed the long foot of the strangely terraced mountain, the river bending away from us in a mile-wide arc toward the crowding forest. A group of chattering magpies, five of them in handsome blue-black-and-white plumage, flew parallel with us, skimming the surface of the little lakes and finally coming to rest in the branches of a small copse set away by itself on an island in a racing stream that snaked away from the foot of the mountain to the now distant river. As if telling us where to make camp. For here, on the mountain side of the stream, facing the little copse where the magpies chattered and fussed, the old man threw up a hand, calling our convoy to halt and dismount. Rowan and Tomoo were running for the stream as soon as their feet touched the ground.

"You know, back home we have superstitions about magpies," I told Tulga as we pulled the saddles off our tired mounts and handed the horses to the guides to take off and tether on the far side of the stream.

"Oh?"

"Yes — 'One for sorrow, two for joy, three for a girl, four for a boy, five for silver, six for gold, seven for a secret never to be told.' You never heard this while you were in the U.K.?"

"No," said Tulga. "I didn't know people in the West *had* stories about animals."

It was true: to the outside eye, Western culture didn't have much to do with nature anymore. I had grown up with it — counting magpies, hunting foxes, fishing for pike and trout in the streams, training young horses — and I was hardly unique in this. Yet the image of ourselves we export is what? MTV, subdivisions, and *Miami Vice*. I smiled, watching the boys play in the water.

"Guys!" shouted Kristin from where she, Justin, and Jeremy were sorting out the saddlebags. "We're getting really worried about Michel. Shouldn't someone go back to see if they're okay?"

"I'll talk to the old man," said Tulga, coming out of the stream. But one of the guides was already shouting, pointing back down the trail to where two figures — Bodo and Michel — were walking, leading a single horse. The guide untethered the horse he'd just picketed, leaped up bareback, and went splashing through the cold stream and off toward the mountain at a fast gallop. He reached the walkers in a matter of seconds. We watched them deliberating, then all three came walking in together, leading the horses behind them. Perhaps a minute later they arrived in camp, Michel white as a sheet, dead on his feet.

"I couldn't stay on . . ." he mumbled. "Need to lie down. Be sick."

Fortunately, Michel's tent was already pitched. We laid him in there, and Justin fetched water from the spring, which he'd found bubbling out of the rock where the last low spur of the mountain's foot came reaching out almost to touch the little copse where the magpies flitted and the horses grazed and kicked out at the evening flies and each other. I prepared a fire. As I struck a match to the tinder, Rowan came running up behind me and threw himself on my back, saying, "How d'you make a fire, Daddy?"

He had never asked a "how" question before.

Then, as Kristin and I were marveling over that, Michel suddenly crawled halfway out of his tent and vomited louder than I have ever heard anyone vomit. It was so loud it rang off the mountainside.

Rowan, alarmed, ran up to where Michel, half dead with nausea, lay spitting into the mess he had thrown up and said, "Michel! Why are you spitting on it?"

He had never asked a "why" question before. Even Michel, wrecked as he was, managed to croak out in a voice like that of the undead, "I hope someone had a camera going. That was the most complex thing I've ever . . . heard . . . Rowan . . . say. Oh, God." And up came more.

A short time later Justin returned from the mountain. While up there he had seen something he was pretty sure wasn't that common — a white ibex.

Now, ibexes are rare enough, and elusive even in places such as this where they are (at least comparatively) plentiful. I had glimpsed one once before, years ago, in the mountains of Turkey. They aren't an animal you see every day. But a white one? Tulga was impressed, and immediately told the old man and his boys. Who immediately went into a quiet huddle, talking among themselves in voices whose tone, low but urgent, suggested that something was up.

That night I slept with Rowan by my side. I heard him talking in his dreams: "Buster, Lily, Blackie." And somewhere in there too the word *ibex*.

There was something about this place.

Next morning we woke to find that three of the horses had disappeared, including Blue and Tulga's horse. And Michel was worse than before. It seemed we could not go on.

18
FARTHER UP AND FARTHER IN

"You know, Ru," Tulga said to me as the old man detailed two of the younger men to go off in search of the strayed horses, "the old man and the others, they were saying that maybe the shamans are testing us. Your accident in the bog. Michel getting sick and losing his horse. Now three more gone. And Justin last night on the mountain — what he saw was so rare, unusual. They are saying that the ibex was the shaman coming down to look at us, to decide whether he will accept us or not."

We were huddling over camp coffee in the morning's chill. My lip hurt like the devil. Michel lay prostrate in his tent, groaning. Should we go on without him, leave him here by the spring with one of the guides and enough food and shelter to let him recover — have Jeremy take the camera? It was going to be a hard, hard ride today, up and over the far-off high pass we'd glimpsed yesterday. Assuming we could even make it over the pass today, for it was at least eight hours of steady climbing.

Anyway, it was a moot point now, unless the four horses could be retrieved.

What had happened to make them run? I'd been asleep, but Tulga and some of the others said they'd heard disturbances in the night — maybe predators coming around. Wolf? Bear? Or maybe just the horses fighting, as horses tethered close together will sometimes do, snapping their tie-ropes in the fray.

"But here is one thing good," confided Tulga, taking a sip of coffee as Rowan and Tomoo chased each other around in the morning sun, the magpies from the little copse across the stream chattering loudly at them. "The old man says he thinks the white ibex is a sign that Rowan has been accepted. If Justin had seen a wolf or a crow or a bear up there, that would have been a bad sign. A sign for us to turn back. So the old man thinks we won't be here long."

We kicked our heels at the foot of the mountain till the sun was high overhead. Stuck. Stuck in beauty, but stuck nonetheless. Around ten or so Michel began to revive, though he looked white as a ghost.

"I think I can do the ride," he croaked as

he emerged from the tent. "The stomach cramps have gone. Maybe it was just a twenty-four-hour thing."

"Or a reaction to the water you accidentally drank yesterday at lunchtime," offered Kristin.

"Don't remind me." He turned to Tulga. "When should we start?"

"We won't start at all unless the guides find the horses we've lost."

"We've lost more? Not just mine?"

"Yes," I said, kicking the dew-sodden grass.

"Oh."

To have come so far — to have to turn back now would be agonizing. Well, I suppose if it came to it, maybe I could just carry Rowan up that mountain and over the pass. To turn back was somehow unthinkable.

Then I heard shouting, hoofbeats; looked up. The younger guides were coming back along the foot of the mountain, grinning from ear to ear, leading Tulga's horse and mine at a gallop. That meant we were still two horses short, but if we left some of our bags here and made one of the packhorses into a riding horse . . .

And so half an hour later we were on the move once more, even Michel, weakened as he was, climbing heroically back into the saddle. We rode single-file along the banks of another stream that tumbled down from the heights, which we now began to climb.

The pass for which we were making, still distant and blue, if not a mere haze on the far upper horizon, was now discernible as a saddle between two jagged peaks, one of them still streaked with snow, even now, with July about to turn to August. Could we really make it? Tulga had given his usual nervous laugh when I'd asked him that morning. We were in the lap of the gods now. Anything could happen — and probably would. So I just concentrated on the ride, giving Blue as much rein as possible as we climbed by stages through forest and natural meadow, crossing and recrossing the rushing river, its cold splashing water a cool relief from the heavy heat of the sun now high overhead.

"Daddy to sing!" So I sang "The Girl I Left Behind Me" again, over and over, in a low voice, as we rode farther up and farther in. "Sing the scubby-boy song!" demanded Rowan as the need for variety kicked in. Thank God he wasn't demanding to get down and play today, but seemed happy to settle in for the long climb. So I sang the scubby-boy song, which went like this:

He was a scubby boy,
A little scubby . . .

And Rowan sang, "Boy!"

He was a scubby boy, a little scubby . . .

"Boy!"

He was a scubby boy, a little scubby . . .

"Boy!"

He was a scubby boy, and his daddy ate
his . . .

"Head!"
At which I had to take a huge pretend bite
of his head, making a big scrunching noise,
as if biting into an apple, and say, "Hmmm,
not bad."

Over and over, up along the rushing river.
"Going to see the reindeer people with
Buster and Lily and Blackie!"

And then we were in the territory of the
reindeer people. We knew, because as we
reentered the forest at a higher elevation,
the last of the flower-strewn riverside natural
pastures behind us, we saw horses' skulls
nailed to the trunks of the great pines and

larches whose overhanging branches cast the trail into a sudden midday dusk.

"Put there for the Lord of the Mountain," said Tulga as we passed the eldritch offerings. "And a request too — the offering is always the head of a good horse. They hope the Lord of the Mountain will send them another just as good if they offer the skull."

I remembered my mother's old copy of Larousse's *Mythology,* the section on Finno-Ugric spirituality, and the reproduction of early photographs of horse sacrifices — skulls and hides on larch poles reaching up to the sky — taken somewhere in Siberia, east of the Urals. The image had made a powerful impression, stirred some ancestral memory. Here we were now, entering that world in real time. And dreamtime. For there was something of dream in this forest, this ride.

"No reindeer antlers on the trees?"

"No — they use horses too," Tulga said matter-of-factly. If he was feeling any dreamtime, he certainly didn't show it. "Actually," he went on, "they don't ride reindeer anymore." My heart sank as he said this. I'd wanted to see reindeer being ridden as they had been since time immemorial, since before the horse was domesticated. I wanted Rowan to be able to ride a

414

reindeer. I'd promised him he would. Well, maybe they'd organize something . . . Tulga was still talking. I quieted my thoughts to catch his words: "They use reindeer for other medicine, I know that."

What medicine? I wondered. Something to do with the shamans? Would the reindeer spirit somehow be harnessed to help Rowan? We rode through a woodland colored purple with rosebay growing taller than the horses' bellies. A hoopoe, a dove-sized bird with white spots and a strange circular crest on its head, swooped low across the trail. We rode in silence, the trail steepening, our pace slowing, the forest at once cool and close with humidity. Would there be a storm to deal with as we tackled the pass? Lightning on the high ground — would that be another shamanic test, like the one the guides seemed to think we had undergone the previous night? Some kind of trickster game to see how serious we were? We didn't even know if Ghoste the shaman would be there when we got to the other side of the pass. And why did we have to come to the bloody other side of the world to see a shaman anyway? Why was this something so far-fetched, so exotic to us as Westerners? After all, we had once had our own shamans.

But we had annihilated them. Or done our best to. The Romans did it first, crushing the Druids of Britannica and Gaul. Then the church, between about 1400 and 1700, did its best to stamp out what vestiges remained. In Western Europe, this was by that time mostly just old village wise women who knew their herbs. Generations of them were put to the stake. There were shamans of the older, pre-Roman kind still living on the outer edges of Europe — among the Lapps, or Saami (also reindeer herders), of northern Scandinavia, the tribes of the Baltic, and some pagan hermits in places like Cornwall, Wales, Scotland, Brittany, and the Basque country. But even these remote areas were aggressively Christianized, many shamans paying the ultimate price for holding on to their traditions. The church, both Protestant and Catholic, did everything it could to burn them all.

By the eighteenth century, when the burnings finally stopped, the physicists and apothecaries of the Enlightenment had to relearn everything: anatomy, natural sciences, herbology — all the things that underpin modern science and medicine. But fundamentalism and fanaticism had not died. Instead they had split into two parallel branches, one for religion, one for science.

Such, it seemed, was our inheritance.

We plodded on, ever uphill, the forest crowding closer. Even Rowan sat quietly now, relaxing against me in a way he hadn't since we'd left Texas, letting his whole body weight rest on my right forearm as it held the reins. My other arm was around his waist, steadying him. On either side of us the forest crowded in, the only noise the sigh of the wind in the pine boughs, the burbling song of the river, and the muffled thump of horses' hooves on pine needles.

My thoughts traveled back to some of the shamans and healers I'd met. Charles Siddle, the horse healer; Besa, calling the leopards out of the night; old Antas, running her hand over Cait's abdomen as she lay supine on the red sand, singing the cancer out of her body. None of it could be explained. Then again, neither could autism.

A story came to mind that Michel and I had been told by a medical anthropologist at George Washington University, Dr. Richard Grinker. Dr. Grinker had an autistic child — a daughter — of his own and had turned his research toward seeing how other cultures viewed autism. While in South Africa, he had come upon a Zulu family whose son had the condition. The grandparents had wanted the child to see the local *sangoma,* or witch doctor. The child's parents, however, being educated and Westernized, had wanted to pursue Western therapies. Eventually, to please their elders, the parents consented to let the *sangoma* see their son. After two days of observation, the *sangoma* said he had found out what was wrong with the child. It was a "white man's disease," he said, called "autism." To the amazement of both the parents and the grandparents, the *sangoma,* who attributed the onset of the disease to ill-wishing on the part of the father's bitter ex-wife, advised that the child be taken away to the city, where he would not only be away from the evil influence of the jilted ex-wife but would get the therapies for autism that he needed. Meanwhile, the *sangoma* conducted rituals to lift the curse. It didn't matter to the *sangoma* which method was better, his or the Western therapists' — the point was to use both, to try every weapon in the medical and spiritual armory.

I looked down at my son sitting in the saddle in front of me, smiling as Blue flexed his hocks and trotted up a steep portion of the trail behind Tulga's horse.

"Whatever works, eh, mate?" I said to Rowan.

He came out of his reverie. "Let's go see

418

more shamans!"

"But of course, m'sieur," I said, adopting a mock French waiter's accent à la Monty Python. "Comin' right up!"

We followed the rushing river. Pied wagtails bobbed on the rocks as the water flowed by them, flicking their tails up and down. Trout jumped. Overhead a golden eagle, larger than the steppe eagles we had seen almost daily since leaving the city, cruised the heights, casting a moving shadow over the bright water. I stole a glance up the long valley, more gorge by now, of the river. The pass we were heading for was still distant, blue, impossibly remote. Hardly any closer than it had seemed when we had started out.

Tulga, riding in front of me with Tomoo, turned and said, "I think the bad bog, the dangerous one the old man was talking about, is up ahead. After that it should be easy to go faster. If we have to camp on this side of the pass because it takes a long time to get to the other side of the bog, we should still be okay. The reindeer people are just on the other side."

"But it'd be better to cross the pass today, in case the shaman's at a farther camp."

Tulga nodded — that much was evident. We rode awhile in silence, the mountains rearing up before us, around us, the going getting deeper underfoot.

"You know," said Tulga after some minutes, "I've noticed, with Rowan, he's been losing his animals but he isn't getting upset like he was at the start of the trip. Remember the first day?"

"The puddles in the rain, you mean? God, trying to find his animals with my toes in the water."

Tulga laughed. "Now he leaves them at all the campsites. On all the mountains."

"I know — and he's stopped tantrumming about it. It's weird."

"I was thinking," said Tulga. "Maybe he's leaving his animals as offerings to the Lords of the Mountains."

We entered the bog suddenly. I was scared as the horse began to sink, slip, and struggle, remembering what had happened the first evening. Rowan showed the first fear he'd shown since the fall we'd taken, whimpering a little as Blue sank down to his hocks a few times. I tried the Code Brown joke; it worked. But soon the bog became so deep, Blue's movements so violent as he and the other horses floundered, belly deep, trying to get through the mire, that talk became impossible. I just gave Blue the reins and let him find his own way, expecting any moment to feel him disappear completely, fall sideways, praying, praying to get through safely, while Rowan, to my amazement, contained his fear, leaned his body back against mine, relaxed, trusting.

When at last Blue and the others pulled clear of the last sucking, holding mire, Rowan calmly turned to me and said, "Daddy to give Rowan a lollipop?"

"You bloody well bet Daddy will give Rowan a lollipop," I said, fishing for one of the dwindling supply in my jacket pocket. "You're so brave."

"A brave little sausage," said Rowan, using an Englishism I had often said to him, but for the first time.

"Oh, darling," said Kristin, riding close behind us. "Oh, darling."

"Rowan is a brave little sausage," he said solemnly, taking the lollipop I had just unwrapped.

"Yes, you are, my darling," said Kristin from her chestnut horse, now black to the belly from the bog. "Yes, you are."

The river valley broadened out into a large gravel shoal, the forest and mountainside rising steeply on either side. Snow and ice, caught in sections of the river where the shade persisted for most of the day, streaked the gray shoals with white.

"Get off and play in the snow!" Rowan wanted to twist down, out of the saddle. But time was so short.

"We'll stop and play in the snow when we come back this way in a few days, okay?" I promised, bracing myself for the inevitable tantrum.

"Okay," said Rowan, his voice quivering a little. But no tantrum. I looked back and caught Kristin's eye.

The track leveled some. We began to find stretches where the horses could trot out or even canter a few steps before a dip or twist of the river forced us to rein in. We started to cover more ground. Following the old man, we crossed the river a final time and put the horses at a really steep section of forest trail — so steep that for one heart-stopping moment I thought Blue, scrabbling for purchase on the near-vertical bank, might tip over backward. I got as far forward as I could without crushing Rowan, felt the horse try once, twice, then find an extra gear to launch himself up the final steep bit. I patted him, praised him, as he kept toiling up, amazed at the strength, the huge heart of this little horse, wishing I had grain to reward him with at the end of the day.

On we went, through more bog, the forest so thick we were bumping our knees against the tree trunks, the larch, pine, and aspen branches brushing our faces. I grabbed handfuls of larch needles, munched them, and gave them to Rowan too. They were high in vitamin C, and that and the sugar from the lollipops I now kept feeding him would, I hoped, keep his energy up. We had been more than six hours in the saddle today, with no end in sight. If Rowan was tired, however, he wasn't showing it.

Unlike the rest of us. We stopped for a breather — and to let the heavier-laden packhorses catch up to us — in a high meadow set in a natural bowl of rock screes leading up to the pass proper. We tied the horses to young trees, sat down on the ground, stretched tired legs, rested sore bottoms on the soft, mossy turf.

"I don't know if I can go on any farther," said Kristin, holding up her knees as she lay, trying to ease her lower back, which always gave her problems but which now, after so long in the saddle, after such a long absence from riding in her daily life, was on fire with pain. I didn't know what to say. The pass, though much, much closer now, still had to be crossed.

"The guide says we still have two hours to go to make it over," said Tulga. Kristin groaned, while Rowan and Tomoo, seemingly tireless, tumbled in the grass. Even the crew was too tired to film. The flies found us again now that we were out of the trees. I lay facedown, to protect my raw lip from them, and reached out a hand to gently rock Kristin's lower back to and fro, to and fro, the scent of mountain flowers and pine drifting over us. Under my hand, I felt Kristin's breathing slow, felt her dropping into sleep. Rowan and Tomoo were under Tulga's watchful eye. I closed my eyes too, pressing my face into the sweet-smelling turf.

Only to feel, a moment later, Rowan jumping hard with both feet onto my back. I rolled over. Rowan and Tomoo were laughing, laughing. *"A monster!"*

So I lay back, pretended to sleep, doing cartoon snores.

They jumped on me again. *"Wake up, Daddy! A monster! Groooar!"*

I fell back again, pretending to sleep once more. Rowan jumped on me. *"Wake up, Daddy!"*

A few moments later Kristin creaked slowly to her feet. I followed. The guide, seeing us rise, immediately went to his own horse and mounted. The packhorses could catch up before evening. I picked up Rowan and plonked him in the saddle, holding my face back out of reach as he tried to swing again at my now very tempting lip. As I did so, I heard a loud *poc,* then a scream.

Kristin was down on her back, writhing, holding her knee, with Jeremy and Tulga leaning over her. "The horse kicked her," they said helplessly as Kristin tried to contain tears.

"Mommy to smile," said Rowan worriedly. "Mommy to not cry."

"How bad?" A kick can shatter a human legbone, no problem. Immediately I was thinking about how we would get a broken-legged Kristin out of this remoter-than-remote place.

"Not too bad," Kristin said between clenched teeth. "I think I'm okay."

She struggled to her feet, limped over to where the guide, his face impassive, held her horse ready, and despite the pain of her back, her leg, hauled herself into the saddle once more.

"I'm so proud of you," I said, somewhat lamely, wishing I could do something to make it better.

"A brave little sausage," said Rowan, right on cue.

The laugh got her up to the foot of the pass.

Which took one hour, not two, as the

guide, perhaps wanting us to feel we were making better time than we were, had predicted. But what an hour. We came up above the treeline, high above the last meadow where we had stopped, and saw a rampart of cold gray granite rearing up before us. The only way up was via a narrow track that ascended a two-hundred-foot-high pile of sand and dirt, originally rock crushed by the winter ice, then piled up against the side of the mountain wall during the short two months of the year when the pass had no snow on it. All around rose the higher peaks, ice and snow still clinging stubbornly to their tops. The track upward was so narrow, so treacherous underfoot, that in a couple of places it disappeared altogether, the horses having to cut a passage in the loose dirt of the slope with their hooves. I tried to keep Rowan's weight centered so as not to throw Blue off, for one false move could send us hurtling down the almost sheer cliff of loose earth.

That was the moment Rowan chose to initiate the let's-swing-around-in-the-saddle-and-smack-Daddy-on-the-raw-lip game.

Part of me wanted to shout at him; part of me didn't want to mess with his upbeat mood, the fact that he was so happy, that he was being such a trouper. So I held my face firmly to the right, as far out of reach as possible, while leaning forward to get our weight off Blue's laboring hocks. It helped not to look down.

And that was how, blowing flies from the red goo of my mouth and holding my face stiffly away from my maniacal son, we reached the top of the pass, reined in, and let the panting horses recover their breath.

We looked back at the way we had come, the mountain gorge and its river sweeping down and away to an unthinkable, unquantifiable vastness of forest, green upon green fading to blue. Siberia. Remote and unconquered. To the north was tundra — the high tops of the mountains above the snowline, like Scottish moorland but vaster, streaked with stubborn snow, little streams and peat hags crisscrossing a moist, boggy terrain of little meres, sphagnum moss, heather, and tough grasses, here and there dotted with stunted pine. The summer pastures of the reindeer people. At last.

The wind up here was intense, whipping at hair, clothes, and the horses' tails and rattling the blue silk prayer scarves on the big *ovoo* of piled stones that had been built at the top of the pass. We walked round it once each in turn, leading the horses. Giv-

427

ing thanks.

As we descended the other side, into the high tundra, faces reddened by the wind rushing up to pour over the pass, Tulga stopped us and suggested that we dismount, because not all horses from the steppe were used to reindeer. "Sometimes when they meet them for the first time they can be scared."

"You mean they might freak out, dump their riders, and bolt?" I asked, knowing what the answer would be.

"Maybe little bit." And then came the nervous laugh.

So we climbed down. I took Rowan on my shoulders once more and led Blue, feet slipping and sinking a bit in the peaty mud of the trail. No matter; it was only a short distance to get around the shoulder of the mountain, on the other side of which, Tulga promised, lay the reindeer people's camp.

So I sploshed on, Rowan sitting sidesaddle on my right shoulder, singing "The Girl I Left Behind Me." We had made it after all, with two hours of daylight to spare. We rounded the turn of the hill, hearts pounding: it isn't every day you come upon one of the most ancient human cultures on the planet.

But there was no reindeer encampment.

Just a long, wide valley of peat bog and moss, ringed by the peaks of the great range on whose high tops we walked, their upper heights streaked here and there with snow. Just that and the wind, sighing in the marsh grasses.

19
THE GHOSTE AT THE
TOP OF THE MOUNTAIN

We walked a mile toward another great arm of moorland that came sweeping down from the broad heights, cutting off the rest of the valley from view. It grew colder, Rowan's weight grew heavier, the going grew muddier underfoot. The late light shone gold on the horses' flanks, picking up the lights in Kristin's long brown hair as she led her horse in front of me.

"See the reindeer people?" asked Rowan.

I sang "The Girl I Left Behind Me" one more time. We rounded the bend in the muddy trail, the water in the peat hags reflecting pink, gold, and orange sunset. No reindeer people.

My shoulder was hurting. If we were going to have to camp tonight and travel another day, as it looked, I might as well let the horse do the carrying. Of Rowan, at least. So I put him back up.

"Ride on Daddy's shoulders!"

"Daddy's shoulders are ouchy. But Blue is strong."

"Blue is strong," my son agreed, or echoed. "Where are the reindeer people?"

"Up here. We're going to find them. Soon."

I prayed to God that I wasn't blowing smoke at him. That these guides had been honest. That they truly did know the reindeer people, and the shaman, as they had said. Or were we simply tourists to them? Eager to see the reindeer people, gullible enough to take anything on trust? We kept walking, the light over the high tops dusting the snow-streaks pink. It would be dark within the hour. Would Rowan tantrum when we made camp without meeting the reindeer people as promised? Would he feel I had broken my word? *Had* I broken my word and dragged him all the way up here for nothing?

The stream that we had followed since coming down from the pass widened to a deeper, stronger flow, cutting its way deep into the peat moss of the moor, a low ridge marching along its farther, northern bank. The ridge rose briefly to the height of a small hill, then tapered gradually off into the thin light between sunset and dusk. I stole a look down at the trail. Deer tracks.

Reindeer tracks.

And there, far away at the foot of the ridge, where it gave out into the wider valley, were three tepees. And out in front of them, silhouetted against the green of the ridge behind him, a great bull reindeer crowned with massive curved antlers.

"Reindeer!" shouted Rowan, spotting the beast and wriggling to get down. "Let's go ride a reindeer!"

Ah, I had promised him that, hadn't I? Rowan was half off already. I looked around and called for someone to give Blue's reins to. Jeremy rode up, dismounted, and took them as the rest of the group congregated around us, the horses shoving their heads down to get at the good green grass that grew by the streamside. Rowan was already down, moving excitedly toward the reindeer bull on the farther side of the stream. I had to marvel at his stamina.

The terrain was deceptive — not level, as it looked, but humped and tussocked, terrain that as soon as you left the trail was designed to trip you, make you stumble, catch your ankle in the deep clefts between one soft, mossy tussock and the next. Rowan fell and got up again, making single-mindedly for the reindeer, which stood and looked at us thoughtfully, chewing on the grass it had been cropping. I expected it to turn and run at any moment. Rowan had now reached the little river. He was clearly going in, so I picked him up and swung him across, and he set off doggedly once more toward the antlered animal, which, suddenly realizing that the two humans were truly approaching it and weren't going to quit, suddenly wheeled around and bolted up the ridge.

And then there came a sound I had never heard before. A strange rushing clicking, like many thousands of knitting needles, or far-off castanets. Rowan and I both stopped, looked up in the direction of the sound. A whole herd of reindeer, many hundreds strong, was coming at a run down along the far side of the stream, being driven by a young man on a gray-white horse. The sound, I realized, was being made by the reindeers' hooves. I had read about this. Reindeer have flexible, movable hooves, which widen, giving greater purchase, as they go across snowy or boggy ground. Travelers' accounts from Arctic and sub-Arctic journeys describe the clicking sound of a herd of reindeer on the move. The young man drove the herd toward the three big tepees, bringing them to pass the night in relative safety from the wolves that, Tulga said, preyed on the reindeer people's herds.

A young man driving his herd of reindeer down from the mountains toward the tepee camp: I was looking back at 40,000 years of human history, back to the ice-age beginnings of my own heritage, my own people, my own culture. Kneeling there with my son, our knees in the spongy, wet moss, I knew I was living a moment that was perfectly timeless, where the ancient past and the present meet. The moon rose higher, and the reindeer disappeared, hooves clicking, in the dusk.

We set up camp, put up tents, got a fire going. As the flames began to grow strong, three visitors appeared: a young man, short, in camouflage army fatigues and rubber boots, and two very graceful, very small young women, beautiful as elves, with long black hair cascading down their backs. One wore a black leather jacket that looked almost tailored, the other a funkier, shorter silk jacket striped in turquoise and gold; both looked incongruously fashionable against the backdrop of high, bare mountains. They were talking with Tulga and the old man while the guides saw to the horses. As Rowan and I came up to the fire, they looked at us with curiosity.

"Hi, Ru," said Tulga. "This is the shaman's

434

son-in-law. I've just been explaining why we've come."

I smiled, we exchanged nods, and the young man spoke.

"He says the shaman, Ghoste, is expecting us. We should go talk to him. I just wanted to wait to tell you before I went. We'll go now, I think, me and the old man, and hopefully the shaman will accept us."

"Let's hope," I said. "I don't know if I could face coming all the way up here just to be turned away."

Tulga laughed his nervous laugh and called to the old man that he was ready to go. "One thing," I said, as the two men walked off into the gloom. "I know the reindeer people don't ride their deer anymore. But I promised Rowan, and he's been so good. D'you think you could ask, if it seems right, whether tomorrow Rowan could at least sit on one? If they have any that are that tame? It means a lot to him."

"I'll ask," said Tulga, and then he was gone, his voice and the old man's sounding low together in the rapidly gathering dusk, a low bass counterpoint to the rushing song of the river.

And so we waited, sitting on our sheepskins, looking at the dancing flames, feeling the fatigue of the long day's ride settle into our muscles, our bones, listening to the tethered horses snort and stamp, crop the sweet mountain grass. Even the two little boys finally came to the end of their energy and laid their heads on our laps — Rowan on Kristin's, Tomoo on his cousin Bodo's — eyelids drooping in the soft firelight and the stars winking overhead.

"I wonder if we should turn in," said Kristin sleepily. There was a general murmur of assent.

But at that moment Tulga and the old man appeared out of the dark.

"The shaman wants to see you," said Tulga.

"Now?"

"Now."

So once more Rowan was scooped up and placed on my shoulders, and in the pitch black, walking slowly so as not to trip on the humped and tussocked terrain, Kristin and I followed Tulga and the old man.

"We're going to see the reindeer shaman," I told Rowan.

"*Whack, whack, whack* on the back," he replied, holding on to my hair and giggling.

"Let's hope not," said Kristin from the dark behind me.

A flat stone slab had been placed across the narrowest part of the stream, where it looped close to the tepees. I lifted Rowan down, swung him across to Tulga's waiting arms, and went up the far bank, above which loomed the large, conical silhouette of the tepee, a small square of light showing from its low doorway, the scent of cooking meat, herbs, wood smoke, and incense emanating into the night.

"Want to go inside?" I asked Rowan.

"Go *inside!*" he confirmed, scrambling down to ground level and scampering into the tepee after Tulga and the old man.

"Wait for me!" I ducked inside too, Kristin close behind me, and entered a scene as timeless as the land itself.

Candlelight, and the orange glow from the small wood-burning stove that stood at the center of the circle made by the great tepee of reindeer hide, twenty feet across, warm as toast inside, everything stored around its sides, helping to shut out the drafts that might sneak in where the tepee met the ground. There were many people inside. I recognized the oldest of our guides, or at least the oldest of the old man's nephews, as well as the young man who had received us when we first arrived, still in his camouflage combats and black rubber boots. But the rest were people I had not seen before — mostly men, some in *deels,* some in ragged Western castoffs. There was one woman, apart from Kristin, a young woman with high cheekbones, fleshy, sensual lips, and a big, handsome face, elegant in her *deel* and with her long hair tight in a bun. She must have been in her early twenties, I guessed. Her son, younger than Rowan, watched as she conducted us to the only part of the tepee where no one was yet sitting. Tulga and the old man had already taken their places next to the group of small, almost pixielike men — considerably smaller, lighter built than the Mongolians we had met before, and more delicate of feature.

The kind of random thoughts that often come unbidden in such situations came in rapid succession as I conducted Rowan across the space to where we were to sit. Here we were with people from the oldest culture in northeast Asia, who lived in tepees. Was it any wonder that people thought that Native Americans, the only people to use similar tents, came from here originally? Though why, then, did no Native Americans herd caribou? And the pixie look — maybe that was a cultural stereotype, but was our British and European folklore about fairies, pixies, in fact a memory of ancient forest peoples long displaced by Celt, Roman, Saxon, Viking? And the fear of pixies, or piskies, who might take your child and replace it with a changeling who would not hear or see, who'd behave oddly, seeming disconnected — was this some early folk explanation for autism? The thoughts rose like bubbles and dispersed. We sat down in our section of tepee, next to the shaman, with thick rugs between us and the mountain turf.

The shaman's face was hidden by the shadows of a wide-brimmed hat until he looked up. He had one of those faces that imprint themselves immediately on the mind, burning itself into the memory. Perhaps sixty years old, but strong and fit. Broken nose, small mustache, eyes set almost too wide apart below a much-lined forehead. Handsome in a beaten-up, ironic, faintly guarded-looking sort of way. Heavy-lidded eyes. Smoking a roll-up and regarding us with an even, measuring gaze. He spoke, words I could not understand, his voice a little harsh-sounding, petering out into a cough.

"He says he'll help the kid," said Tulga as Rowan crawled freely around the tepee, over people's laps, saying, "Hello, I think it's a person!" over and over, making them laugh, until he made his way back to us. "But,"

Tulga went on translating, "no cameras. And it will be expensive." He paused, looking nervous again. "Five hundred dollars?"

I was taken aback. "U.S. dollars?"

That uncomfortable laugh. "Yes. I think it is a lot."

I looked at the shaman. Before leaving Ulaanbaatar, Kristin and I had taken out exactly that amount in local currency from the ATM at one of the larger hotels, for contingencies. We hadn't used a nickel of it, not a penny. Now we were being asked for this amount exactly. I looked at the shaman. The laughter and low conversation in the tepee had died down. Were we being tested?

"Sure," I said. "Tell him no problem."

I was used to healers charging. The Bushmen healers do the same, though seldom that much. And of course if someone can't pay, he gets healed anyway. But we *could* pay, so why shouldn't we? A part of me was taken aback by the straight-up directness of the demand. Another part reasoned that we'd pay a therapist for any services rendered, so why not a shaman too? In this land he was considered a professional, as much as any therapist was in ours. I looked at Kristin. She shrugged.

The shaman got up. He too was wearing the *deel,* the long robe. In his wide-brimmed hat, his eyes hidden from view by its shadow, he reminded me of an image from an old book of Norse myths I had had as a boy, of the god Odin, who hung for nine days on the tree of life, a raven pecking out one eye, in order to gain knowledge. Odin, who also wore a wide-brimmed hat. Like a shaman — *one who knows.* I was tired, letting my romanticism run away with me.

Rowan was making the rounds again. I was surprised how comfortable he was with all this. Impressed that he was still awake, still going.

The shaman went to the space immediately behind him, a place hidden by a low curtain, reached inside, and drew out some dried herbs, which he then placed on the hot plate of the wood stove, scalding them so that their scent — astringent, familiar somehow — went smoking out into the gloom of the tepee. Then he knelt in front of Rowan, who was now back in Kristin's lap, and began to tap him gently with the scorched sprig. Rowan started to scream, but I could tell it was only a reflex. A moment later he was quiet, giggling, trying to grab the herbs as the man tapped him about the head, neck, and shoulders.

"Can you feel that?" said Kristin out of the side of her mouth.

"No." I kept my voice low while the shaman tap-tapped. "What?"

"Pins and needles. All up my arms. Really strong. You can't feel anything?"

"No."

The shaman, Ghoste, stopped his business with the herbs, turned to Tulga, and asked some abrupt-sounding questions.

"He wants to hear Rowan's story — from you."

So we told him. About the autism, trying to describe how it was to have a child who seemed not fully there, the neurological firestorms that would course through his body, the tantrumming, the impossibility of toilet-training, the feeling of being completely shut out. We told him about Betsy and what had happened between her and Rowan. We told him about Rowan's exposure to the shamans we had met when we had brought the Bushmen over to the United States from Africa soon after his diagnosis. How he had seemed to lose some of his autism symptoms for a few days but had then regressed. How his middle name, Besa, was for a shaman, a healer from the Bushmen whom I was close to. How Betsy, of all the things we had tried, both orthodox and not, had seemed to affect him the most strongly.

The shaman said, through Tulga, "Tonight I will make a journey. To America, where you come from. To work with Betsy, the horse, because she is his protector. Tonight I want you to notice how Rowan sleeps. And tomorrow — you must be very honest — tell me how he slept. Anything unusual, or anything at all. You must tell me. Then tomorrow night I will work on him. You should go now."

And so we went, back out into the dark, Rowan on my shoulders once more, trying to feel our way safely over the broken ground, the slippery stone bridge, the humps and tussocks between the stream and our camp. The night had turned pitch dark. Stars and moon were hidden by cloud; it smelled like rain.

We did the nightly ritual with the vodka, the crushed herbs, Rowan now crying, "Go to sleep! Cuddle with Mommy. Time for a cuddle-cuddle!"

I did the honors. Kristin's hands and fingers were still numb from the pins and needles.

And so we went down to sleep, here at the top of the mountain, at the end of perhaps the longest day of our lives, wondering what was to come.

20
A HAWK
IN THE HOUSE

Somewhere around dawn — a cold, wet dawn with rain spattering on the tent wall — I heard Rowan scream. Heart sinking, for I could tell by my own dry eyes that we hadn't slept that long, I roused myself. It was cold. Was that why he had woken? He was screaming loudly enough to wake the camp; Kristin's attempts to calm him were failing. I unzipped their side of the tent. He was thrashing, unhappy, short of sleep, exhausted.

"Maybe he needs to pee," I wondered aloud. I certainly did. So I hoisted him, still crying, out into the cold gray drizzle and took him behind the tent. Sure enough, he needed to. Would he ever be able just to ask to go like a normal kid? Would we always have to unlock the cause of every tantrum with a process of deduction in the face of screaming and thrashing?

I took him back to the tent. God, but it

was cold up here. I climbed in next to Kristin, Rowan between us, giving him extra warmth. He was asleep again in seconds. As were we.

We didn't wake until the sun was high — at least momentarily so, before another rain front came pouring in over the mountains. The others were up already, sitting in the cover of their tents drinking tea, watching the rain fall over the tepees across the river.

Rowan kept sleeping. Deeply, powerfully, not waking even when Tomoo came running over and put his face in, smiling. I made tea on the little gas stove we had brought up on the packhorses, along with the other kitchen supplies, and took it back to where Kristin still lay next to our sleeping son.

"He's really out," she said, almost wonderingly. He never slept this late, with the daylight playing on his face.

"Well, after yesterday, I'm not surprised."

"True. It's still unusual, though."

I nodded, sipping tea, watching the rain.

"I had a dream," said Kristin suddenly. "After we all went to sleep again."

"Oh?"

"Betsy and a leopard were lying down in a field together."

"Really?"

Ghoste had said he was going to work with Betsy last night. Was this the power of suggestion? Kristin knew about my time with the healer Besa and his gift to me of the leopard as a kind of totem. After that first time I'd seen him dance and the leopards had circled the fire, whenever I was with him I saw leopards, close to his hut or crossing the road at night as we went to another healing. You don't see leopards that often, even if you live in the bush.

"A leopard and Betsy lying down together in a field," repeated Kristin. "Interesting, no?"

"I guess." I didn't want to give it too much credence. Not yet. Just because we had met the shaman didn't mean I couldn't maintain a healthy skepticism — for now, at least. Until you see results you have to, whether it's a shaman, a therapist, or a Western doctor. Of course I wanted her dream to mean that Betsy and I, or some essence of us, were protecting Rowan in some way. I wanted it so much that I said nothing but watched the rain until Rowan finally woke.

"Go see the tepees," he said immediately, clambering out of the sleeping bag with a record fourteen hours of sleep behind him, and set off barefoot for the river, oblivious to the rain. "Let's go see the reindeer. And the shamans!"

"Hey! Wait! You need to have some breakfast first!"

Rowan's face crumpled, tears starting. *"Tepees! Go see the tepees!"*

"Don't you want some bacon first? Daddy will make it fast."

"Then we'll go see the reindeer."

"Yes, Rowan, and the tepees."

"And the shamans."

"First bacon, then reindeer, then tepees, then shamans, okay?"

He weighed this a moment. "Okay."

Somewhat mollified, he consented to come back to the small fire that the guides had kindled. Tomoo joined him. Seconds later they were wrestling and laughing as usual, while I chased an industrial-sized load of bacon around the pan, intent on getting as many calories into him as possible after his grueling ride. And who knew what demands this day might bring?

But in fact the day brought relaxation and delight. The rain cleared; a warm sun came out, lighting up the high tops and making the river sparkle. A day of wonder. Almost on cue, once Rowan had done eating, we heard the telltale clicking sound again and saw a rider — a lone male rider — approaching us from farther down the valley.

On a reindeer.

"So they *do* ride reindeer still!"

"Reindeer! Ride a reindeer!"

A minute later the man, small, slight, reined in the gentle-eyed, huge-antlered creature at the fireside where we all still sat. Rowan and Tomoo were both jumping up and down with excitement. The man, who had come from another reindeer camp farther down the valley, had brought crafts to sell: exquisite reindeer carved from antler; homemade hunting knives with wicked blades and horn handles; pendants made from the incisors of a maral, which Tulga said were used to ward off bad dreams; reindeer-skin bags decorated with scenes of bears, foxes, deer, hunters, people riding reindeer, all embroidered in colored threads. And a little white ibex carved in bleached bone. Just like the one Justin had seen on the mountain.

Not that the boys noticed, as Tulga and I lifted them onto the reindeer together. They were ecstatic. They hugged each other and ran their fingers through the soft coat of the reindeer while the smiling man led them around in wide circles on the turf, their laughter pealing in the air like birdsong. Then Rowan rode the reindeer alone, sitting on it and thoughtfully, gently feeling the soft summer velvet that covered its antlers.

"Are you happy or sad?" I asked him.

"Happy. Look, he's got antlers. So soft."

A short time later we heard the rushing clicking sound, like thousands of distant castanets, of the main reindeer herd being brought down from the mountain toward the main camp. Rowan was off the reindeer he was riding in a moment and heading for the tepees.

"Do you think it's okay?" I asked Tulga as I trotted behind him, unsure whether I should stop him.

"I think so, yes. Go on," he said. So we did, crossing the river by the little stone bridge once more to find that, in a large cleared area between Ghoste's tepee and the two others and a little apart from where the main herd was corralled, several fluffy gray-brown baby reindeer lay contentedly enjoying the sun, tethered to small wooden posts. Rowan just about left his body in delight.

He threw himself down next to the nearest of the five or six impossibly cute creatures, which, far from exhibiting any alarm, merely batted its Marilyn Monroe eyelashes at him and let him snuggle close. His fingers moved over the little creature with the delicacy of butterflies dancing. He squinted into its eyes, holding its head close. It gave him a lick. "Look," he said softly, his fingers still moving with delicately exquisite touch. "He's got a nose . . ." His fingers drifted over the little creature's nose, making it sneeze. "He's got eyes." He fluttered over the liquid globes, which blinked. "He's got a little butt . . ."

"Hey, don't —" I began, then stopped myself. This was no time to interfere. Rowan's joy was intense, perfect, innocent. No scolding adult voice needed to intrude.

Instead Rowan sat up and began to sing, his hands marking gentle time on the baby reindeer's back (it closed its eyes in apparent bliss at the touch).

He was a little reindeer
Little, little cute
He had a little face
And he had little hooves
And eyes and ears and a little butt butt

"What's his name?" I asked when the song was done.

"Abracadabra," said Rowan, then got to his feet and pointed at each of the tethered baby reindeer and named them in quick succession: "That's Abracadabra, and Daisy

450

and Pink, and Nellie and Zoo-Zoo, and Wilbur."

Kristin and I looked at each other, collectively melting under the barrage of cuteness.

Wilbur was the smallest baby reindeer of all, and almost pure white. "With a pink nose," whispered Rowan, plonking happily down next to it. "Wilbur has a little pink nose. And a tongue," he added, as Wilbur licked him. The corralled adult reindeer looked on from under their forest of curved, sculpted antlers, their hooves clicking as they shifted weight, their strong scent (not good, not bad, just deer) carrying over the mountain breeze. Though we could hear voices from the tepees, both adults and children, no one approached us, interfered with us, even came to sit with us. Whether from absolute lack of curiosity about who we were, a mistrust of strangers, or a deep respect for our right to our personal space — or all three — we were left alone while Rowan sang his song to Wilbur, and despite myself I felt the tears well up.

So the afternoon passed, Rowan eventually drifting away from the baby reindeer ("Bye-bye, baby reindeer, we'll see you again very soon") to the second two tepees, wandering into them with his usual genial trust, surprising the families there while I shrugged and smiled apologetically. Everyone must know why we were here, so any breaches of etiquette were forgiven, I hoped. Anyway, what could we do? Finally Rowan, remembering, said "Tomoo?" and flitted back across the stream and over the rough ground to the camp, where several other reindeer herders from down the long upland valley had now gathered, also intent on selling crafts. Some had arrived by horse, others by saddled reindeer. Rowan rode on a reindeer again, then, under the frankly curious stares of the children, suddenly jumped off and ran at Tomoo, shouting, "Wrestle!"

It was all going so well. So then, inevitably, depressingly, came the Code Brown. And with it yet another back-arching, alarmed tantrum, the shrieks echoing off the mountainsides as Kristin and I struggled to clean him yet again. And off I went with his soiled pants to find a boggy spot far enough from the river in which to scrub them clean. How many thousands of times had I had to do this? I was so used to it, so trained. And yet today I realized that I had had it. I found myself on my knees, scrubbing away at the mess, praying out loud: "Please, God, please let this end! Let this end! He'll be six in a few months, for chrissakes! Six! Please let this end! I'm so sick, sick, sick of this! Please end it!"

It wasn't just me. Early the day before, in the camp by the spring, I had found Kristin sitting with her head in her hands, having just done her turn cleaning Rowan up — for we were taking his accidents, as we always did, fifty-fifty. "I don't know if I can keep doing this, Ru," she said. "I know it's futile to talk about it like this. But sometimes I wonder if I can go on, you know?"

Something had to give. Please, God.

Back at the camp, the sale of crafts laid out upon the turf was still going full swing, and Rowan — clean once more, and eschewing crowds as always — had wandered off a short distance to play with his toy animals on a piece of cleared ground high above the tent. I looked at him. Would anything ever really change?

Then movement caught my eye from across the river. A young reindeer — not one of the babies — had been tethered apart from the main herd. As I watched, one of the young women, the one with the elegant black jacket who had come to greet us the evening before with her friend and the young man, Ghoste's son, came out of one of the tepees and led the beast away around the bend of the low, rocky bluff that stood above the Dukha camp.

"They will slaughter it." Tulga had appeared at my elbow. "Out of sight."

"For meat?"

"For medicine. It's part of the ceremony for Rowan, the old man told me."

I looked across at the old man, who was busy trying to wrestle Michel, waddling after him, laughing while the guides, Jeremy, Justin, and the reindeer people who'd come to sell us their crafts all looked on, grinning. "Why me?" Michel was pleading as the old man, arms outstretched, chased him around the camp. "Why me?"

"Part of the ceremony?" I pictured blood, animal parts. "Is that good?" I concluded, a little lamely.

Tulga, getting my drift, was quick to reassure me. "No, it's to make a medicine. To drink. You'll see. Part of what you are paying for with the ceremony is to buy this young reindeer."

"Oh, I see." In that light, the steep price seemed less outrageous.

"And half the money will be paid to the other two families here," Tulga went on. "The old man's been explaining it to me. It's to prevent any jealousy. And to make sure everyone benefits."

"So Ghoste himself only gets a small part?"

"That's what he said."

There was a roar of laughter, and we turned to see Michel leap high into the air, just avoiding a low grab at his crotch from the old man's hamlike hands.

"Why me? Jesus! Why me?"

I looked away, over to the bluff around which the reindeer had been led for its discreet slaughter, and repeated my prayer. *Please, God, let this work. Please. And* — to the reindeer — *thank you. And sorry. Truly. But if your death helps my son in some way, then I'm in your debt.*

Apologizing to a dead reindeer on a Mongolian mountainside before going to see a shaman in a tepee. God, but I must be desperate.

We had gotten up so late that day — or at least Rowan had — that the afternoon was already far advanced. The weather turned cold again, and several new lines of rain blew in, driving us back into our tents and the visitors away on their reindeer to take shelter in the tepees. We read Rowan his books, and he played *Lion King,* made Kristin sing the Carpenters song about a hundred times, and came and jumped on me, shouting, "Yak attack!" and "Raspberry attack!" As the light died, I made farty noises on his belly while he laughed uproariously and the rain beat down on the tent and Kristin and I wondered, in between raspberry attacks, tickles, and stories, what the ritual would be like. Would it be traumatic and difficult like the long ceremony outside UB had been?

"Once upon a time." Rowan came and put his face up to mine, wanting a story. "Once upon a time . . ."

"There was a little boy called Rowan," I continued. "Who went to a place called Mongolia to see some shamans, and he had friends there, Tomoo and Buster —"

"And Blackie and Lily the little girl rabbit!"

"And they got on horses."

"And got a bit *upset!*"

"But then it was okay again, and they went to a lake, and a spring, and traveled in a van, then got on horses again, and the horse was called . . ."

"Blue!"

"And they went up a mountain . . ."

"And Michel got sick!"

"He did, yes. Wow — that's amazing, Rowan. Good talking. Really. They went up the mountain and saw the reindeer people and Rowan rode on a reindeer!"

Rowan grabbed my hair and gave it a delighted yank.

"And he saw some baby reindeer too, and cuddled with them." More delighted hair yanking. "And the smallest baby reindeer was all white and Rowan gave him a name. He called him . . ." I sucked in my breath.

"Wilbur!"

"That's right!"

"Wilbur's *so* cute!" Another good hair yank.

"Want me to go on with the story?"

"On with the story!"

"Okay. Well then, after Wilbur, Rowan went to the tent to play, and to wait for the shaman . . ."

"Whack whack whack on your back!" He giggled.

"Well, I hope not, I have to say. And after the shaman . . ."

Kristin and I looked at each other. After the shaman, what?

Michel appeared at the tent. Apparently the old man, who'd taken something of a shine to Michel, had persuaded Ghoste to allow him to film. "Which is good news," said Michel. "But I'm only allowed a small light, so I don't know what I'll get."

"I'm pretty amazed he's allowing any filming. Most of the Bushmen healers I know don't. Or not unless they know the film-makers. You're lucky."

"So what do you think is going to happen?"

"I don't know, mate. I just don't know."

Sunset turned to dusk. "Go see the shaman?" Rowan asked several times.

"Soon."

Well, at least he seemed to want to. That was good.

Rowan and Tomoo were playing sword fight again, the rain having cleared once more, the first stars coming out overhead. The waxing moon came up above the pass, washing the streaked snow and ice on the high tops with pale blue light. But you could see almost as clearly as at dusk. The boys tumbled about. I watched them, marveling at how normal it now seemed to watch Rowan playing with a peer. Ten days ago he'd been incapable, uninterested, unreachable.

As I sat there on one of the saddles to keep it dry, Tulga loomed up at my side. "I think it's time."

One last check-in with Rowan, just to make sure his voice was heard. "Rowan, shall we go see the shaman now? Yes please or no thank you?"

"Yes please!"

I scooped him up on my shoulders, and off into the dark we went, all of us, the guides too. No one was going to miss the ceremony. We had just reached the river and were following its bank to the little stone slab footbridge when the wave hit me.

"Jesus," I said, staggering, Rowan's weight lolling as I righted myself and put him down on the ground, unable suddenly to bear his weight.

"What's the matter?" Kristin stopped.

A wave of nausea — no, not quite nausea, a sort of extreme dizziness. Sudden, unexpected. A great wave of saliva welled up in my mouth, forcing me to spit.

"Oh, God," I said, doubling over. "Listen . . . You may have to do this without me. I . . . uurgh." I spat again as another great gob of saliva came inexplicably into my mouth. There was some kind of white noise in my head.

"Shaman! Go see the shaman!" Rowan protested, hating the delay.

"Everything okay?" asked Tulga.

"Don't know. I think I might have what Michel had. Or food poisoning." I spat again. Where was this saliva coming from? The only thing I'd ever experienced that was similar was once years before in South Africa, when someone had offered me a drug called mandrax to smoke. Curious, I'd tried it, and had promptly lost the use of my limbs for an hour, shuddered violently, and experienced the same massive saliva production. "I'm going to try," I said, getting control of myself. "But I may have to . . ." I paused to spit yet again. "I just may not make it."

"Shaman! Shaman!"

So we went on, me holding Rowan's hand now, as I didn't trust my balance. The dizziness washed over me in waves. Across the stone slab bridge we went once again, me going slowly like an old man, afraid of tumbling in, spitting every few feet as the saliva just came gushing up like oil from a well.

No sooner had we scrambled up the stream's far bank and come level with the tepees than the dizziness ceased. The saliva stopped. My head cleared. I was myself again.

"It's gone," I said, wondering. "It's okay."

"You sure?" Kristin was worried.

"Yes. Whatever that was" — my mouth was dry, normal — "it's passed."

We were outside the lighted doorway of Ghoste's tepee.

"Go inside!" shouted Rowan excitedly, bouncing up and down.

"Oh," said Tulga from next to me, "we have to go first and give money to the other two families. Then we go to the shaman. That is the way it is done."

That meant Rowan would have to wait — never his strong suit, especially when it came unexpectedly. "Listen, Scubby," Kristin was already explaining. "Daddy just has to go visit the other two tepees quickly, then he'll come back and *then* we'll go see the shaman. Okay?"

"Okay," said Rowan.

Tulga and the old man, who had materialized out of the night, took me to the two tepees, both of which were full of people — small, huge-eyed, delicately featured, so different from the burly folk of the steppe. Were the tepees so full of people because the visitors from down the valley had decided to stay while the shaman worked? No one explained. Instead, as instructed, I removed my shoes, bowed, accepted and drank a bowl of hot, salty, milky tea — the reindeer milk tangy and sharp on the palate — and counted out bills to the head of each household. Owl-eyed, impassive, they nodded as they accepted the money. After a few minutes we were back outside Ghoste's tepee, everyone still waiting for us, Rowan included, patient, unworried, not his normal self at all.

I looked at Tulga. "Shall we?"

He turned and asked the same question of the old man, who nodded, leaned down, and lifted the door flap. We stepped through, into the square of yellow light.

It was as before — a full house, or full tepee, Ghoste's handsome niece welcoming us into an already fairly crowded circle around the warm stove, which occupied the middle of the space. The older two of our guides were already seated, along with several of the Dukha, but space was found for Michel and Justin, with their equipment, as well as for Kristin, Rowan, and me, in the same spot we'd sat in the previous night, next to Ghoste.

The requisite reindeer-milk tea was served, and Ghoste asked how Rowan had slept. We told him — the first part of the night soundly, then a strange distressful wake-up at dawn, then back to sleep for the longest time we'd ever known him to sleep, at least since he was a small infant. We also told him Kristin's dream about Betsy and the leopard lying down together. Ghoste nodded as all this was translated, then got to his feet. The half-light cast by candles, stovelight, and the one portable filming light that Michel and Justin had brought made almost a dream figure of the shaman, who put out his arms for the heavy, beribboned shaman's coat that his niece now helped him don.

The coat hung from his powerful shoulders. Ghoste next reached out for the headdress and mask, made of hawk's or eagle's feathers. As he placed it on his head, hiding his face, transforming himself into something not quite beast, not quite human, Rowan — who'd been sitting unusually quietly — said, "Wow! Look! Look at that! A hawk. A hawk in the house!"

Tulga translated for the old man, and a quiet chuckle went around the circle. It died as Ghoste was handed his large round drum and fur-clad drumstick. Suddenly he seemed massive, the transformation complete. As if he had one foot in the spirit world already. A solemn moment.

"I'm a baby elephant!" shouted Rowan, getting on all fours and marching up and down in front of where the shaman stood, impassive. *UURWUUUURRR!* he trumpeted, happy as a clam. Ghoste, undisturbed, cocked his drum at the ready and, softly at first, then louder, began to tap out the rhythm on which he would ride to whatever other place he went to when his business was to heal.

Rowan stopped to listen. "Look, he's drumming. The shaman is drumming!" He giggled. "Baby elephant!" And around Ghoste's legs he scooted, trumpeting once more, grinning from ear to ear.

The drumming continued, growing louder, faster, Ghoste whirling suddenly, his feet instinctively avoiding Rowan the same way a horse instinctively avoids a fallen rider prone on the ground. I reached forward, grabbed Rowan, and brought him into my lap. The drumming grew louder still, faster. And with that Michel's film light suddenly, inexplicably died, leaving only the pale light of the fading dusk.

The drumming ceased. Ghoste was singing, chanting. He barked an order. A hand — presumably his niece's (it was hard to see in the gloom) — offered him a small, shallow bowl like the ones the shamans had used in the ritual outside Ulaanbaatar. He reached down and handed it toward Rowan. I could see it was filled with reindeer milk.

"Good bloody luck," I thought as Rowan, quiet in my arms till that point, flinched away and threw out an arm, which caught the little bowl and sent it flying.

But as if expecting this, the feathered, masked figure that was Ghoste deftly flicked out the arm that held the drum, caught the bowl on the drum's taut skin surface, and tossed it back down onto the ground at our feet. Ghoste stooped, peering at it, then picked it up, handed it back to his niece's hand in the gloom, and resumed his dance.

He stopped suddenly, put down his drum, doffed his headdress, leaned down, and offered it to Rowan. Delighted, Rowan reached out, took it, put it on his own head, then reached back and put it on mine.

And with that the ritual was over.

We didn't realize it at first. But a moment or two after Ghoste had taken the headdress back, he shrugged off the shaman's coat and handed it to his niece, along with the headdress, sat down, and reached into his pocket for a cigarette. He said something to the circle of faces and lit up.

"He says it's done," said Tulga.

I looked at Rowan, rolling happily around on the rug at my feet, being an elephant again. We'd been in the tepee perhaps twenty minutes. That was it? Kristin and I looked at each other. Ghoste was speaking again.

"He says," translated Tulga, "that we shouldn't stay here too long. That there is a lot of spirit activity here now and too much might be bad for Rowan. We must go back to the camp. He asks that you and Kristin come to see him in the morning."

"With Rowan?"

Tulga relayed the question to Ghoste. "He says yes, with Rowan, but that even tomorrow the spirit activity here will be very high. After you have come to see him here, we should pack up. He will come to say good-bye to us, and after that we should camp just a little way over the mountain, on the other side of the pass. Not here."

"Okay." It seemed so sudden, so truncated. So low-key after the high drama of the first ritual near UB.

"Go now," said Tulga, translating once more. "He says it isn't good to stay much longer here where the center of the spirit has been."

So up we got. "Come on, Rowan," I said. "Time to go back to camp."

In the tepee Rowan had found a cookie tin with cartoon animals on it that said *Huggy's School* and, lolling happily on his back, holding the tin close to his chest, he looked at me with horror. "Shamans!" he shouted, bursting suddenly into tears. "Stay here! *Stay with the shamans!*"

But Ghoste was adamant. So out we went, Rowan screaming, crying, *"Shamans! More shamans!"* into the frosty air. There was an unusual note to his distress. He sounded really heartbroken and was sobbing as if he'd been separated, say, from me or from Kristin. Back to the tents we went, walking slowly in the dark, Rowan sobbing on my shoulders. "More shamans! Shamans! Shall we go see the shamans? Okay, let's go see the shamans! *There they are, there's the shamans!*" He was trying to comfort himself, poor little guy. But why?

21

INTERVIEW
WITH A SHAMAN

The morning dawned misty and mild, a light fog covering the ground with sunshine overhead. From the clicking sound that carried through the tent walls I knew the reindeer herd was grazing close today. Sure enough, antlers were showing above the light mist not a hundred yards away. We had been here long enough now for the usually shy beasts to want to investigate us. I got up, greeting the day, and went off a little ways to piss, the mist lifting visibly, the nearer reindeer, scenting my urine, lifting their heads to snuff. The reindeer people's little wolflike dogs were prowling around the edges of the camp. Every now and then they would get too close to one of the tethered, grazing horses and an angry hoof would fly out, narrowly missing the dogs as they furtively ate the horse droppings. I could hear voices — our guides were stirring. We'd have to pack up this morning, and that would be a long process, I knew. Kristin's and Rowan's gentle snores still sounded from their side of the tent.

The ceremony the night before had been the complete opposite of what I had expected. No drama. No histrionics. So low-key it had left me a little perplexed. And then there had been Rowan's heartbroken reaction to having to leave.

I wandered over to the fire, where the old man and the other four guides were cooking venison, its smell delicious in the morning air. The previous evening a large quantity of meat from the young reindeer that had been slaughtered as part of the ceremony (though for quite *what* part of the ceremony I couldn't yet tell) had been delivered to us. Now, as it cooked in its own juices in a pan on the open fire, its rich scent made me salivate. No wonder the wolflike dogs were hanging around. The old man, supervising the cooking, looked up and smiled as I came over and handed me a piece. It tasted of the forest, the mountain. After so long on noodles and mutton fat, the reindeer was . . . I was too busy gulping to think of words.

"Go see the shamans?"

I looked around to see Rowan already heading for the river and the tepees beyond it. Was it too early?

"First bacon, then shamans!" I called after him. To my surprise, he stopped what he was doing and, though a little whiny and teary, came over while I went to the kitchen tent to find some breakfast for him.

Kristin appeared at the fireside. "Talk about dreams," she said, squatting down to warm her hands by the small flames. "I had another one last night. I have to tell you now, before it fades. My grandmother — you know, my mom's mom. I saw her and her son walking away, hand in hand. He was grown, a man, not a little boy like he'd been when he was killed. But it was him. Then I woke up."

I handed her some tea. "I've been praying," I said.

"Me too."

"Go see the shaman!" wailed Rowan.

Several times over the next hour or so Rowan tried to make his way over to Ghoste's tepee. Each time we delayed him, not wanting to go barging in on the shaman too early in the day. And though Rowan wasn't happy about it, he didn't fly off the handle as he usually did when gratification was delayed. He was adamant, though. Finally he just left his game with Tomoo and started stomping toward the stone slab bridge. Feeling that he'd held himself together long enough, we called for Tulga to come help, and a minute or two later we crossed the stream once more.

"Shaman! Let's go see the shaman! Let's go inside!" chirped Rowan, barging his way past the tepee's flap.

"Rowan, wait!" It was futile. We entered behind him, making apologetic noises.

As before, Ghoste's handsome, silent niece received us, conducted us to the spot where we had sat the previous two nights, and handed us a bowl of salty reindeer-milk tea while Ghoste, his wide-brimmed hat partly shading his deep-set eyes, cast a professional-looking eye over Rowan, who went straight for the Huggy's School cookie tin with the cartoon animals on it. For some reason there were captions on it in English: a cartoon bear saying "Be clean and cool," a cartoon kitten saying "Be happy and help-ful," and so on.

"Be happy and helpful," said Rowan, read-ing the caption. Kristin and I looked at each other. Not bad.

"So," said Tulga, translating as Ghoste began to speak. "He says there are some things you should know before you head back."

"Okay."

"First, Rowan must have these." Ghoste leaned across and gave me three small stones. "Take these home and add four from your own place and put them under his pillow at night."

"Okay." I took the stones and secreted them in a small inner pocket of my coat. "Any significance to the number seven?"

Tulga asked the question for me, but if there was an answer, Ghoste didn't give it. Instead, he said, through Tulga, "Last night was good. Rowan accepted the healing. That was the important part. When I offered him the milk in the bowl and he rejected it, it was because of his condition, not a real refusal. I could tell because when the bowl fell, it landed right side up. That was very important. Then when I gave him my headdress, he took it and put it on his head. Better still, he then put it on yours, and then gave it back to me. If he had refused to take it, then the healing would not have worked. In fact, it worked better than I expected."

"Be smart and special," said Rowan, happily reading the Huggy's School tin.

"You know that Rowan will be a shaman — that's what Ghoste is saying," Tulga went on. "Unless you, both of you, do something . . ." Tulga fished for the words. "Something, er, *deliberate* to stop it. Unless

472

you do that, then a shaman is what Rowan will become. Ghoste is saying that . . . that he was like this himself as a child. He was a baby in his mind until about nine years old and he had . . . falling down?"

"Epilepsy?" suggested Kristin.

"Yes! Yes, I think so. I think that is it. Epilepsy, yes. He had this, er . . . *condition* until he was twenty-five. Ghoste says that a child like this, like Rowan, is marked out to be a shaman. A part of him is already in the spirit world."

"Does that mean we have to try to become shamans ourselves?" I asked. "I mean — well, I mean, do I have to train to become a shaman in order to help Rowan learn? Is that what Ghoste means?" Tulga translated the question.

"No, you don't have to do that. But every year from now until he is nine, you have to do at least one good ritual like this. It doesn't matter where, but with strong shamans. Somewhere in there Rowan will meet the shaman who will train him. Or later. It doesn't matter. It's no big deal if you do stop him from becoming a shaman. Nothing bad will happen. It's just . . . this is his" — Tulga paused, trying to find the right word — "destiny."

"I see."

473

I thought a moment, watching Rowan play. He was happy here. Such a complete contrast to the nervous anxiety he'd started the trip with. "The number nine," I said. "This keeps coming up. The shamans outside UB also said Rowan would need a good ritual every year till he turns nine. You've talked about nines too — ninety-nine gods and all that. What is the significance of the number nine?"

Tulga translated. Ghoste just smiled.

"Well," I went on, realizing I wasn't going to get an answer, "can you tell him that I have a relationship with the Bushmen in Africa? In fact, Rowan is named for a shaman, a healer there, that I'm very close to, named Besa. Rowan's middle name is Besa."

Tulga translated. Ghoste replied.

"He says that if you have this kind of contact, and if Rowan already has . . . what he is calling it is a 'shaman father,' then you must either take Rowan there to see him or bring this shaman to you."

"The only problem is that I'm banned in Botswana. Can you tell him I did some human rights work there for the Bushmen, helped them win a land claim, and now the government has banned me."

Tulga translated and then, when Ghoste

had given his answer, said, "You will find a way. It's very important. If Rowan has a shaman father already, then he must go to him. It will help a lot. Also, he says that the shamans here, they have heard about the Bushmen through some of the NGO workers that come through here. And also in their spirit journeys. They know the shamans in Africa are the most powerful."

He paused while Ghoste went on. "He's asking how the shamans in Africa, the Bushman shamans, do their healings."

Ghoste listened, smoking his roll-up as I told him stories about the Bushman trance healings I had seen. "As far as I know," I told him, "the healers there use an energy they call *nxum*. Which I think is similar to what the Chinese call *qi,* or *chi.* They've described it to me as a sexual energy, a life energy, that resides at the base of the spine. With the right system of training, of exercises, a healer can bring this energy around into the stomach and make it boil. It's very painful — I've seen them bleed, collapse, great streams of mucus coming out of their mouth and nose. Then they go into a more blissful state, which they call *nxaia,* which means, I think, 'to see.' What they see then is an interconnecting web, connecting everything. Some of the strands have differ-

475

ent colors. There are green ones, which you can take if you want to physically travel somewhere to heal someone far away. Then there are red ones, which have to do with black magic and have to be avoided. You can't get the Bushmen healers to do black magic, though there are other medicine men from other tribes down there who will. And finally there are the white or sometimes silver lines, which come down from the sky. They call these 'the ropes to God.' When they see them, they use a song that's been given to them while in a trance when they were young, to climb or swim or fly up these ropes.

"When they get to the top, they find a village where all the ancestors live. The biggest hut in the village is God's. God can appear as a person or an animal or something in between, or a light, or a fire, or a voice — whatever is relevant to that situation, I guess. The healer and God then sit down and bargain over the dilemma, the soul of the sick one, whatever, and then, when they're done, the healer goes back down the rope, back to the fire, and puts his hands on the people who need healing, pulling out the bad stuff and throwing it away. That's about as much as I can say."

Tulga, manfully translating this esoteric

diatribe, came to a halt too. Ghoste nodded, spat, took a drag of his cigarette.

"Much the same here," he said. "Take him to his shaman father in Africa. It'll come clear how to do that. Oh, and he can take that if he wants." Ghoste indicated the cookie tin, which Rowan had evidently fallen in love with. He also gave me a small bundle of herbs wrapped in an old piece of plastic. "Keep this with you, in something you wear a lot, when you get home."

"Okay," I said, secreting it away with the little stones he'd given me earlier. "Tulga, did you tell him about Justin seeing the white ibex on the way up here? Does he think that's significant at all?"

Tulga translated. Ghoste's face gave nothing away as he replied. "That mountain, it's a sacred mountain. You can see anything there."

"Okay."

"And when we go back down, on our way home, he says we mustn't camp at the foot of it like we did last time. You know, where the spring was. Too much spirit activity again. We have to make sure we go on a mile or so."

"Okay. I guess you'll tell the old man that, Tulga?"

Tulga nodded as Ghoste spoke again.

"And now he says we should go," said Tulga, getting to his feet. "He says there is also still a lot of spirit activity from last night here. We should move over to the other side of the pass as soon as we can. We must pack up — he'll come in a little while and wish us goodbye."

"All right. Please tell him thank you from us."

"Yes," agreed Kristin, "please tell him that."

As we were halfway out the door, Ghoste said something more.

"He says . . ." Tulga looked nervous. "He says that yes, Rowan will be getting gradually less and less autistic till he's nine. After that you, Rupert, will take over from Betsy as his main . . . protector."

"What does that mean exactly?" I interrupted.

"I don't quite know. I'm sorry. But he also says the bad behaviors, the stuff that drives you crazy, you know . . ." Tulga reddened like a schoolboy. "The toilet problems, the tantrums. Those will stop now."

"Now?"

"Yes."

"Now, like today now?"

Tulga relayed the question. Ghoste nodded.

"Now. From today. Yes."

Kristin and I looked at each other, not knowing what to say.

Back at the camp a little later, Rowan started to get upset because I wanted him to put on an extra coat (more rain clouds were coming in over the pass). I threw my bread at him in frustration. He stopped, the whine dying on his lips. "I'm sorry," he said. I looked at him. He'd never said that to me before.

As the guides began the long process of packing up the horses once more, Rowan took his dwindling supply of animals off to a cleared space a short distance above our camp. With the little wolf-dogs still hovering about the edges of the camp, I kept a weather eye on him while helping Kristin pack up the tents and saddlebags for the guides to tie onto the horses. As always, it took a good hour before the loading was done to their satisfaction. A good thing too, as any misplaced weight could send a horse tumbling down the cliffside on our way back down the pass. As the last ropes were being tied, the last boxes and bags lashed onto the still-tethered horses, Tomoo said, "Shaman!" And we looked over to see Ghoste, his niece, and her little child walking over the rough ground toward us, already on our side of the little river.

The old man and the guides stoked up what was left of the fire and brought a kettle and tea, purposely packed on top of the outside box on the horse that carried the kitchen provisions. We all sat. Ghoste looked over to where Rowan lay playing with his animals and said, "That was my camp last year. Where my tepee was."

Interesting. Rowan seemed as comfortable there as he had in Ghoste's tepee. So much so, that when, at Ghoste's request, I went to fetch him to say goodbye, he cried and struggled, shouting, "Mountain! Stay on the mountain!"

"Don't you want to go see the shaman? Say goodbye to the shaman?" This seemed to get through. "First say goodbye to the shaman, then come back and play on the mountain?" I suggested. "Yes please or no thank you?"

"Yes please."

"Okay. Come on, then, take my hand."

So back down to the fire we went. I remembered that once I'd wondered if Rowan would ever do something as simple as hold my hand while walking. We'd come a long way, all of us.

Once at the fire, Rowan happily clambered

into Ghoste's lap and let the shaman run his hands in a light, feathery touch up and along his spine, from his pelvis to the crown of his head and back, all the while chatting casually with the old man, the guides, and Tulga. Watching his hands, I noticed that every time he completed a cycle of spine to crown and back, his fingers would make little flicking motions to the north and west, as if flicking something away. I'd seen the Bushmen healers doing similar things when pulling sickness out of someone during the gentle final stages of a trance dance, toward dawn, when the high drama was done and a peaceful feeling had settled around the fire. There was something of that same feeling now. The easy, relaxed chatter, Rowan happily eating a chocolate cookie, Jeremy snapping Polaroids to pass around.

When the time to take formal leave finally came, Rowan gave Ghoste a hug and didn't make so much as a squeak as the man and his family walked back to their side of the river. When we finally came to mounting up and I said, "Okay, Rowan, say goodbye to the reindeer people," he said, "Bye to the reindeer people" without a qualm.

"Trot!" he ordered as Blue's hooves squelched through the peat and mud. "Trot!"

So we trotted, Kristin jogging along behind us on her chestnut gelding, the afternoon sun warm overhead. Upward, along the long miles until the gradient of the slope pitched sharply up toward the lip of the pass, where the wind blew hard and cold and all Siberia stretched out below.

"Snow! Get down and play in the snow!" Rowan eyed the frozen white strip up on the highest top. *"Get down and play! With the animals in the snow!"*

It was time to dismount and walk once around the *ovoo* to ask the Lord of the Mountain for protection on our way down the treacherous pass. "We'll go and play in the snow farther down the mountain," I said, not really expecting him to take it in. "Come on, up on Daddy's shoulders. Let's lead Blue round the *ovoo.*"

"Okay, we'll play in the snow later on, down the mountain."

No tantrum. Not even a whine.

Down the steep side we went, down the earthen cliff with the treacherous narrow path. I led Rowan, thinking it safer than for both of us to sit on Blue's back as he negotiated the tricky path.

"Daddy to get up!" said Rowan.

"It's safer if I lead you. Here," I said. "Why don't you hold the reins?"

"Daddy to get up!"

"Just give it a try, just till we get down the really steep stuff." My heart was in my mouth — this was the most dangerous part of the mountain. Not forgetting the river, of course. And the bogs.

"Buster says, hold the reins." His temper, having risen, evaporated out of him like steam.

"Yes," I said, bemused, pleased. "Buster holds the reins. He's a very good rider. Do it like Buster does it. Yes, that's right!"

Rowan was holding the reins, sitting upright in the saddle, not slouching or holding on but riding. Dangerous as the trail was, I let go of the bridle and walked out in front.

"You're riding, Rowan!"

"Just like Buster."

"Look, love!" I called over my shoulder to Kristin. "Look!"

We made camp in the same high meadow we had stopped in on our way up the mountain, before making our final assault on the pass — where Kristin had been kicked (she now sported a fine crescent-shaped bruise on her inner thigh as a mark of her heroism). A natural amphitheater set between the rocks of the upper pass and the forest below, the little meadow was awash with flowers. Purple, orchidlike pedicularis, yellow cowslips, blue columbines carpeted the ground. Bees, drunk on nectar, buzzed unsteadily from bloom to bloom. We dismounted, our horses suddenly shattering the stillness with a series of whinnies and squeals as Michel's horse, riderless, came thundering down the mountainside behind us. Had he fallen off again? The horse, white as snow, came hurtling downhill so fast that when it put its foot into a ditch or gulley hidden by bushes, it suddenly turned head over heels. It somehow righted itself and went galloping on down the mountain trail, past the meadow, with one of the younger guides in hot pursuit.

I looked at Rowan, who was lying on a rock in the center of the meadow, playing *Lion King* with his animals. He watched the drama with mild interest. No sign of any distress, even though the horses were screaming loud enough to start rocks tumbling down from the cliffs above.

A short time later, Michel having come in on foot, with only his pride injured, we pitched the kitchen tent. Rowan appeared just as I was busy preparing his bacon. "Water?" he asked. "Daddy to give Rowan some water?"

Just out of curiosity, to see what he'd do, I

said, "Sure, you can have some water. The water bottle is in the side pocket of your bag, which is in our tent, in the middle section, between the two sleeping compartments. Why don't you go get it?"

A minute later Rowan tapped me gently on the back as I squatted down to put his bacon in the dented frying pan. "Daddy to open it?"

Damned if he hadn't gone and got it. That had been the most complex set of instructions I'd ever given him, and he'd just trotted off and done it. I unscrewed the bottle cap, looking at him carefully, wondering what other surprises might be in store.

That night he went to bed without a murmur. Everyone was tired and turned in early, leaving only Tulga, Justin, me, the old man, and Michel to sit up under the bright moonlight. The meadow was drunk with it, and soon so were we; we'd kept a couple of bottles of vodka, and I'd gone to crack them open. I felt like celebrating. Something had lifted from Rowan. I could feel it. Something had changed up there on top of the mountain.

I took another drink, toasted the moon, the mountain. Next to me Michel yawned. "Well, I think I'll be turning in." He rubbed his thigh where a bruise was coming up.

The old man looked at Michel, rubbing his leg and laughed drunkenly, and slapped him hard on the back.

"Yes, well." Michel got up. "I *really* think I'll be turning in now. Good night."

He wandered off toward his tent. A moment later the old man got up and followed. Tulga, Justin, and I looked at each other in disbelief, then burst out laughing as a girlish shriek erupted in the night.

"Guys! He's trying to wrestle me!" Michel's voice went up a notch from girl to choirboy. "Guys! I'm serious! Guys! *Guys!*"

"Thanks for not helping me," said Michel next morning. He was half joking; either the old man hadn't been serious, or Michel's hasty retreat into his tent after the old man had grabbed him in a wrestling hold in the dark had been taken as a no. Or perhaps the old man was just winding Michel up. Either way, our attention was elsewhere, for the time had come to take the reindeer medicine.

The fee for the healing had not just included the purchase of a half-grown reindeer for meat (we were breakfasting on the delicious venison again, sitting around the fire in the morning sunlight); it had also included the recipe for a soup, a medicinal

486

soup, that Ghoste had told the old man how to make.

So here we were, looking at the thing. It had been brewed inside the reindeer's stomach, or one of them anyway, and was a kind of menudo that Tulga — translating for the old man as he held the stomach up between finger and thumb — told us was composed of a piece of every organ of the reindeer's body and . . .

"And also a piece of . . ." The nervous laugh again. "Feces."

"You're kidding!" Kristin looked at the stomach, which was bulging ominously.

"Shit soup?" We were all incredulous. Tulga gave his nervous laugh. The old man, still holding the steaming stomach up for view, smiled wryly at our evident squeamishness, as did the rest of the guides, who had wandered over, attracted by the laughter.

"It's no joke, then. That really is the medicine?"

"Yes." Tulga laughed again. "It really is."

"All right," I said, taking a breath. "In for a penny. Rowan has to drink this too?"

"If possible."

Kristin and I exchanged looks, then laughed outright.

"Maybe you could cook his bacon in it,"

suggested Justin, who had just joined us, having spent the morning collecting specimens of the incredible wildflowers that dotted the meadow. Daava, the old man's son, had been schooling him in their medicinal uses — the white, lily-looking one for coughs and chest complaints; the deep royal purple, orchid-looking one for menstrual cramps and constipation; and a selection of differing green herbs for bringing down fever.

"Genius," I said, going to fetch a pan. "Still," I asked, over my shoulder, "think we should try to get even just one spoonful neat into him?"

"Maybe it would be good to try," said Tulga.

Kristin was skeptical. "Good luck."

So into the pan went seven strips of bacon. We were running low again but had just enough to see us through three or four more days. Soon it was sizzling away in a liquid soup of reindeer medicine, poured in by the old man.

"Okay." I cleared my throat. "Who's going to try it first?"

Everyone looked at me.

At Tulga's order, the old man poured some out into a spoon, brought from the kitchen tent for the purpose. I took it, looked dubiously at the brown liquid, then took a deep breath, put it in my mouth, and swallowed.

"Yup," I said, trying not to gag. "Totally disgusting. Better have another while I'm on a roll."

I took three more. The liquid was luke-warm, rancid-tasting. I choked the last one down. "Who's next?"

"Me," said Kristin.

I gaped at her. She had been a vegetarian for more than twenty years. "Now that's heroism," I said, meaning it, and nodded for the old man to pour some more of the noisome liquid into the spoon. She took three of them.

"Sure you're not going to divorce me?" I asked as she swallowed the last one.

"Talk to my lawyer," she joked as Michel stepped up to take his turn.

In the end we all took it — no one wanted to chicken out. And Rowan, quiet and happy on his rock, playing *Lion King,* chomped his medicine-infused bacon down. Still, it nagged at me. If this was truly medicine, maybe we should try and get at least one spoonful into him. Kristin was of like mind. So, quaking inwardly at the inevitable explosion, we filled up a spoon with one more squirt from the now almost empty stomach and crossed the meadow to his rock, me holding the brimming spoon at arm's length so as not to spill.

He took one look, guessed what was coming, and erupted, screams ringing off the mountainside above. As we had gotten used to doing with regular medicines, I grabbed the arms to minimize the flailing while Kristin tipped the spoon into his mouth. He gagged and spat most of it over his body, but some went down. We held him, crooning, while he thumped and kicked us, the pitch of his screams rising, rising . . . and then, quite suddenly, stopping. The outburst had lasted a minute, tops, and Rowan was back to his game.

As we walked back to the tents, leaving him be, Kristin asked, "Hasn't that been the first tantrum since —"

"Since yesterday morning, when he didn't want to put on his jacket. And even that one didn't really count." I had had the same thought.

And even this last one was, to be fair, more protest than tantrum proper. It seemed hardly credible. Our lives *were* tantrum. Tantrum and the spaces in between. Twenty-four hours without one: it was unheard of.

22
MIRACLE
AT THE RIVER

Farther down the mountain, at the wide
stretch of river where the snowbanks still
clung to the shady side of the wide, wolf's-
willow-grown banks, Rowan asked to get
down and play. We sat, letting the horses
graze as he and Tomoo set up the few
remaining toy animals on the white crystals,
which in truth were more ice than snow.
After a while I joined them, gathering snow
into scrunchy little balls that I tried to throw
but that vaporized in the sunlight almost as
soon as they left the hand. Not that it mattered to the boys, who knew an invitation to
fight when they saw one. Both tackled me
at once. I went down under them, tickling
and pushing snow into their laughing faces
as Rowan thumped his head on my midriff
and Tomoo, a good little wrestler in training, tried to lift my legs to prevent me from
getting up.

When we were done and it was time to

mount once more, we gathered up Rowan's toys. Simba, the *Lion King* toy, the most treasured one of all, was missing. Somewhere in our rough-and-tumbling, we must have kicked it off the snowbank and into the river.

"It's gone," I said, bracing myself for the storm.

"It's gone," said Rowan wistfully. "Gone into the river."

And with that — *that* — he trotted up to where one of the guides held Blue at the ready. Shaking my head, I followed, lifted my son on board, and swung up into the saddle behind.

The mountain was so beautiful. Perhaps it had rained more on the days since our ascent, because the flowers were more intense than before. At Rowan's orders we trotted and cantered through great swaths of purple rosebay, the warm wind in our faces, while in a strange, guttural voice, Rowan recounted disconnected phrases about Buster, Lily, Blackie, and Lee Lee the baby elephant and Asha the baby rhino at Whipsnade Wild Animal Park, sounding like a humorous version of *The Exorcist,* arms pumping the air as if he were a crazed soccer fan as the horse moved beneath us. There was an ecstasy in this — Rowan's happiness, the leggy rhythm of Blue's fast-moving trot, the colors, the wind. I even forgot about the cold sore that was my lip.

We crossed and recrossed the fast-flowing river, the same golden eagle that had tracked us on the way up now doing so again. Our party became strung out over some miles, the guides, slowed by leading the pack-horses, falling gradually behind as we flew at a trot or canter across the great meadows and through the forest glades. We came under the shadow of the sacred mountain, the one where Justin had seen the white ibex, which Ghoste had told us not to camp on. On we went, up and over a low saddle until at last we were looking down on the wide, wide valley of the River Belchir once more, its great loops reflecting the mountains and sky, the grassy floodplain stretching lazily in the sunlight along the near shore, the forest, the great taiga, crowding close on the other like a dark green army of pine, fir, and aspen.

The last long hillside between us and the river was covered with royal blue flowers of a type I had never seen before — spherical, like thistledown, but not like any thistledown I had ever seen. The petals, stirred by the warm south wind, lifted and rippled across the meadow.

"It's like riding through fairy land," said Kristin, cantering level with me, dark and beautiful on her gelding.

"Look at the clouds," said Rowan, pointing upward as we rode. "Look! Just like a giraffe!"

We drew rein at the river. The sun was hot now, so as the guides tethered the horses in the shade of the willows, we stripped down to underwear and splashed into the clear, crystal water of the shallows. The water lapped off our backs, shoulders, washing away the tiredness and the dirt. The sand was soft and fine underfoot. Rowan waded in waist-deep, letting the water play over his outstretched, submerged fingers. I lay on the two or so feet of a sandbank, letting the water flow over me, dunking my head, watching the boys play.

Rowan rose out of the water like a little river god and began to run up and down on the sandbank, stretching his arms out. "Fly like a bird! Fly like an eagle!" Until all of a sudden he stopped, went up on tiptoes, and began to quiver: the Code Brown stance. I got up, ready to grab him and move him off into the willows so he could do it more privately. Then I changed my mind.

"Come on, Rowan!" I found myself shouting. "Come on! You can do it! You *can*. Just squat and let it go!"

And there and then I squatted down in my sopping underwear, make-believe pooping. Rowan looked at me with that deer-in-the-headlights look I knew so well.

"Ro-*WAN!*" Tomoo had come out of the water and was squatting down too. "Ro-*WAN!* Look!"

"Come on, Rowan, you can do it!" Michel and Jeremy were out of the water now, squatting down in their boxers too, shouting encouragement — a ludicrous sight. I caught a glimpse out of the corner of my eye of three of the guides standing in the willows watching, scratching their heads. Rowan, confused, stood and quivered on his tiptoes, hands flapping autistically.

"Come *on,* Rowan!" There was desperation now. "Come *on!*" I yelled, trying to temper my urgency with pretend humor. "Code Brown! Come on, you remember! Code *Brown!*"

Rowan ran off. Away up the sandbank, overwhelmed, scared, confused, putting distance between us and him. My heart sank.

Then he suddenly stopped. Squatted. And let fly.

"No way!" Jeremy's voice was loud on the water.

"GOOD JOB!" I screamed over the hundred or so yards that separated us. "Oh, Rowan! Good bloody *job!*"

"Oh, my God!" Kristin said.

I was jumping up and down, whooping. "I can't believe it! It's like watching England win the World Cup!"

Jeremy turned to me. "Well, mofo, I guess you got your wish."

We looked back again. Rowan moved to the water's edge, bent down, and splashed himself clean. By himself. His first intentional bowel movement, and then cleaning himself. Not thirty hours after old Ghoste had said it would happen.

"Incredible," said Tulga quietly to himself.

"I'M SO PROUD OF YOU!" I roared across the distance, the words echoing slightly from the water. "ROWAN! YES, *YOU!* MY SON! I'M SO PROUD!"

That evening Rowan asked me to take him riding. So, still barefoot from the river, I resaddled Blue and climbed back on board, and together through the meadow of wildflowers we ran and ran, to the foot of the mountain and back again, over and over, laughing, laughing, as the evening turned to dusk.

We made it to the river crossing in record time next morning, flying along at a gallop beside the broad brown water at Rowan's behest. Any vestiges of fear were totally gone, as he laughed, shouting, "Run! Run! *Chuh! Chuh!*" Then doing his weird *Exorcist*-voice commentary on Buster, Lily, Blackie, and Lee Lee the baby elephant and Asha the baby rhino.

"I'm wild and crazy and I just don't care!" I joked, imitating his devil-boy voice.

"I'm wild and crazy and I just don't care!" growled Rowan in echo as we rounded the wide bend, Blue flying along underneath us, the ground a green blur, the sun warm on our faces, and my son laughing in the sunlight, even as we forded the wide river, the horses floundering on the stones and dipping belly-deep. It seemed nothing could shake his mood.

Not even the unexpected six-hour wait on the other side of the river. The night before, Tulga had had the bright idea of sending the old man's son, Daava, and the other youngest guide on ahead to find the vans and drivers where we had left them near Ulaan-Uul and tell them to come to the riverbank and meet us by another road. It seemed like a good idea at the time. Being fast riders, the youths could cover the distance much faster than we could. But when we got to the river, no vans awaited us.

All through the humid afternoon we waited, while thunderstorms crashed and broke on the distant mountains and the heat grew intense. We swam, staying out as far into midstream as we could because the flies, thick around the forest margins, would not venture out over the water.

Despite the disappointment, the wait, Rowan did not tantrum. Did not even complain.

As he and Tomoo waded quietly in the rushing shallows, Rowan found an old section of fishing rod. Some tourist passing through must have dropped it.

"What's that?" I asked him.

"A fishing rod. Look, I'm a fisherman. I'm fishing."

"That's right. Good language!"

Then he turned to me, pointed the rod, and said, "It's a magic wand. I'm a wizard."

My jaw dropped. "Okay," I said, amazed, wondering how to get my head around this new son with his complex language, his ability to start being conversational, his emotional continence. "Um . . . what are you going to turn me into?" I asked lamely.

"An elephant!"

I gave a pretty poor imitation of a trumpeting pachyderm. Rowan waved the wand again.

"What are you turning me into this time?"

"A mouse!"

I crouched down in the water and in a tiny, squeaky voice said, "Oh no, Mr. Elephant, you're too big! Please don't tread on me!"

Rowan's laughter pealed out above the babble of the water. He waved the wand again.

"What am I now?"

"A ring-tailed lemur!"

"Is Daddy *really* a ring-tailed lemur?"

"No," said Rowan, after a pause. "Daddy's a friend."

"Oh God, Rowan." I leaned down to hug him. "I love you so much!"

He leaned against my shoulders. And whispered — very softly, almost inaudibly — "I love you, Daddy."

The sublime and the ridiculous always go together. When the drivers and vans finally turned up, it became clear that the two young guides (who still had not shown up) had only recently found them, having spent the whole night and most of the morning drinking at a *ger* compound somewhere close to Ulaan-Uul, and that in fact we had been waiting for nothing. Tulga was furious, the old man embarrassed. However, the time had come to say goodbye, and Rowan — not to be denied now that his beloved leopard-skin pimpmobile had suddenly re-appeared — had already ensconced himself with his animals on the passenger seat. So we hugged the old man, without whom we'd never have made it up the mountain and back, and his two older, more responsible guides, while the old man vowed vengeance upon the younger guides and wished us luck. "May the good changes in your son continue."

And with that we were off, bumping and lurching once more inside the tumble-dryer ride while Tomoo and Rowan scrambled excitedly, playing at being monsters.

"So did the old man cop a feel?" I asked Michel flippantly, knowing he'd been anxious not to spend another night in camp with him.

"Nah," Michel joked. "I guess he was fickle after all."

We laughed.

"He copped a feel on me," said Kristin

matter-of-factly.

"For real?"

"I'm not kidding. I went to hug him good-bye and he totally felt my breast."

"Why didn't you say anything?"

"Oh, you know. We were leaving anyway. What was the point?"

"Hey, Tulga!" Jeremy raised his voice over the roar of the engine to reach Tulga where he sat in the front passenger seat. "Did you hear what the old man did to Kristin? Is that normal?"

Tulga laughed his nervous laugh again. "No. Not normal at all. No."

I looked at her. "Do you want us to turn the van around and go make him apologize?"

"No, it's just funny is all. We go up the mountain, guided by this wise old man, and then at the end he totally cops a feel. Kind of perfect, don't you think? Sublime with the ridiculous."

"You're sure?"

"Hey, listen, he took us to see Ghoste. We've got a kid who's toilet-trained, or almost. Who hasn't tantrummed in, what — ?"

"A day and a half," said Justin from the back. "The guides were commenting on it too back there."

"So if that's what it takes — I don't know." Kristin shrugged, looking out the window at the forest, the meadows full of grazing yaks and sheep. "Given what's happened, I kind of can't find it in me to get that upset about it, you know?"

Two nights we camped on the road to Moron. Two hot days of lurching, bumping travel over the high mountains, stopping to give thanks at the *ovoos;* two days of heat, of cramped limbs, of bad jokes and worse smells, for none of us had washed in an age. Both nights on the road, when everyone had at last fallen asleep, I went and looked at the moon rising big, almost full, over the mountains and gave thanks, breathing in the herb-scented air and praying for these amazing, amazing leaps forward Rowan had shown us to continue.

Though neither Kristin nor I had uttered it aloud, there was still a fear lurking behind our wonder at what had happened since Ghoste had worked his magic — if that indeed was what it was. Both of us remembered that when Rowan had been exposed to the shamans at the Gathering, he had also appeared to shoot forward, but then he had regressed. Would that happen again now? I tried not to attach myself, to prepare myself for a regression so as not to be crushed, heartbroken, when and if it happened. But who was I kidding? I was desperately attached. If he regressed now, after leaping forward what felt like three years in just three weeks, I'd be devastated. So I looked at the moon and the mountains and prayed.

The second night on the road, we camped in the foothills just three hours or so from Moron, so as to have plenty of time to make the journey next day — for then we'd fly to "the Mongolian city," as Rowan called UB, for the last part of the journey before heading back to the West. A small wood of delicate young pines hugged the hilltop below which we had pitched the tents. Perhaps half a mile distant stood a pile of huge boulders, rearing up on the crest of the hill.

"Want to take a walk up there?" I asked Kristin, on a whim.

"What about Scubs?"

"Let's see if he'll let Tulga and the others look after him. Hey, Scubs," I called. Rowan's head snapped around. "Mommy and I want to take a walk to those rocks up there." I pointed to where they crowded on the hilltop, two large hawks circling on the thermals above them. "Is that okay? You can stay here for a bit with Tulga and

Tomoo, okay?"

"Okay," said Rowan. So up the hill we went.

At the top, we looked out over the endless rolling steppe.

"So," said Kristin quietly, "do you think this really is it? I do. I think our lives are going to change now. I feel it. I really do."

I looked across at her — tall, beautiful, impossibly elegant. Tears were welling in her eyes. Below us the vast steppe rolled away to infinity, its grasses moving in the ever-blowing wind.

That night, as Rowan slept, she came to find me in my side of the tent. Climbed astride me. Claimed me as her husband once more.

Later, much later, the pain from my lip woke me. Lying there in the darkness, Kristin breathing beside me, I suddenly heard Rowan's voice, high and clear. He must have noticed that Kristin was gone, and was calling for her. But no. He was talking. To himself. In his sleep? I could not tell. Instead I lay there and listened, not getting every word. But he was telling a story. Not about Mongolia or the shamans. One completely made up, involving Buster and Blackie and Lily and Lee Lee and Asha and someone new called Crazy Crocodile, who all went to Whipsnade Wild Animal Park, then went home and broke into the kitchen "and Mommy said naughty and they stole the cookies and then Mommy came in again and got very angry and they all ran away."

I drifted to sleep, lulled away from pain by the sound of my son's bedtime story.

Next morning it rained hard. Justin offered Rowan his headphones as the van slushed through the rain and mud. To my surprise, Rowan, who usually could not tolerate anything on his head, took them and listened intently to the music on Justin's iPod. "Big business monkey!" he suddenly shouted, in time with the song, sung by a Texas eccentric called Daniel Johnson. "He runs his house like a Burger King manager!"

We drove through sheets of water, down tracks and turf roads indiscernible to any but the most trained eye, back to the main road to Moron. Rowan climbed into the front seat with Tomoo and Tulga and tried to talk to the driver.

"Hello. My name's Rowan! Shall we go to the Mongolian city?"

"He doesn't speak English, Rowan!" said Kristin from her seat next to me.

So Rowan tried using sign language — the same signing that he had learned months before at Greenbriar. What connections were being made in his brain? Whatever they were, they kept happening. Once at Moron, back at the *ger* camp on the edge of town, where Rowan had suffered the agonies of being denied the wrestler's guinea pigs, he began to play chase with a whole group of children, running up and down playing tag just like a normal child.

Then, because I couldn't very well have Rowan squat down in the compound, I tried taking him to the toilet. He resisted, crying. Kristin came in to see how we were doing. Heart sinking, I shook my head at her. "He's clammed right up again," I said dispiritedly. "Maybe I've tried too much too soon. I hope I haven't blown it."

"Off! Get off! Get down! Off!" Rowan was chanting it like a mantra. Kristin knelt down.

"Hey, Rowan," she said gently. "Can you tell us *why* you don't want to go poopy on the potty?"

"Go outside!"

"Is it because you're mad? Or is it because you're scared?"

He looked up at her. Again it was like seeing a light bulb suddenly come on behind the eyes.

"Scared!"

"Oh, don't be scared, Rowan." She knelt

forward and hugged him, just as I was hugging him, the three of us linked, arms about each other, in a cramped toilet in a guest camp in the middle of Mongolia.

That's when we heard the first *plop*.

Kristin and I looked at each other. "Oh my God!"

Rowan, sitting there, looked as astonished as we did.

"You're brilliant!" I told him.

"You're brilliant," he echoed back.

I ran outside, shouting, "Indoor poopy! We have indoor poopy!"

It was like winning the lottery. Unable to contain my joy, I did a little jig, causing the daughter of one of the *ger* camp women, who happened to be passing by, to cover her mouth and giggle. Rowan — Kristin had cleaned him up — came rushing by. Immediately the girl set off in laughing pursuit, Tomoo appearing from around the corner to join them.

Indoor poopy; Rowan playing with other kids just like a normal child. Truly our prayers had been answered.

That evening we kept the beers coming from the *ger* camp's bar, watching as Rowan ran back and forth with Tomoo and the children of the women who ran the place — joyful, happy, included. At last, in the dying light, the sky streaked with sunset, they came marching back from their game, four of them all hand in hand, swinging their arms in unison, singing some song that only children, who know the common language of children, understand. There was a honking sound from the sky. I looked up. Seven cranes were flying over, heading west into the sun's last rays.

The next day we had to hang around for hours waiting for the flight to take us back to UB. Still no tantrums. We killed time in what from a distance looked like a children's park, but we found the grass strewn with broken glass, the slides, climbing frames, and swings barbed with sharp pieces of metal just waiting to skewer a kid.

"Christ, they're like psychic black holes," said Justin, clicking away with his camera as we took turns sitting on the concrete animals that someone, sometime back in the Soviet era, had thought fit to erect amid the broken bottles and stinging nettles. He was right — it was as if Mongolia's rural heart was instantly poisoned the moment it tried to be urban.

Once we were at the airport, there were more delays, the kind of thing that a few weeks back — no, a *week* back — would have sent Rowan into conniptions. Instead he sat quietly. A different child. He even used the airport potty for another indoor poop. Who was this boy?

We flew over mountains, over the steppe, looking down at the vastness. When we touched down in UB, Rowan wanted to be taken to the Natural History Museum immediately. But Tulga's wife, Naara (who was shocked to see how her husband's beard had grown out these past few weeks), had booked us into a *ger* camp way out on the other side of the vast city, which looked shocking — so ugly, so raw — after our long sojourn in the vastness of the countryside. It began to rain, then to pour, as the driver took us there down roads that seemed to snake endlessly through dismal industrial suburbs. When we finally arrived at the camp, it was long after dark. Rowan was exhausted, hungry. He went straight to bed in the *ger* that had been allotted to us.

Sitting up, listening to the rain on the roof of the *ger,* Kristin and I counted all the usual triggers to tantrum that Rowan had had that day and came up with twenty-two. But he'd taken the bait of none. "So what do you think?" asked Michel. "All these changes in Rowan. Do you think it's the shamans?"

Kristin smiled. "I'm not even asking how things are working. Or why they're working. I don't know if I believe in shamanism or not, or whether it's just a metaphor. But I do know Rowan is doing things he's never done before. Right now that's enough for me."

23
FOUR MINUTES AND FIFTY-TWO SECONDS

We woke to find ourselves in a slice of heaven: a mountainside leading down to the great Tuul River, the same sacred river on whose banks we had conducted that first ritual with the nine shamans. It seemed an age ago. Poplars, beeches, and aspens clustered along the banks, grew on islands amid the flow. Sometimes the riverbanks ran softly down to the water's edge in great sweeps of pasture, grazed here and there by herds of horses. Elsewhere they reared up to great cliffsides, the ledges covered with little trees. Mountains towered behind. A gentle rain still fell, softening the light, bringing out the depth, the subtleties of the greens. A man rode up with a horse for me and Rowan. Interested to see whether Rowan would reject the horses again now that he knew he was on his way home, I asked him if he wanted to ride the animal, a cremello with pink nostrils and pink around its blue eyes.

"Yes, let's go riding!"

So off we went with the horse herder, fording the river, following him toward the herd that grazed on the far bank. By signs, the man indicated that he wanted us to help him herd the mares and foals onto the side of the river we'd come from, and that my horse, a stallion, might get excited, so Rowan should share his saddle, not mine. So, in part to see what Rowan's reaction would be, I passed my son across to sit in front of the herder. No problem, no fuss. When we reached the herd, my stallion began to scream challenges at the alpha male in charge of the mares and foals. A couple of times it even rose up on its hind legs and kicked out with its forelegs. Rowan never batted an eyelash. We drove the herd back through the river, Rowan joining in as we shouted *Chuh! Chuh!* and the herder galloped, wheeled, stopped, turned, the two stallions screaming all the while and Rowan just plain loving it.

I looked at him, excited, happy, living his adventure, and never wanted to leave.

But there was one final piece of the journey left to complete. I had arranged weeks before to go to one of the places, Hustai, where the original wild horses of Mongolia, known as the *takhins,* or "honored ones," still grazed the steppe. Grandfathers of the domestic horses we'd ridden here, and indeed of domestic horses the world over, the *takhins* are to the modern horse what, say, the timber wolf is to the dog. I wanted to take Rowan back to the source — the source of horse, as it were — and give thanks to them in some way for all that horses had given us. A pilgrimage of sorts. So off we went in the van once more, back onto the awful roads that were not roads, west out of the great, falling-down city and back onto the steppe for our final journey.

It was strange to be back on the road once more, when it felt in many ways as though the journey were complete.

"Do we really have to be doing this?" asked Kristin irritably as we bumped and juddered our way through another rainstorm, westward toward Hustai National Park, some three hours or so from UB. "I'm so exhausted. Couldn't we just chill out in UB for a little before going home?"

She had a point. Perhaps this was overkill. Yet some nagging voice — the same voice that had pushed going to Lake Sharga — said that we ought to make this journey to the last wild horses — truly wild horses, that is — of Mongolia.

"I'm sorry," I said, meaning it, for I was heartily sick of the van too. We all were. And this section of road was some of the worst we'd encountered. Moreover, the dynamic had changed subtly. Tulga, after spending so long out in the sticks with us, had had to go meet another group of travelers off a plane from the U.K., so he had assigned a freelance guide, a woman called Daava, to look after us. She was perfectly pleasant, but the easy banter of the last few weeks was missing. As was Tomoo, who had had to stay home with his mother. We were just going to see the wild horses for one night, then back to UB; then, the day after that, we'd be leaving for good.

By the time we had gone an hour and a half or so, Kristin began to feel nauseated. Michel too. In fact, by hour two, the same wave of sickness that had engulfed Michel on the way up to the reindeer people had overcome them both completely. Both lay there, heads lolling as the van bumped over the endless, merciless ruts, making them feel worse with every mile. I was hating it too. Of all of us, only Rowan was happy, in his element, watching the landscape pass, enjoying the pitch and toss of the van's movement, the sense of forward motion, just as he always did.

At last we turned south off the main road, with its many scrapes and cuts desecrating the steppe, and into drier country. Sand hills, tall grass, no trees; occasional gullies with scattered bushes growing thick where the water ran in times of rain. Horse country, for sure. Soon after that we entered the national park.

A small herd of non-*takhin* horses milled about, grazing near the entrance as we drove through.

"They don't stray into the reserve," said Daava. "The wild horses attack them. They know to stay outside."

We parked in a small parking lot set among the tall grasses, where various other tourist buses and vans had already parked before us, and were shown to a *ger* camp clustered around a two-room log cabin *cum* tourist lodge. European, American, and Chinese tourists bustled about, busy with cameras, bags, each other. It was the first time we had really been around other travelers, other tourists, since arriving. The effect was unsettling.

Not that there was much time to be freaked out. Kristin was wilting visibly. And Michel could barely walk. Both were ensconced in bed in our two allotted *gers* more or less immediately, while Justin,

515

Jeremy, and I held a powwow about how best to film. Rowan, happy to have his own *ger,* played quietly on the carpet with his new plastic train set as we talked. On the way out of UB we'd stopped at the city's old Soviet department store — an extraordinary place where you could buy everything from wolf skins to antique Buddhist reliquaries to perfume, toys, and books — and bought him this train set as a reward for being so good. We chuckled as we walked out through the children's shoe section, where the leading kid's shoe brand was Stabi-foot.

"It's a zoo train," Rowan said, laying out the animals at intervals along the track. "Just like at Whipsnade."

When the time came for us to go to the van and look for the wild horses (Kristin rallying and coming too, despite her nausea), he didn't want to leave the train set. Torn between not wanting to end his pleasure and that nagging gut feeling that somehow we had to offer some kind of prayer to the wild horses, the original horses, in person, I insisted.

So it was that we had our first tantrum in three days, in a packed van, driving to try to find the wild horses.

"Wow." Daava, unused to this (as were the game guide the park had hired for us and the new driver), had to raise her voice above the screams. "You really let him do anything."

I almost hit her. For the fist had closed around my heart once more. Rowan was really going for it — a back-arching, full-on autism *Gi-RAFFE*, back-to-square-one, eardrum-splitting, just-ain't-going-to-quit, shrieking, brain-shredding tantrum. Was this the beginning of a regression? I felt myself start to panic, fought the panic down.

"Rowan!" I said, thinking of Ghoste, what he had said about the "bad behaviors" going away. "Rowan! The screams are ouchy on Daddy's ears. They make Daddy sad. But talking is nice."

He turned his eyes on mine, and again I saw that light bulb come on somewhere behind the retinas. He understood. He *understood*. And he stopped.

"Let's go see the wild horses," said Rowan, drying his eyes. "Then let's go back to the *ger* and play with the train set."

"Okay," I said. "That's exactly what we'll do."

As so often happens in wildlife reserves, we spotted our game by first spotting a group of vans parked by the side of the road, their passengers — Westerners all — disgorged onto the steppe and looking off across a wide gully toward a long hillside. We pulled up, got out, and saw them: a herd of nine stocky tan horses with stiff white manes, white noses, black stripes on their backs and on their legs, and muscled compact bodies. Completely unlike any domestic horse I had ever seen. They moved slowly down the gully toward us, grazing a little, herded from behind by a large stallion. Two little foals skipped at their mothers' sides. The tourists, looking through binoculars, murmured their delight.

"Look!" said Rowan. "So *cute!*"

And suddenly he was *being* a horse, galloping up and down the sloping grassland, neighing and whinnying, laughing and shouting to me to join in: "Daddy be a horse too!"

So up and down we went, galumphing together behind where the tourists had gathered. The wild horses, flicking their ears toward the noise we were making, began to approach at a faster walk. Daava and the other Mongolian guides (each tourist party had its own) told us to give ground; by law, two hundred meters had to be maintained between humans and the wild horses. So back we went with the others, cantering and snorting like fools at a fair.

"Rowan to ride Daddy!"

So I took him on my back and galloped in circles. I was fitter now, much fitter, than I'd been at the start of the trip. All the same, within a minute or two I was blown and let him down.

Almost immediately a baby grouse came rocketing up from a tall grass clump in front of us, then landed on the ground again, being unable to fly far, and scurried off into a further clump. Rowan gave a happy halloo and began to chase it. Together we knelt down and peered into the grass. There it was, within reach, its dark eyes regarding us with animal caution, its soft, variegated feathers blending perfectly with its cover. I remembered the baby snipe that had appeared right in front of us when Blue had gone down underneath us in the bog, that first day of riding up to see the reindeer people. How chasing it immediately after our fall had saved Rowan from his fright.

"Hold it!" said Rowan, reaching into the grass stalks.

From behind him, I restrained him. "The baby grouse is scared, Rowan. If we grab it, we might hurt it. Let's just look at it, shall we?"

Back went the head, out came the train-whistle scream. A dozen tourist heads whipped around. *"BABY GROUSE! BABY*

GROUSE!" His back was arching now. But I remembered what had just happened in the van on our way here. "Rowan!" I leaned close to his ear. "Do you want to shout and scream and see no baby grouse? Or do you want to be nice and quiet so the baby grouse can stay?"

The screams cut off abruptly, replaced by sniffles.

"Be nice and quiet so the baby grouse can stay."

So we stayed, crouching on our knees, peering at the wild bird, which stared back at us, while behind us the nine wild horses grazed, drifting gradually closer, till Rowan finally decided he'd had enough and fetched his toy animals from the van.

It seemed a good time for Kristin and I to say our final prayer. She was back in the van, however, holding her head as another wave of nausea washed over.

"Do I have to?" she said wearily when I suggested it was time.

"Are you feeling that bad? Should we go back to the *ger?*"

She sighed. "No, I guess I can do it. All right, then. Let's get it over with."

"Wow, that's pretty negative."

"Yeah? Well, this whole thing is your idea anyway. So deal with it."

"Okay," I said, biting down the urge to hit back. Now was clearly not the time to fight.

So, standing together on the steppe, hand in hand if not heart to heart, we faced the wild herd, eyes shut, conjuring our internal prayers. I tried to push my irritation from my mind and concentrate. *Thank you, Lords of the Mountains, Lords of the Land, for healing my son. He's so much better I can't believe it. Thank you. I know I shouldn't be attached to its continuing. I know that's always a mistake. But I can't help it. Please let him go on getting better like this. You've given us so much. Please keep the healing going. Wild horses, if there's anything you can give him, care to give him, on top of what he's had already, then please do. I don't know what I can offer in return. I know it's maybe wrong to want more. But if there's anything, anything more you see fit to give him, then please do. He deserves it. I love him. And thank you. For everything.*

I let Kristin's hand slip from mine, put my hands together, and, feeling a little self-conscious, bowed three times toward the horses. Kristin, her own silent prayer done, did likewise and went back to the van, waves of irritation still coming from her. I felt a great answering anger surge up inside me. We'd fight later, I knew, and fight hard. But why now? In such a sublime moment. Why?

Rowan saved me from picking the fight there and then by appearing suddenly at my side and demanding, "Rowan to ride Daddy the horse!"

So we did, up and down, up and down, his delighted laughter ringing off the steppe. The horses were clearly intrigued by this odd human behavior; presumably most humans they encountered simply stood silently and stared at them through binoculars. They raised their heads, pricked their ears, and gradually approached closer. Cameras clicked and whirred, some of them using flash in the now rapidly dying light. We were down to the last minutes of daylight.

Daava came up: "It's time to go. It's forbidden to be out in the reserve after dark."

"Okay," I said, putting Rowan down. "Okay, Rowan, shall we go back to the *ger?*"

"I'm gonna get you!" he shouted instead, and went off at a run, shooting a chase-me look over his shoulders. So I chased him, making monster noises, trying to herd him back to the van. That's when I heard the man saying, in a thick German accent, "Excuse me! Excuse me! Yes! I want to talk with you!"

I turned. A tall man, about my own age, was approaching from one of the tourist vans that had not yet left. I grabbed Rowan, put him on my shoulders.

"Sure," I said. "What is it?" Though I knew full well what was coming.

"I want to ask you why you are letting this . . . this *child* behave like this!" he said, his accent stiff and stilted. "We are in a place for the nature! Not a playground for the children! We have come here for the quiet and the peace! Not to listen to kids yelling. Why do you let him do this?"

"Are you familiar with the term *autism?*"

Light dawned on the man's face. For a moment I saw compassion there, embarrassment even. But only for a moment. "Yes," he said. "But that is not the point."

I looked at the man, fighting down the urge to hit him. He did have a point. Not that Rowan had been that bad. We'd kept our distance from the other tourists as best we could. If anything, the wild horses had come closer because of his antics. All the same, I could understand the man's annoyance. Perhaps it would be better to try to explain. In front of the camera — if only I could get him there.

Why? Because finally, here was someone censuring us in public — but with a way to record it. I wanted to punish him, punish all the people who had done this to Kristin and Rowan and me over the past three years. Juvenile perhaps, but human — and another part of me was simply curious to see how he'd justify himself. To my amazement, and perhaps his own, I managed to get him to come down to where Justin had the camera rolling.

"Well," he said — not to the lens but rather to me where I sat, Rowan wriggling and laughing in my lap — his tone suddenly somewhat more polite. "Well, I think, if you have a child like that. With a certain . . . *condition* — by which it is very *noisy*, it's not very sensible to be around here, where a lot of people come to be in a quiet environment. That's my point."

"Can you tell us who you are and where you're from?" I asked, putting on my journo's voice. He bridled instantly:

"Why?"

"For interest's sake."

"No . . . why . . . I should be at fault? I know what film can do, and how you can cut things. So you can do anything with this comment. Which I think is a very reasonable comment" — his politeness was giving way to smugness. "So, I mean . . ." He waved an authoritative hand: "I'm a psychologist myself."

This floored me. "What branch?" I asked.

"Ah . . ." Here he had the grace to look just a little sheepish. "Diagnostics."

"And you didn't . . ."

"Oh — you think I should have known that he was autistic?"

"Well . . ." It did surprise me. "What would you have expected to see, in an autistic kid?"

"I would have expected . . ." He thought a moment. "I would have expected him to be very quiet. Afraid."

This was a professional opinion. That was scary. How many other professionals thought as he did?

"Do you think he shouldn't be here?" I asked, indicating Rowan, now back at the marmot hole, singing to his animals.

"No, no." The man didn't sound too convincing. "I think he should be here also. But . . . maybe not, like, half an hour!"

"You think it should just be, like, a quick in and out?"

"No, look. You're trying to get me . . ."

"So if we were to bring him to a place like this, what would be the best way to do it, do you think?"

"Maybe he don't stay so long. Not a half hour . . . maybe . . ."

"What do you think the optimum would have been? An hour? Two hours? Twenty minutes? Five?"

The man gave an impatient snort. "Four minutes and fifty-two seconds."

The trouble was, I thought, watching him as he walked back to his group, he meant it.

He'd had a point, but his desire to stick to that point at all costs had completely blinded him to any compassion. What a short jump it was from there to deciding that loud, problematic children should not be anywhere that adults might find them troublesome. From there it was a short jump to sticking them in special schools, and then special institutions when they grew bigger. No integration. No community.

We drove back through the dark toward the *ger* camp, me seething with anger. At the bastard psychologist. At my wife. At myself, for . . . For what, exactly? For once more being the person who had the embarrassing child in public? After all Rowan's breakthroughs, it seemed unworthy. It was like bile coming up from the stomach. I felt ashamed.

Two more wild horses loomed up out of the dark, a pair of bachelor males, not yet having won their own harem of mares, sticking together out there on the wolf-hunted nighttime steppe.

"So cute," said Rowan, watching them cross the road. "The wild horses are so very cute."

For our last night in Mongolia, instead of a hotel in the middle of the polluted city or another *ger* camp far out on the edge of town, Naara had booked us into a private residence for expats under the sacred Bogd Khan mountain, not far from where Rowan had had his first healing. It was a strange meeting of worlds, this place — modern-built, like a big hotel, but full of separate apartments. And kids — wealthy children, children of diplomats and executives of multinationals: American, Chinese, European, all wandering around in a big pack, riding bicycles, playing basketball, playing on the climbing frame and swings, under the watchful eyes of their Mongolian nannies. Rowan went straight to them. Within an hour he had them all charmed. The older boys began trying to teach him basketball, holding him up so he could dunk the ball in the basket. When Tomoo arrived, some time after we'd settled in, the two of them went running about amid the pack like regular kids. I kept a watchful eye all the same, alert for any sign of teasing, bullying, or rejection when they realized that Rowan was not quite as normal as all that. But the moment never came.

Kristin had taken to her bed after grumpily asking to be left alone. "I don't know why I'm being like this," she admitted in a moment of clarity. "It's not just the nausea. It's like some black, negative energy's got hold of me. I don't know why. I know I'm being negative. Everything has gone so wonderfully. It's like I can't help it. Like sinking into black goo. I know it's not fair I'm taking it out on you. I know you're having to watch Rowan. I just . . . I just can't fight it right now. I'm sorry."

So I left her and, the other kids having gone off to their apartments, took Rowan walking on the mountain. There was an *ovoo* up there on a bluff looking down on the apartment building and the great, strange, ugly city beyond. Behind us, dry hillside led up to wild pine forest. Horses were grazing on the mountain. Caught between worlds, we watched the sun go down over mountains, trees, high-rises, smokestacks.

"We're going back to London tomorrow," I told Rowan, though he knew it well enough. "Did you like Mongolia?"

"Yes."

"Did you like the shamans?"

"Yes."

"Do you want to go home?"

"Yes. Yes, I do."

And so to bed, to sleep briefly but soundly before Naara, Daava, and Tomoo came back, just before dawn, to take us to the airport.

As we stood in line for the check-in, Rowan and Tomoo perched together on the luggage cart like two brothers. When it was time to go, they embraced and then, with the feral, almost animal way of just accepting things that children have, they let each other go.

As the plane lifted over the mountains, the sheer vast emptiness of this land that had given us so much, Rowan turned to me and smiled. "A brave little sausage," he said, his voice muffled by my jacket. I caught Kristin's eye. She was back from the dark place. We reached out for each other's hands as the plane banked, climbed, and pointed its nose to the West: home.

EPILOGUE

When we got back to London, en route for Texas, Rowan began to slip almost immediately into his obsessive behaviors. Several big tantrums followed. On the third day in the city, waiting for the plane that would take us to Austin, while we were walking up the busy main road close to my parents' house, Rowan began to stim, flapping his arms and babbling. Regressing. As I stood there on the street, watching him flap and shake his head as the traffic thundered past, I felt my heart would break.

That evening Kristin and I took Rowan on the train from my parents' house up to Hampstead Heath, that wonderful wilderness in the middle of North London. Once the haunt of highwaymen and harlots, shepherds and deer, it is now a large piece of protected countryside, still magically wild. Perhaps, I thought, clutching at straws, if I got him back into nature, the regression might stop. I prayed hard, watching him look out the window of the train at the passing London rooftops — prayed that all he had accomplished would not be for nothing.

Under the great spreading oaks, I watched Rowan trot ahead of me, chasing the handsome black-and-white magpies that hopped along the path before him, giggling when a gray squirrel darted up a tree to chatter at him from a branch. Suddenly my son came running back to me, the old devil grin on his face: "Time for a tickle!"

Relieved that he was speaking lucidly again, I asked, "A tiny little mouse tickle, or —"

"A great big elephant buffalo rhino blue whale tickle!" he interrupted, and with a great roar of laughter he ran head-first into my stomach, squealing with frenzied delight as I tickled his ribs, scrobbled his head, and did my best to keep my fear at bay, not make it his problem.

We walked long into the evening, looking at birds, watching the sun set over the great London basin. Here in nature, he was calm once more.

But for how long? I wondered. How long?

For good, it turned out. That last episode of

tantrumming and stimming in London, a week after coming down the mountain from Ghoste's summer camp, was the last truly dysfunctional behavior we ever saw. Rowan's toilet-training continued unabated. For a while we had to keep a watch on him in order to avoid accidents. Then even the accidents stopped. By the time we got back to the United States, my son was starting to take himself to the potty. Soon after that, neither Kristin nor I was even involved anymore. And the tantrums, the hyperactivity and anxiety — those ever-present demons that had squatted like gargoyles on Rowan's shoulders for the past three years — had left him completely by the time we'd been back in Texas a month.

We had come back with a completely different child.

Just before we left England for home, Kristin and I traveled up to Cambridge to interview Dr. Simon Baron-Cohen, probably England's leading autism expert. I didn't agree with all his theories; for example, he felt that the current pandemic of autism was a result of increased diagnosis, not of environmental pollution, as many other scientists think. Kristin, donning her psychology professor's hat, pointed out that if increased diagnosis were in fact the cause, then surely one would see a decrease in diagnosis of other types of mental condition that might previously have been considered autistic. They agreed to differ. But one thing that Dr. Baron-Cohen said did resonate. "Perhaps in the future," he said, "it is going to be increasingly controversial whether autism is something that needs to be cured or not. Perhaps it is more a personality type."

When Rowan got back, his academic status was reassessed. At age five, he was reading at a seven-year-old's level. Three months later he had reached an eight-year-old's level and started reading himself to sleep at night.

I had also worried whether Rowan's connection with Tomoo might have been a one-off. But within a week of our returning to the States, a friend brought her young stepson, Gavin, to ride with us. Rowan and Gavin became fast friends immediately. A few weeks later, half the neighborhood kids were turning up for riding playdates. By Rowan's sixth birthday, a few short months after returning from Mongolia, he had so many friends that we had to throw a proper party — his first ever birthday party — for a whole gaggle of kids, all of whom counted themselves as his friends. And only one of whom was also on the autism spectrum.

Rowan's social life was now like that of any other child.

Then there was the riding. A fear had long been lurking in the back of my mind: that our short few years of riding together on Betsy would end up being a kind of golden time that would end when Rowan got too big to share a saddle comfortably with me. Which was more or less around his sixth birthday.

When we first got home, Betsy greeted Rowan with the same spontaneous obeisance that she always did, and as before we rode together through the fields, pastures, and wild pecan groves around our home. Some weeks after our return, however, I started making a point of no longer getting back onto Betsy after climbing off to open the gate before the final quarter-mile back to the barn. Instead I walked alongside them, not holding the reins, motioning to Betsy with subtle flickers of my finger to tell her that she should walk alongside me, with Rowan perched on top.

Rowan wasn't happy about it at first. "Daddy to get up!" he kept insisting. I made a joke out of it, pretending not to hear, saying, *What? What?* in my mad old English colonel voice and tickling him where he sat in the saddle, making him giggle as Betsy plodded patiently along, flicking her ears back and forth between my son and me. When we got back to the barn I suddenly stopped and said, "Pull the reins and say *whoa.*"

Startled, Rowan did it. "Whoa," he said. Betsy stopped dead.

The next day we repeated the exercise, but at the end I ducked to the left and said, "Pull the reins to Daddy!"

Rowan looked confused. "Pull your hand toward Daddy!" I said instead. He did. Betsy turned toward me, quiet as a lamb.

Next day we repeated both exercises again, but this time added a turn to the other side.

And so we built it, with no more than five minutes or so of alone-time for Rowan in the saddle each day, so as not to make it a chore for him. By the end of a month he was stopping and turning Betsy with confidence while I moved ever farther and farther away. When one day she tried to put her head down to graze, I called out, "Pull the reins up and kick her on." He did. She obeyed. I turned to see Uncle Terry walking up. "Rowan just rode by himself!"

"Rowan," said Uncle Terry, grinning, "now you're never gonna give that poor Betsy any peace, are you?"

Later that evening, I told Stafford what had happened, over a celebratory beer.

"Rupert," he said, clinking my bottle, "I believe that soon you ain't gonna have nothin' more to complain about."

I looked at this kind man, my neighbor, my friend. Had he not allowed us access to his horse, his land, my son would never have come this far.

Around this time I bought another horse, a Texas quarter horse called Clue, who had a penchant for jumping. I bought him partly to take some of the pressure off Betsy — he was also known to be good with kids — and partly to reclaim my own riding career, to have a horse I could jump once more. I wanted to set off by myself when time allowed and take the country as it came, without an autism or child agenda. At first when I offered, Rowan did not want to ride Clue, being loyal to Betsy. But after a week or two he was riding the new horse too, each day a little more, while I — or Kristin and I, out for a family walk while our son rode — sauntered alongside.

As for me, freed now from riding only as part of Rowan's therapy, I discovered a whole new direction with horses. I found a trainer who specialized in high school dressage, the most complex form of equestrianism, where you train the horse quite literally to dance underneath you. I'd always hankered to try this most esoteric of riding disciplines but had also always thought, somewhere in the back of my mind, that I wasn't quite good enough. Perhaps Mongolia had given me a little more faith in myself. Whatever the reason, I put my insecurities aside, started training, and found, to my delight, that not only could I do this most difficult style of riding — riding as an art form — I could even do it well enough to compete. By immersing myself in this deeper, more connected form of riding, I began to discover my own inner horse boy.

By New Year's Day, Rowan was riding by himself for up to two hours at a time, stopping and turning the horses when I did the gates, kicking them on when they tried to stop and graze, even piloting them around twisting courses of traffic cones I put up for him in the field. Riding as the nomads had said he would.

Kristin and I were able to reclaim our romantic life. With the arrival of playdates in Rowan's life came the arrival of babysitters in ours, which enabled us to take evenings out together, on actual dates. The revelation of finding myself sitting across a restaurant table from my beautiful wife again, looking into her dark brown eyes — so dark as to be almost black, with those little lights dancing in their center — was just that: a revelation. It had been so long.

"You know, Ru," she said over dinner, both of us marveling at the newness of it all, "that black mood I got into when we came back down from the reindeer people, when I got so irritable and sick and depressed? I don't know — we went to the shaman and asked for healing, and I think I got some myself. It was as if all this old negativity, years of it, was seeping out of me. Part of that was about destroying, clearing away old stuff. Now I feel like there's this new creative energy rising up in me." That same month she began writing a book on her self-compassion work, and a few months after that she found an agent and a publisher. Never have I seen her so fulfilled.

As for us, we are still a work in progress, as all couples are. Rowan's recovery has given us the room to look for the next place to go together. No longer do we have to think 100 percent about Rowan and his autism. We have time to think about us — one of the gifts of Rowan's recovery.

Is *recovery* too strong a word? Perhaps *healing* is better. Healing rather than *cure*.

Rowan is still autistic — his essence, his many talents, are all tied up with it. He has been healed of the terrible dysfunctions that afflicted him — his physical and emotional incontinence, his neurological firestorms, his anxiety and hyperactivity. But he has not been cured. Nor would I want him to be. To "cure" him, in terms of trying to tear the autism out, now seems to me completely wrong. Why can't he exist between the worlds, with a foot in both, as many neurotypical people do? Think of immigrants to the United States, living with one foot in their home language and culture, the other in the West, walking in two worlds. It is a rich place to be. Can Rowan keep learning the skills necessary to swim in our world while retaining the magic of his own? It seems a tangible dream.

Upon our return from Mongolia, I managed to raise money to buy land to start an equestrian program for PDD kids. Fifteen acres of gorgeous land, shaded by big pecan, elm, and mulberry trees, that catches the breeze even on the hottest of Texas days. An old, falling-down farmhouse sits on it. It is a place where children can play and ride and learn and be happy. Perhaps appropriately, the road it sits on is called New Trails.

As I sit here writing on my back porch,

the bright red cardinals singing around me, the Texas spring rain spattering on the tin roof, the woods bursting into new green leaf, a construction crew is remodeling the old farmhouse, putting the final touches together. The horses and other animals are being bought, and staff is being hired. Part of the proceeds from your purchase of this book will enable us to offer scholarships to families who cannot afford equine therapy.

At the same time, I am sending e-mails and fielding phone calls to and from Africa. As I write, I am making arrangements to take Rowan to the Kalahari this summer, just as Ghoste told us to do. I'm still banned from Botswana, so Besa, Rowan's "shaman father," is going to travel out of Botswana for the first time and meet us in neighboring Namibia to see "little Besa." What will happen there? What other healings will occur?

Rowan himself has just appeared at the door of the screened porch where I sit writing. He wants to see his friends — Adelina, Gavin, Honor, Ariella, Annie, and Bessie (none of them autisitic, by the way) — whom we usually see on Tuesday afternoons for a riding playdate with Betsy, Clue, Taz, and an old black horse named Chango.

"We've had to cancel because of the rain,"

I just told him. "But we'll see them in a few days."

"I want to see them now!"

"Rowan" — I make a silly face — "do you want to whine and . . ." I rack my brains for something funny rather than simply punitive. ". . . and have to sit upside-down in a tub of lard for thirty-six years with someone you don't like very much . . ."

This gets a giggle. *"Or . . ."* he prompts me, knowing the game.

"Or do you want to be nice and quiet, see your friends next time, and then go ride bicycles on the moon?"

This gets a peal of laughter. Rowan rushes off to make a zoo train. But a few moments later he's back. "Hey, Daddy."

I look up. He's peeping round the door, that devil-boy grin on his face.

"Let's go ride bicycles on the *moon!*"

We went riding that same April night. Me walking, Rowan riding, sitting up straight on Betsy's broad brown back. I followed behind, barely keeping up.

"Hey, Rowan," I said. "Pull the reins and make Betsy stop while I do the gate."

He did. Betsy stopped.

"Now pull the reins to Daddy, so she turns."

He did, and rode her over to stand behind me while I bent down to refasten the chain.

"Now ride her home. Say 'Come on, Betsy,' and give her a kick."

"Come on, Betsy," said Rowan, clapping heels to her sides.

She took off at a gentle jog-trot, back toward the barn. My son sitting up in perfect balance. Riding away from me. Free.

ACKNOWLEDGMENTS

It all began one summer afternoon at my friend Ginny Jordan's cabin in the Colorado Rockies. "What do you really want to do?" she asked as we looked up at the moving clouds from where we lay on a wooden dock above a mountain pond whose black waters — strangely — held dozens of axolotyls drifting close to the surface. Axolotyls are one of the wonders of nature: the embryonic form of salamanders, which never achieve full salamanderdom but instead mutate (no one knows why) into an adult form of embryo, retaining their feathery gills, growing up to a foot long, and achieving sexual maturity in this, their supposedly embryonic form, thus able to reproduce their own strange kind. As far as I know, they are found only in the Americas. I read once that the Aztecs considered them to signify transition, the death of old selves, the beginning of new. I had never seen one in the wild before. Nor had my friend Ginny, even though this was her pond. And now suddenly there were dozens of the things, all floating, silent and still, just below the surface. Why? Something to do with climate, or the change of the season? Something to do with their strange reproductive cycle? Ginny and I were both a little freaked out, but also honored, as you always are when you find yourself a sudden witness to one of nature's secrets.

"So what do you want to do?" Ginny repeated as we lay there looking upward, away from the black water and its strange denizens. I replied that I wanted to write this story. And in the single most supremely generous act anyone has ever made to me, Ginny made me a gift that allowed me to put aside the incessant scramble for freelance work and concentrate on this, the work in hand. Words cannot express my gratitude.

Stafford O'Neal, Betsy's owner: a gentleman in every sense of the word. You didn't have to let me bring my son onto your property, day after day, week after week, year after year. You didn't have to put up with my constant invasions of your privacy, the risks of litigation which we all know accompany the permission to ride a horse on one's land; you didn't have to generously offer up your land, your horse, your heart. But you did. Few men are cut from your cloth. It's an honor to be your friend and neighbor, and my debt to you is incalculable. And to Daphne-Ann, your wife, endlessly welcoming, and Uncle Terry, endlessly kind. I'm also grateful for your lethal mustang grape wine and your bon mots of philosophy. "I'd rather be stupid than rude" should be the mantra by which we all live.

The other landowners who let us range across their broad Texas acres: the Arbuckle brothers, Mr. Powell of Powell Lane, Keith and Sarah Macneill, the Martin family. The wild pecan groves, cattle pastures, and woods of your land provided the backdrop against which my son learned how to communicate with the world around him.

It is hugely misleading that most books carry only the name of the author on their spines; in reality, all books are collaborations. In this case, everyone involved brought creative talent to bear in the most effective way possible. Elizabeth Sheinkman, my agent: you are the master alchemist. Judith Clain at Little, Brown: finally I know what it is to work hand in hand with an editor of vast, rare talent. You make it seem deceptively easy, and you make the creative process breathless, dynamic, fun (I didn't know you were allowed to have fun when editing a book).

My wife, Kristin, who doesn't let me send anything to the editors before it has ceased to activate her irritometer (when there are no more sighs from the couch where she's reading, I know the kinks are ironed out). Seriously, darling, you're a superb editor, and you and I both know I couldn't do it without you.

Felicity Blunt, thank you for always having my back. Betsy Robbins, my foreign rights agent, is another worker of magic. Everyone at Curtis Brown, my agency: thank you for bringing your considerable talent and dedication to this project. I'm lucky to have you. Similarly Eleo Gordon at Viking Penguin in the U.K. and Michael Heyward at Text in Australia: thank you for helping to shape the book into its final form. Jamie Byng at Canongate, again thanks for your unselfish support. John Stewart of Haehnel Stewart Advertising, grateful thanks for building us an amazing Web site.

Tulga: you held our hands across the steppe and up into Siberia. You kept us alive. You found the shamans. You took us to Ghoste. I owe you a lot. Naara, if you had not decided to send your son with us on the trip, Rowan would not have made his first friend. Tomoo, for being Rowan's first friend, there are no words to express how grateful to you I am.

To Ghoste: thirty hours after I brought my son to you, he became physically continent, emotionally continent. To the nine shamans of the Bogd Khan: my son made his first friend in the middle of your ceremony. It took huge courage to keep your traditions alive under the iron fist of the Soviets, when even possessing a shaman's drum was cause for arrest. Had you not possessed that courage, I could never have brought my son to you. Lords of the Mountains, Lords of the Rivers, I salute you and offer my thanks.

And Betsy. How do I thank Betsy? Suffice to say that I have never been as indebted to another living being as I am to you. Perhaps, in another life, it'll be my turn to carry you. It would only be fitting.

For more information about equine therapy centers, please visit the following Web sites:

www.narha.org
www.horseboyfoundation.org

ABOUT THE AUTHOR

Rupert Isaacson was born in London to a South African mother and a Zimbabwean father. Isaacson's first book, *The Healing Land* (Grove Press), was a 2004 *New York Times* Notable Book. He lives in Austin, Texas, with his wife, Kristin, and their son, Rowan.

We hope you have enjoyed this Large Print book. Other Thorndike, Wheeler, Kennebec, and Chivers Press Large Print books are available at your library or directly from the publishers.

For information about current and upcoming titles, please call or write, without obligation, to:

Publisher
Thorndike Press
295 Kennedy Memorial Drive
Waterville, ME 04901
Tel. (800) 223-1244

or visit our Web site at:

http://gale.cengage.com/thorndike

OR

Chivers Large Print
published by BBC Audiobooks Ltd
St James House, The Square
Lower Bristol Road
Bath BA2 3SB
England
Tel. +44(0) 800 136919
email: bbcaudiobooks@bbc.co.uk
www.bbcaudiobooks.co.uk

All our Large Print titles are designed for easy reading, and all our books are made to last.